ENVIRONMENTAL PRINCIPLES AND POLICIES

PROFESSOR DR SHARON BEDER is in the School of Social Sciences, Media and Communication at the University of Wollongong and has held a number of appointments at Australian universities over the past two decades. Beder has written six books as well as some 140 articles, book chapters and conference papers. She is a qualified professional engineer and worked in this field until a career shift into researching and teaching environmental politics. Her website is <http://homepage.mac.com/herinst/sbeder/home.html>

Her earlier books, some of which have been translated into other languages, include: *Suiting Themselves: How Corporations Drive the Global Agenda*, Earthscan, London (2006); *Power Play: The Fight for Control of the World's Electricity*, Scribe, Melbourne and the New Press, New York (2003); *Selling the Work Ethic: From Puritan Pulpit to Corporate PR*, Zed Books, London and Scribe, Melbourne (2000); *Global Spin: The Corporate Assault on Environmentalism*, Green Books, Devon, UK and Scribe, Melbourne (1997 and 2002); *The New Engineer*, Macmillan, Melbourne (1998); *The Nature of Sustainable Development*, Scribe, Melbourne (1996) and *Toxic Fish and Sewer Surfing*, Allen & Unwin, Sydney (1989).

ENVIRONMENTAL PRINCIPLES AND POLICIES

An interdisciplinary introduction

SHARON BEDER

EARTHSCAN

First published by the University of New South Wales Press Ltd in 2006
Published outside Australia, New Zealand and Oceania by Earthscan

ISBN-10: 1-84407-404-8 paperback
1-84407-405-6 hardback
ISBN-13: 978-1-84407-404-4 paperback
978-1-84407-405-1 hardback

Typesetting by Ruth Pidd
Printer Everbest, China
Cover design by Di Quick based on photographs by Sharon Beder

For a full list of publications please contact:
Earthscan
8–12 Camden High Street
London, NW1 0JH, UK
Tel: +44 (0)20 7387 8558
Fax: +44 (0)20 7387 8998
Email: earthinfo@earthscan.co.uk
Web: www.earthscan.co.uk

22883 Quicksilver Drive, Sterling, VA 20166-2012, USA

Earthscan is an imprint of James and James (Science Publishers) Ltd and publishes in association with the International Institute for Environment and Development

A catalogue record for this book is available from the British Library
Library of Congress Cataloging-in-Publication Data

Beder, Sharon.

Environmental principles and policies : an interdisciplinary introduction / Sharon Beder.
p. cm.
Includes bibliographical references and index.
ISBN-13: 978-1-84407-404-4 (pbk.)
ISBN-10: 1-84407-404-8 (pbk.)
ISBN-13: 978-1-84407-405-1 (hardback)
ISBN-10: 1-84407-405-6 (hardback)

1. Environmental policy. 2. Science and the humanities. I. Title.
GE170.B43 2006
363.7'05--dc22

2006021876

Printed on chlorine-free paper

CONTENTS

PART IV • ECONOMIC INSTRUMENTS FOR POLLUTION CONTROL

PART V • MARKETS FOR CONSERVATION

INTRODUCTION

This book discusses six major principles of relevance to environmental issues and uses them to evaluate a set of environmental policies. The principles chosen include three that are specific to environmental matters – ecological sustainability, the polluter pays principle and the precautionary principle – and three more that have wider social application – equity, human rights and public participation. While these six principles are by no means comprehensive, and different scholars, policy analysts and environmental groups have recommended others as also relevant to environmental policies, they were selected because they were developed over the past half century and have the broadest acceptance around the world. Each has, to varying degrees, been incorporated into international treaties and national law.

While these six principles can and should be used to evaluate all environmental policies, this book focuses on one set of policies. This set of policies forms the new wave of economic instruments and market-oriented environmental policies that seek to utilise economic incentives and market forces in protecting the environment. These economics-based policies are being progressively applied at the national and international level, and have been embraced by business, government and many environmental groups.

The following brief historical context should be useful in better understanding the political significance of the principles and environmental policies around which this book has been written.

PRINCIPLES

The sustainability principle

The first wave of modern environmentalism was associated with the counter-culture movement of the 1960s and 1970s. It grew out of traditional nature conservation concerns into an awareness of the potential for a global ecological crisis, and introduced the world to the concept of 'sustainability', of systems in equilibrium. Environmentalists and others argued that exponential growth was not sustainable – that it could not be continued forever because the planet was finite. In other words, there were limits to growth. They argued that the exponential growth of populations and industrial activity could not be sustained without seriously depleting Earth's resources and overloading the planet's ability to deal with pollution and waste materials.

Between 1965 and 1970 environmental groups proliferated, and the protection of the environment, especially through the control of pollution, rose dramatically as a public priority in many countries. *Time* magazine labelled environmental protection a 'national obsession' in America. A 'sense of urgency – even crisis – suddenly pervaded public discussion of environmental issues. The press was filled with stories of environmental trauma ...' (Vogel 1989: 65).

Despite controversy at the time over whether economic growth was a help or a hindrance to the achievement of ecological sustainability, the essential role of the planet's ecosystems in providing life-support systems for humans as well as ensuring their health and wellbeing was widely recognised, as was the fact that human activity had the potential to irreparably damage those ecosystems.

The polluter pays principle

Governments worldwide responded to this early wave of environmental concern with new forms of comprehensive environmental legislation and the establishment of environmental regulatory agencies. The new environmental laws were part of a general trend in legislation aimed at regulating corporate activities and constraining unwanted business activities.

The polluter pays principle was introduced in the 1970s because of concerns that pollution control laws might disadvantage the industries of some nations. The first international agreement on the polluter pays principle was incorporated in a 1972 Organisation for Economic Cooperation and Development (OECD) Council recommendation. Its main goal was to prevent governments from subsidising pollution control and thereby giving companies from their own nations an unfair advantage in competing for international trade with firms from other nations which did not subsidise pollution control. The idea was that the costs of pollution control should be reflected in the cost of goods and services that required such controls.

It was only later that the goal of providing an incentive to prevent pollution by making firms responsible for paying for its prevention and consequences became widely accepted. The notion of the polluter pays principle as an ethical principle, a principle of fairness and responsibility, also developed later.

The precautionary principle

The precautionary principle as an official principle guiding policy also dates back to the 1970s, when it was incorporated into German and Swedish environmental policy. The first recognition of the precautionary principle in an international agreement came in 1982 when it was incorporated into the World Charter for Nature and adopted by the United Nations (UN) General Assembly (EC 2000a: 11).

Until the 1970s environmental protection existed mainly in the form of remedial action. Governments were reluctant to do anything to protect the environment unless demonstrable harm had already occurred. In this context, uncertainty was frequently used as a reason to postpone government intervention, which all too often meant that death or serious harm occurred before anything was done; witness the case of asbestos, which caused the deaths of thousands of people before it was banned (Harramoës et al. 2001).

The inadequacy of the reactive approach became undeniably apparent after a series of unpredicted environmental disasters, including the discovery of the hole in the ozone layer and the chemical contamination of various marine environments such as the North Sea. It became evident that the ability of the oceans and the atmosphere to soak up and dilute and assimilate a variety of pollutants without detriment was limited. The precautionary principle seemed particularly relevant to marine pollution, 'where an abundance of ecological data on pollution yielded little understanding but much concern', and during the 1980s it was integrated into a number of international treaties beginning with the North Sea Treaties (de Sadeleer 2002: 94; MacGarvin 1994: 69).

Modern environmental regulations are more anticipatory than earlier such regulations. Although their introduction was in most cases forced by evidence of environmental harm, they seek to prevent further harm by considering the environmental impacts of human activities in advance, evaluating risks and preventing activities known to be harmful. They are based on the idea that it is safer, and often less expensive, to prevent damage rather than attempting to fix it up later. The precautionary principle, which goes even further than this, says that even where it is not certain that serious or irreversible harm will be caused, if it is likely, action should be taken to prevent it.

The participation principle

Many governments introduced requirements for the environmental impact of certain proposed activities to be assessed in the 1970s and 1980s. Environmental impact assessment (EIA) is required to ensure that environmental impacts are considered before certain developments and projects that are likely to have a detrimental affect on the environment are given approval.

Environmental impact assessment often included a limited form of public consultation, an early recognition of the right of the public to participate in environmental decisions that might affect them. An environmental impact statement (EIS), usually prepared by the project proponent, is publicly displayed for a few weeks, and interested persons and organisations have the opportunity to make submissions about the proposal. The EIS and the public submissions are then assessed by a government authority – sometimes a local council, sometimes a government department – and a decision is made about whether the project should go ahead.

Freedom of information legislation was also introduced into many countries as the right to know became established. This legislation covered the right to know about environmental matters with respect to government agencies and in the 1980s began to be applied in a limited way to information about polluting companies. Inventories of pollutants have been established in a number of countries, including the USA, Canada, the United Kingdom, the Netherlands, Norway and Australia, as a contribution to fulfilling the public's right to know.

The right to participation, often interpreted as the right to be consulted, did not spread far beyond EIA until the 1990s, when various international agreements acknowledged its importance to achieving environmental goals.

The equity principle

During the 1980s the concept of ecological sustainability was married with the idea of equity (or fairness), and particularly intergenerational equity, that is, the idea of justice and fairness to future generations. The 1980 World Conservation Strategy, produced by the International Union for Conservation of Nature and Natural Resources (IUCN) in collaboration with the UN Environment Programme (UNEP) and the World Wildlife Fund (WWF, now the World Wide Fund for Nature), called for:

> the management of human use of the biosphere [the thin covering of the planet that sustains life] so that it may yield the greatest sustainable benefit to present generations while maintaining its potential to meet the needs and aspirations of future generations. (IUCN et al. 1980)

The World Commission on Environment and Development (WCED), otherwise known as the Brundtland Commission, which played such a prominent part in popularising the notion of sustainable development, defined it in equity terms as 'development that meets the needs of the present without compromising the ability of future generations to meet their own needs' (WCED 1990: 85).

The Earth Summit in Rio in 1992 reaffirmed the centrality of equity in its Rio Declaration. Since then the rhetoric of equity has been incorporated into numerous sustainable development strategies and policies.

Human rights principles

It was not until the 1980s that the most important and basic principle for guiding human affairs, that of human rights, was seriously applied to environmental issues. The Universal Declaration of Human Rights was adopted in 1948, well before environmental concerns were as pressing as they later became, and does not specifically mention the environment. It has since become clear that environmental protection is necessary to support some of the most fundamental of human rights, such as the rights to life, health and wellbeing (UNHCHR 2002).

Environmentally damaging activities that result in death, injury and disease obviously breach human rights. For example, 'almost a fifth of all ill health in poor countries', according to the World Bank, 'can be attributed to environmental factors, including climate change and pollution'. Twelve million people die each year from contaminated water and inadequate sanitation. More than 2 million die from air contamination within their homes and 800 000 from outdoor urban air pollution. Some 4000 die from outdoor air contamination in the Brazilian cities of San Pablo and Rio de Janeiro alone (CEDHA 2002; Vidal 2005).

It is clear from these statistics both that environmental protection is essential to safeguard human rights, and that human rights principles need to guide environmental policy. Other relevant human rights include a person's 'right to a standard of living adequate for the health and well-being of himself and of his family', the right to participate in governance decisions and, in later human rights documents, the right to self-determination and the right to peaceful enjoyment of property.

In 1984 the OECD agreed that the right to a 'decent' environment was a fundamental human right (Bosselmann 2005). In 1994 the UN's Special Rapporteur on Human Rights and the Environment proposed a Draft

Principles on Human Rights and the Environment. These have yet to be adopted. The right to a healthy environment has nevertheless been incorporated into the constitutions of more than 90 nations since 1992.

POLICIES

Environmental legislation

The first wave of environmental legislation effectively reduced many of the most obvious sources of pollution in developed nations, and many of the most environmentally insensitive developments. However, by the late 1980s its shortcomings were becoming apparent, while local pollution events, such as medical waste washing up on New York beaches and sewage pollution on Sydney beaches, also contributed to the public perception of an environment in decline. Not only was the environment continuing to be degraded, but new global concerns such as ozone depletion and global warming were also emerging. The World Commission on Environment and Development noted in 1987:

> Each year another 6 million hectares of productive dryland turns into worthless desert ... More than 11 million hectares of forests are destroyed yearly ... In Europe, acid precipitation kills forests and lakes ... The burning of fossil fuels puts into the atmosphere carbon dioxide, which is causing gradual global warming. This 'greenhouse effect' may by early next century have increased average global temperatures enough to shift agricultural production areas, raise sea levels to flood coastal cities, and disrupt national economies. Other industrial gases threaten to deplete the planet's protective ozone shield to such an extent that the number of human and animal cancers would rise sharply and the oceans' food chain would be disrupted. Industry and agriculture put toxic substances into the human food chain and into underground water tables beyond reach of cleansing. (WCED 1990)

The shortcomings of the first wave of legislation were partly due to the unwillingness of governments to risk economic growth and confront business. Enforcement of environmental legislation and standards in most nations had been particularly weak and regulatory agencies poorly resourced and staffed (Gunningham & Sinclair 2002: 31). To be effective, regulations need full political support so that regulatory agencies have the financial and human resources to monitor and enforce standards properly.

Industry in many countries opposed environmental legislation, claiming the costs involved hindered economic development and detracted from the ability of private enterprise to operate efficiently and effectively. However, Douglas Costle (1981), an administrator of the US Environment Protection Agency (EPA) in the 1970s, found that both industry and the EPA tended to overestimate rather than underestimate the costs of complying with environmental regulations. He tells of how the chemical industry overestimated the costs of a proposed vinyl chloride standard by two hundred times, and how the automobile industry overestimated the cost of a shoulder harness in a car by five times.

There was also little evidence that environmental regulation had an adverse effect on the economy in general. The Pearce Report (Pearce et al. 1989: 26) found it difficult to locate examples of cases in which environmental regulations had hurt the competitive position of a country. Some business people admitted that environmental protection could bring benefits to industry by reducing costs for raw materials, energy, water and waste disposal.

Nevertheless, most governments went out of their way to accommodate business interests. For example, when water pollution legislation and standards were established in New South Wales the government was careful to ensure that the legislation would 'cause minimum hardship to industries and services which need to use areas of water for waste disposal' (*Sydney Morning Herald* 12/3/69). There was, therefore, no goal of ridding the waterways of pollution – rather, the strategy was to keep pollution 'to a level where it will cause the least possible harm'. In introducing the legislation the Minister said: 'Where a degree of pollution is unavoidable because of the need to dispose of sewerage and industrial wastes, it is permitted in a controlled fashion designed to meet the needs of the community as a whole' (Jago 1969).

Environmental concern peaks

Worldwide, when public concern about the environment rose in the late 1980s, reinforced by scientific discoveries regarding phenomena such as ozone depletion and weather patterns that seemed to indicate that global warming had already begun, the obvious solution was to tighten environmental regulations.

A 1989 *New York Times*/CBS poll found that 80 per cent of people surveyed agreed that 'protecting the environment is so important that standards cannot be too high and continuing environmental improvements must be made regardless of cost'. Greens parties in Europe attracted 15 per cent of the vote. Sixteen per cent of Canadians surveyed said the environment was the most important problem in Canada – more important even than unemployment – and most people felt that solving environmental problems required government action. A poll in 1990 found that 67 per cent of Australians thought the government should 'concentrate on protecting the environment even if it means some reduction in economic growth' (Doern & Conway 1994: 118; McIntosh 1990; Rowell 1996: 22; Winward 1991: 107).

The heightened public awareness of global and local environmental problems in many countries drew attention to the inadequacies of existing political, economic and regulatory structures. There were increasing demands from environmental and citizens groups for tightened environmental standards and for increased government control of private firms and corporations. Greens political groups challenged traditional political parties with varying degrees of electoral success.

In response to this public pressure, regulatory agencies in various countries got tougher and new laws were enacted. In the USA, environmental convictions recorded by the EPA reached a new peak in 1989, with half of those convicted receiving jail sentences. Environmental indictments by the Justice Department increased by 30 per cent in 1990 over the previous year (Harrison 1993: 6).

In New South Wales, an *Environmental Offences and Penalties Act*, introduced in 1989, provided for jail terms and million-dollar fines for senior executives of polluting companies.

The perceived environmental crisis brought with it calls for a new environmental ethic and changes in the moral values that govern the relationship between nature and humankind. It appeared as if the free market economic system was unable to provide economic growth *and* environmental protection. Business leaders feared that the environmental benevolence of the profit motive itself would be questioned, and that the corporations responsible for pollution would be labelled as villains.

Economic instruments

It was in this political context of demands for a new environmental ethic, political change and tighter environmental regulations that business groups and economists looked for market solutions to environmental problems that would accommodate economic growth, harness and exonerate the profit motive, and avoid further legislation and regulation.

They saw economic instruments as meeting these requirements. There are two main types of economic instrument. There are those that use prices to provide an incentive to reduce environmental impact, by way of imposing fees, charges and taxes. And there are those that create property rights for the use of environmental resources and a market in which those rights can be traded.

Governments have traditionally favoured legislative instruments over economic instruments for achieving environmental policy.

Economic instruments were at first thought to be too indirect and uncertain because they are aimed at altering the conditions in which decisions are made rather than directly prescribing decisions. Governments also believed that additional charges would fuel inflation and might have the undesirable distributional effect of most severely hitting low-income groups. They were additionally concerned that the public might see charges as giving companies a 'right to pollute' because they had 'paid' to do so.

Businesses had also preferred direct regulation, partly because they feared that charges would increase their costs, and partly because of the perception that they would have more influence on legislation through negotiation and delaying tactics. The threat of a new wave of environmental regulations in the early 1990s caused businesses to rethink this preference, however.

Business-funded conservative think tanks in the USA and other English-speaking nations, which were pro-market and anti-regulation, disparaged environmental legislation – labelling it 'command and control' – and recommended using the market to allocate scarce environmental resources like wilderness and clean air. They argued that legislation should be replaced with voluntary industry agreements, reinforced or newly created property rights, and economic incentives. The Washington-based Cato Institute, for example, stated that one of its main focuses in the area of natural resources was 'dismantling the morass of centralized command-and-control environmental regulation and substituting in its place market-oriented regulatory structures ...' (Cato Institute 1995).

According to the Heritage Foundation's policy analyst, John Shanahan (1993), the free market is a conservation mechanism. He urged the use of markets and property rights 'where possible to distribute environmental "goods" efficiently and equitably' rather than legislation, arguing that 'the longer the list of environmental regulations, the longer the unemployment lines'.

Think-tank economists emphasised the importance of market processes in determining optimal resource use. Anderson and Leal (1991) argued that the political process is inefficient, that it doesn't reach the optimal level of pollution where costs are minimised:

> If markets produce 'too little' clean water because dischargers do not have to pay for its use, then political solutions are equally likely to produce 'too much' clean water because those who enjoy the benefits do not pay the cost.

Under pressure from business groups and influenced by think tanks, various governments began to reassess the use of economic instruments as a supplement to direct regulation. They were concerned that tighter pollution control measures might inhibit economic growth. They believed that economic instruments could achieve environmental goals at less cost, providing new sources of finance and allowing industry to find its own cost-effective ways of reducing pollution. Another reason was dissatisfaction with the effectiveness of direct regulation and a perception – promoted by business groups – that industry would not stand for stricter regulations (OECD 1989: 24–5).

The changing consensus wrought by conservatives meant that economic instruments, once associated with market economists and conservative bureaucrats, became widely accepted. Government sustainable development policies today embrace economic instruments and market policies. Such thinking has spread throughout the world.

> Over the last decade and a half, environmentalists in a variety of non-governmental and governmental organizations, multilateral financial institutions, and corporations have sought to fashion and to implement a new family of environmentalism based on markets, commodity flows, incentives, and the idea that people are fundamentally economic creatures. (Zerner 2000: 3)

But how well do these economic instruments and market-based policies fit with the basic environmental and social principles that have been developed over the last 50 years? This book seeks to examine these policies and evaluate them in terms of the six widely accepted principles described.

PART I

ENVIRONMENTAL PROTECTION PRINCIPLES

1

THE SUSTAINABILITY PRINCIPLE

The idea that Earth has unlimited capacity to provide for human desires and absorb human wastes was undermined when the first pictures of the planet from outer space were published. The US Ambassador to the United Nations, Adlai Stevenson, stated in 1965:

> We travel together, passengers on a little spaceship, dependent on its vulnerable reserves of air and soil; all committed for our safety to its security and peace; preserved from annihilation only by the care, the work and, I will say, the love we give our fragile craft. (quoted in Hardin 1977)

In 1966 Kenneth E Boulding (1966), a professor of economics, used the same analogy in his classic essay, 'The Economics of the Coming Spaceship Earth'. In it he described the actual economies of industrialised countries as 'cowboy' economies, 'the cowboy being symbolic of the illimitable plains and also associated with reckless, exploitative, romantic, and violent behavior, which is characteristic of open societies'. He wrote of the need for a 'spaceman' economy which recognised the planet has limited supplies and a limited capacity to extract wastes. In this economy people would have to find their place 'in a cyclical ecological system which is capable of continuous reproduction of material form'.

While a cowboy economy maximises production and consumption as desirable goals, and success is attained by continually increasing the throughput of materials and energy, a spaceman economy tries to minimise throughput in a closed economy. In such an economy the aim would be to:

- limit extraction and pollution
- decrease consumption

- continuously reproduce the material form
- increase stock maintenance – goods would be built to last as long as possible.

Economic success in a spaceman economy would be measured by the 'nature, extent, quality, and complexity of the total capital stock, including in this the state of human bodies and minds'.

LIMITS TO GROWTH

Early warnings

In the late 1960s and early 1970s many scholars and thinkers observed that continual economic growth was causing environmental decline, and argued that it could not be sustained forever. One of the most famous studies done at this time was commissioned by the Club of Rome, which was formed in 1968 by scientists, educators, economists, humanists, industrialists and civil servants under the leadership of Italian businessman Aurelio Peccei. The study was undertaken by a team of scientists at the Massachusetts Institute of Technology (MIT) in the USA and published as a book called *The Limits to Growth* (Meadows et al. 1972). The study used a computer model of the world economy to show that the existing exponential growth rates of population and economic activity could not continue indefinitely on a planet that had only limited natural resources and limited ability to deal with pollution. It found that:

> If the present growth trends in world population, industrialization, pollution, food production, and resource depletion continue unchanged, the limits to growth on this planet will be reached sometime within the next one hundred years. The most probable result will be a rather sudden and uncontrollable decline in both population and industrial capacity. (Meadows et al. 1972: 23–4)

Although this has often been characterised as a doomsday scenario, the study was optimistic in its assertion that it 'is possible to alter these growth trends and to establish a condition of ecological and economic stability that is sustainable far into the future'.

The Limits to Growth 'made headlines around the world and began a debate about the limits of the Earth's capacity to support human economic expansion' (Atkisson & Davis 2001: 165). It was translated into 29 languages, and 9 million copies were sold. While the idea of limits to growth appealed to the layperson's common sense, it 'seriously perturbed Western intellectuals' and angered economists, conservatives and politicians alike, who viewed any criticism of economic growth as a direct attack on capitalism. Socialists, who were also attached to economic growth as essential for progress, disliked it as well (Ekins 1992: 270; Norgaard 2001: 167; Suter 1999).

In the same year as *The Limits to Growth* was published, the magazine *The Ecologist* (Editors 1972) devoted an entire issue to arguing that economic growth could not continue into the future without disaster. Their argument was supported by 33 eminent academics. The issue was also published as a book – *A Blueprint for Survival* – which stated:

> The principal defect of the industrial way of life with its ethos of expansion is that it is not sustainable ... By now it should be clear that the main problems of the environment do not arise from temporary and accidental malfunctions of existing economic and social systems. On the contrary, they are the warning signs of a profound incompatibility between deeply rooted beliefs in continuous growth and the dawning recognition of the earth as a space ship, limited in its resources and vulnerable to thoughtless mishandling.

In 1973 economist Herman Daly (1973) published a book of papers entitled *Towards a Steady-State Economy*. Daly, like Boulding, argued for an economy in which the numbers of people and goods were stable and the throughputs of materials and energy were restrained.

Backlash

These publications and others unleashed a wave of controversy. There was a major counter-attack on the whole idea of limits to growth. Economists and others argued that technological change and the invisible hand of the market meant that there were no limits or, if there were limits to particular resources, humans could outsmart them by finding alternatives.

One well-known response to the limits to growth thesis was *The Doomsday Syndrome* by John Maddox, the editor of *Nature*, a leading science journal. Maddox (1972: 21–2) argued that there was no forthcoming crisis, that environmental and associated problems could be and were being fixed through legislation and through scientific and technological innovation:

> Tiny though the earth may appear from the moon, it is in reality an enormous object. The atmosphere of the earth alone weighs more than 5,000 million million tons, more than a million tons of air for each human being now alive ... It is not entirely out of the question that human intervention could at some stage bring changes, but for the time being the vast scale on which the earth is built should be a great comfort.

Another well-known refutation came from economist Julian Simon, professor of business administration and senior fellow at the libertarian think tank, the Cato Institute. Simon (1981) wrote a book entitled *The Ultimate Resource*, in which he argued that human resourcefulness would ensure that resources would never run out because, if a particular resource became scarce, either new sources would be discovered, people would learn to do more with less, or substitutes would be found.

A team of scientists at Sussex University re-ran the model used in *The Limits to Growth* but with the assumption that instead of there being absolute limits on food and resources, resources could be increased exponentially through discovery of new resources, recycling and pollution controls. Not surprisingly, they did not come up with the pessimistic results of the original model (cited in Ekins 1992: 270).

One analyst noted that neither outcome was certain, and that what separated the resource optimists from the resource pessimists was that

> [the] optimist believes in the power of human inventiveness to solve whatever problems are thrown in its way, as apparently it has done in the past. The pessimist questions the success of those past technological solutions and fears that future problems may be more intractable. (Lecomber quoted in Ekins 1992: 270)

The pessimist also believes there are certain physical constraints that mean that resources cannot continue to grow exponentially, no matter how much recycling is achieved or how clever technology becomes (Ekins 1992: 272).

Complete recycling, in fact, is not possible, since some materials are always lost through wear and tear, and corrosion and energy are required to make the transformation from waste product to new product. Moreover, according to limits-to-growth advocate Ted Trainer (1985), even if the pollution generated by manufacturing could be cut by 30 per cent, this gain to the environment would be soon lost if more manufacturing was undertaken as the result of economic growth. If the manufacturing sector grew at 3 per cent per year, it would only take 13 years before there was just as much pollution as before the cuts, and 23 years for there to be twice as much.

The merits of economic growth

The debate was not only over the question of whether human ingenuity, the market and technological change could overcome the physical limits of the planet but also over the merits of economic growth. Herman Kahn (1989: 178–9), and the US Hudson Institute, argued that while economic growth might not be able to continue indefinitely, there was too much to gain from economic growth to attempt to reduce it in the shorter term:

> In our view, the application of a modicum of intelligence and good management in dealing with current problems can enable economic growth to continue for a considerable period of time, to the benefit, rather than to the detriment, of mankind. We argue that without such growth the disparities among nations so regretted today would probably never be overcome, that 'no growth' would consign the poor to indefinite poverty and increase the present tensions between the 'haves' and the 'have-nots'.

Economic growth was put forward as the solution to problems such as poverty: the poor would be better off as the economy grew. Without such an argument politicians would have little answer to demands for more equitable redistribution of wealth (Norgaard 2001: 167). But economic growth does not necessarily eliminate poverty. The economic growth that has occurred worldwide over the last three decades has not decreased the poverty within developing nations; and the richest nations in the world still accommodate some of the poorest people. Much poverty results from distributional problems rather than from a nation's lack of wealth. This was already evident in 1973 when the president of the World Bank, Robert McNamara, said that although the world had just experienced ten years of unprecedented economic growth, 'the poorest segments of the population have received relatively little benefit … the upper 40 per cent of the population typically receive 75 per cent of all income' (Sachs 1992a: 6)

The need for growth in high-income countries was even more controversial. US economists Paul Barkley and David Seckler (1972: 18) wrote that:

> the more developed nations of the world have now reached a state where all reasonable and rational demands for economic goods have been or can be satisfied. As a result, the virtues of added economic growth may be an illusion because growth does not come free. In fact, the costs of added growth are climbing quite rapidly as the pressures against certain resources, and on the environment as a whole, increase. The developed countries may have reached a level at which the costs of additional growth in terms of labor and loss of environmental quality exceed the benefits …

Similarly, economist EJ Mishan (1967) argued that the costs of economic growth outweighed the benefits:

> The uglification of once handsome cities the world over continues unabated. Noise levels and gas levels are still rising and, despite the erection of concrete freeways over city centres, unending processions of motorised traffic lurch through its main thoroughfares. Areas of outstanding beauty are still being sacrificed to the tourist trade and traditional communities to the exigencies of 'development'.

> Pollution of air, soil and oceans spreads over the globe ... The upward movement in the indicators of social disintegration – divorce, suicide, delinquency, petty theft, drug taking, sexual deviance, crime and violence – has never faltered over the last two decades. (quoted in Ekins 1992: 273)

The limits to growth debate did cause more conservative economists 'to incorporate natural resources and pollution' into their growth models. Such models had completely ignored the ecological basis of production before this time. However, the technological optimism of the 1980s came to dominate economic thinking, and faith in the ability of markets and technological change to overcome natural limits was reaffirmed in economic circles (England 2000: 425–6).

In 1980 the administration of US President Carter published a report entitled *Global 2000* which predicted that 'if policy everywhere continued unchanged, the world in 2000 would be more crowded, more polluted, less stable ecologically and more vulnerable to disruption than the world in 1980'. As one of the report's authors noted at the end of 2000, 'this conclusion has, unfortunately, met the test of time' (Barney 2000).

Initially, however, the trend seemed to be more hopeful. The oil crisis of 1973 provided a large incentive for companies, governments and individuals to use energy more efficiently, and between 1973 and 1985 the intensity of energy use declined in most developed nations while economic growth continued. This was taken as proof that economic growth and resource use were not linked (Ekins 1992: 275).

The limits-to-growth argument was readily dismissed during the 1980s, even by many environmentalists. This was partly due to the exaggerated pessimism of some of the early writers, who had prophesied imminent disaster that did not occur (at least in the short term); partly due to their focus on the depletion of resources such as oil and minerals rather than environmental degradation; and partly due to the success of well-financed think tanks in refuting their arguments. The debates over whether there were limits to growth were no longer found in the mainstream discourse of the 1980s.

SUSTAINABILITY IN THE 1980s

Sustainable development

In the 1980s the idea that continuous economic growth could not be ecologically sustainable was replaced by the notion of 'sustainable development', which argued that ways could be found to sustain economic growth without creating too much pollution or environmental degradation. The gloom and doom scenario was replaced with one of optimistic faith.

The environmentalists of the 1970s had used the term 'sustainability' to refer to systems in equilibrium: they argued that exponential growth was not sustainable, in the sense that it could not be continued forever because the planet and its resources were finite. In contrast, sustainable development sought ways to make economic growth sustainable, mainly through technological change. In 1982, the British government began using the term 'sustainability' to refer to sustainable economic expansion rather than sustainable use of natural resources.

Many of the ideas associated with sustainable development were articulated in the 1980 World Conservation Strategy (cited in the Introduction), which argued that while development aimed to achieve human goals through the use of the biosphere, conservation aimed to achieve those same goals by ensuring that use of the biosphere could continue indefinitely. National conservation strategies based on this World Conservation Strategy were adopted in 50 countries. The Australian National Conservation Strategy, like many others, argued that development and conservation were different expressions of the one process and that economic growth could be achieved through a more appropriate use of resources. It called for sustainable modes of development, a new international economic order, a new environmental ethic and population stabilisation (DHAE 1984) – but the World Conservation Strategy and its national equivalents had little impact on the wider public or on national policies.

In the mid-1980s, however, the World Commission on Environment and Development (WCED 1990) rejuvenated the concept of sustainable development in its report *Our Common Future* (also referred to as the Brundtland Report, after the commission's chair, Gro Harlem Brundtland, who was prime minister of Norway at the time). In October 1987, the goal of sustainable development was largely accepted by the governments of one hundred nations and approved in the UN General Assembly.

The Commission defined sustainable development as 'development that meets the needs of the present without compromising the ability of future generations to meet their own needs'.

Promoting economic growth

In the foreword to the report Bruntland said, 'What is needed now is a new era of economic growth – growth that is forceful and at the same time socially and environmentally sustainable' (WCED 1990: xvi). This call for economic growth was made in the name of the developing countries, but the notion that affluent nations might reduce their own growth to make room for the growth of poorer nations was not entertained. Jim MacNeill (1989: 106), secretary-general to the Brundtland Commission, argued that:

> the most urgent imperative of the next few decades is further rapid growth. A fivefold to tenfold increase in economic activity would be required over the next 50 years in order to meet the needs and aspirations of a burgeoning world population, as well as to begin to reduce mass poverty. If such poverty is not reduced significantly and soon, there really is no way to stop the accelerating decline in the planet's stocks of basic capital: its forests, soils, species, fisheries, waters and atmosphere.

Although the Brundtland definition of sustainable development is the one that is most often quoted, there are many other definitions of sustainable development, and while it has been argued that interest groups define sustainable development to suit their own goals, they are nearly all premised on the assumed compatibility of economic growth and environmental protection.

Sustainable development aims to achieve economic growth by increasing productivity without increasing natural resource use too much. The key to this is technological change. The Australian Commission for the Future (Commission for the Future 1990: 27) argued:

> Rather than growth or no-growth, as the debate about environment and development has sometimes been cast, the central issue is what *kind* of growth. The challenge of sustainable development is to find new products, processes, and technologies which are environmentally friendly while they deliver the things we want.

Instead of being the villains as they were in the 1970s, technology and industry were now seen to provide the solutions to environmental problems. The International Chamber of Commerce (ICC 1990) launched a Business Charter for Sustainable Development that stated:

> Economic growth provides the conditions in which protection of the environment can be achieved, and environmental protection, in balance with other human goals, is necessary to achieve growth that is sustainable.
>
> In turn, versatile, dynamic, responsive and profitable businesses are required as the driving force for sustainable economic development and for providing managerial, technical and financial resources to contribute to the resolution of environmental challenges ...

> Business thus shares the view that there should be a common goal, not a conflict, between economic development and environmental protection, both now and for future generations.

The conflict between economic growth and environmental protection was thus being denied, even when energy use per unit of GDP began to increase again in the late 1980s. The concept of sustainable development enabled a new breed of professional environmentalists to partner with economists, politicians, business people and others to achieve common goals rather than confronting each other over whether economic growth should be encouraged or discouraged. By avoiding the debate over limits to growth, sustainable development provided a compromise that on the face of it suited everyone.

More radical environmentalists continued to resist this win-win mentality, Wolfgang Sachs (1992b: 21), for example, arguing that by 'translating an indictment of growth into a problem of conserving resources, the conflict between growth and environment has been defused and turned into a managerial exercise' that forces development planners to consider nature.

CARRYING CAPACITY

While the concept of a limit to economic and population growth is seldom found in recent economic or political texts, it is still alive in ecology and environmental science where, rather than being discussed in terms of limits to growth, ecological sustainability is discussed in terms of carrying capacity and ecological footprints.

The idea of carrying capacity comes from animal husbandry and ecology. It refers to:

> the maximum number of a species that can be supported indefinitely by a particular habitat, allowing for seasonal and random changes, without degradation of the environment and without diminishing carrying capacity in the future. (Hardin 1977)

Resources can be renewable, conditionally renewable, fixed or non-renewable. Resources such as water, timber and food can be *renewable* if not overused. Resources such as fish and soil are *conditionally renewable*, that is, these resources are currently being overused in some cases and therefore are close to not being renewable. Resources such as land are *fixed* in quantity and once used for one purpose, often cannot be used for another. Then there are *non-renewable* resources such as fossil fuels and minerals (ECOTEC–UK 2001: 2–3).

Global human carrying capacity is generally calculated by choosing one of the limiting resources – land, energy, biota – and estimating how much there is of it in the world and how many people that it will support.

Garrett Hardin (1977) promoted the use of the concept for human populations, noting that 'carrying capacity is a time-bound, posterity-oriented concept'. He pointed out that when animals exceed the carrying capacity of their habitat the environment is rapidly degraded and the animals 'become skinny and feeble; they succumb easily to diseases. The normal instincts of the species become ineffectual as starving animals struggle with one another for individual survival'.

Hardin (1986) later argued that although carrying capacity could not be accurately determined and there were inevitably differences of opinion about it, the concept should nevertheless be taken seriously because exceeding carrying capacity results in 'serious and, more often than not, irreversible' consequences, that is, irreversible 'on the time scale of human history':

> Because transgression is so serious a matter, the conservative approach is to stay well below the best estimate of carrying capacity. Such a policy may well be viewed by profit-motivated people as a waste of resources, but this complaint has no more legitimacy than complaints against an engineer's conservative estimate of the carrying capacity of a bridge. Even if our concern is mere profit, in the long run the greatest economic gain comes from taking safety factors and carrying capacities seriously.

Cultural carrying capacity

For people, carrying capacity goes beyond merely populations and the resources necessary to feed them.

Humans require quality foods beyond subsistence, clothing that is more than just functional, comfortable housing, transportation, heating, and other items that constitute a reasonable standard of living. Hardin (1986) referred to this as 'cultural carrying capacity'. While many more people could be supported by the Earth if they subsisted on a minimum of food and not extras, this would be neither desirable, nor a socially stable situation (Richard 2002).

The impact of humans on the environment, as noted by Paul Ehrlich and John Holdren (1971: 1212–7), is a combination of population, resource use per person (affluence) and environmental damage per unit of resource used (technology) (see figure 1.1 on the next page).

Figure 1.1 The factors determining environmental impact

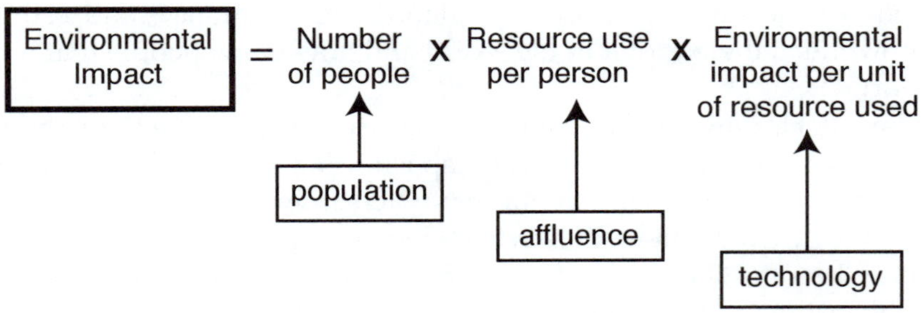

Because humans are consuming more resources per person each year, the 'world is being required to accommodate not just more people, but effectively "larger" people ...' (Catton quoted in Rees 1996). The planet not only has to provide a life-support system for its human population but also has to support our industrial metabolism, which in turn requires natural resources as inputs and produces outputs that must go back into the environment. William Rees (1996) cites rising daily energy consumption as an example: in 1790 the average American used 11 000 kcal of energy compared with 210 000 kcal used by the average person in 1980, some 20 times more. Rees defines human carrying capacity as:

> the maximum rates of resource harvesting and waste generation (the maximum load) that can be sustained indefinitely without progressively impairing the productivity and functional integrity of relevant ecosystems wherever the latter may be located. The size of the corresponding population would be a function of technological sophistication and mean *per capita* material standards.

Technological solutions

The resources required to produce a reasonable standard of living have varied throughout human history. Economists still argue that technological change and international trade will ensure that there are always enough resources to meet cultural or human carrying capacity. They argue that humanity can in fact increase carrying capacity through technological innovation, for example, by increasing the food that can be obtained from a given area of land through the use of synthetic fertilisers. If a resource runs out, people will find another way of meeting their needs. In other words, 'necessity is the mother of invention'.

Technology can change the amount and type of resources that are required to produce a reasonable standard of living.

But the technologies that extend carrying capacity often come at a price. For example, the agri-chemicals used to increase crop yields have significant environmental impacts. Our ability to continue to increase the carrying capacity of the planet may therefore be limited – and there seems to be evidence that such limits are already being reached (see below). Modern advocates of the concept of carrying capacity still argue against economic growth:

> Our dominant culture continues to celebrate expansion in spite of its heavy toll on people and nature. In fact, we desperately try to ignore that much of today's income stems from liquidating our social and natural assets. We fool ourselves into believing that we can disregard ecological limits indefinitely. (Chambers et al. 2000: 47)

Rees (1996) argues that when technology makes resource use more efficient, it may encourage greater use rather than result in less use. For example, as energy use became more efficient, more energy, not less, was used because we used it for more things. Technological changes that enhance productivity often result in increased exploitation of natural resources. For example, modern fishing technologies enable catches to be increased and depletion of fish stocks to be accelerated (see chapter 14).

Biological diversity

One of the consequences of exceeding human carrying capacity is the loss of biological diversity. Biological diversity (or biodiversity) refers to the variety of ecosystems and species of plants and animals that is found in nature. There are three levels at which biodiversity is important: the gene, the species and the ecosystem. Jeffrey McNeely and his colleagues (1990: 17) describe these levels:

> Genetic diversity is the sum total of genetic information, contained in the genes of individual plants, animals and microorganisms that inhabit the earth. Species diversity refers to the variety of living organisms on earth and has been variously estimated to be between 5 and 50 million or more, though only about 1.4 million have actually been described. Ecosystem diversity relates to the variety of habitats, biotic communities, and ecological processes in the biosphere, as well as the tremendous diversity within ecosystems in terms of habitat differences and variety of ecological processes.

When people talk about preserving biodiversity they generally mean that a full and diverse range of plant and animal species should be maintained. It has been argued that current human activities are causing the mass extinction of species at a rate never before experienced. Several species become extinct each day, while scientists estimate that the extinction rate in pre-human times was just a few species per thousand years. In the past, technologies were relatively harmless, and population patterns and cultural customs and taboos prevented overexploitation, so species were less likely to be under threat.

The rate of extinction of native mammal species in Australia today is particularly high compared with other countries. As in other countries, extinction has been caused by the removal of forests and bushland for agriculture, forestry and urban development; competition from introduced and cultivated plants and animals; and pollution of and changes to waterways. The state of species worldwide is shown in table 1.1.

Table 1.1 Numbers of extinct and threatened species in 2004

	Species extinct	Total number described	Species threatened	Percentage of species threatened
Birds	133	9917	1213	12
Plants	110	187 655	8321	3
Mammals	77	5416	1101	20
Insects	60	15000	559	0.06
Amphibians	35	5743	1856	32
Reptiles	22	8163	304	4
Crustaceans	8	40 000	429	1
Fish		28 500	800	3

Source (Baillie et al. 2004: 7; Worldwatch Institute 2005)

Environmentalists argue that the destruction and modification of habitats that results from economic activity is threatening the ability of life forms to evolve and therefore to survive through adaptation. They differentiate between *conservation*, which means maintaining the ability of species to evolve, and *preservation*, which provides only for the maintenance of individuals or groups of species, not for their evolutionary change. Preservation considers the setting aside of representative samples of biodiversity to be all that is required (Harris 1991: 8).

ECOLOGICAL FOOTPRINT

The ecological footprint, a different way of expressing carrying capacity, was developed by Mathis Wackernagel and William Rees in the early 1990s. Instead of working out how many people a particular area can take, the idea is to work out how much land and water is necessary to support a particular human population – a nation, a city, a company, a product, or even an individual – given their current levels of technology and consumption. This water and land – divided into categories such as arable, pasture, built or degraded – is not necessarily all in one place but may be spread all over the globe (Chambers et al. 2000: 60–3).

> The Ecological Footprint is a tool for measuring and analyzing human natural resource consumption and waste output within the context of nature's renewable and regenerative capacity (or biocapacity). It represents a quantitative assessment of the biologically productive area (the amount of nature) required to produce the resources (food, energy, and materials) and to absorb the wastes of an individual, city, region, or country. (Venetoulis et al. 2004: 7)

Such analyses highlight the way that human populations, particularly cities, are dependent on environments well beyond their political boundaries. It also shows that the area of land and water outside their boundaries necessary to support them – the appropriated carrying capacity – is getting larger and larger. To be sustainable the ecological footprint must remain within the Earth's limits. If those limits are exceeded – a situation called 'overshoot' – then resources are used faster than they can be renewed, the environment becomes degraded and the ability of Earth to sustain life and economic activity is further reduced (Rees 1996; Venetoulis et al. 2004: 7).

In 2000 a joint analysis of national ecological footprints by WWF International and Redefining Progress found that although the footprint per person had been falling over the previous 20 years because of increased efficiencies in resource use, the total footprint had been increasing (Venetoulis et al. 2004: 7–8). More recent studies show that humanity's ecological footprint had exceeded the planet's ecological limits by the 1980s and is continuing to rise. As a result there is evidence of major environmental degradation in every part of the world and land-use conflicts – for example, between agriculture, mining, urbanisation and forests – are increasing as land becomes more scarce (Chambers et al. 2000: 38–9).

Box 1.1 Glossary of ecological footprint terms

Appropriated Carrying Capacity: The biophysical resource flows and waste assimilation capacity appropriated per unit time from global totals by a defined economy or population.

Ecological Footprint: The corresponding area of productive land and aquatic ecosystems required to produce the resources used, and to assimilate the wastes produced, by a defined population at a specified material standard of living, wherever on Earth that land may be located.

Fair Earthshare: the amount of ecologically productive land 'available' per capita on Earth, currently about 2.2 hectares (2000). A fair seashare (ecologically productive ocean – coastal shelves, upwellings and estuaries – divided by total population) is just over .5 ha.

Ecological Deficit: The level of resource consumption and waste discharge by a defined economy or population in excess of locally/regionally sustainable natural production and assimilative capacity (also, in spatial terms, the difference between that economy/population's ecological footprint and the geographic area it actually occupies).

Sustainability Gap: A measure of the decrease in consumption (or the increase in material and economic efficiency) required to eliminate the ecological deficit. (Can be applied on a regional or global scale.)

Source (Rees 1996)

Partial measure

Footprint analysis is generally a conservative estimate, that is, it tends to underestimate the amount of land and water required to support human populations. It does not take account of toxic pollutants; in fact, the only pollutant it generally considers is carbon dioxide. Nor does it take account of species extinctions although it sometimes includes an allowance for natural habitats. It does not take account of the scarcity of different types of land. It cannot deal with details such as whether land in a region is farmed sustainably or unsustainably, or of where in the world the impact of overshoot is felt. It includes the use of non-renewable resources only by taking account of the land and energy associated with mining, processing and consumption, but does not consider their exhaustibility. It does not address social issues such as income distribution, education or unemployment. It 'intentionally says nothing about people's quality of life' and it does not analyse who is responsible for a community's increasing footprint (Chambers et al. 2000: 31; ECOTEC – UK 2001: 17, 27; Lenzen & Murray 2001: 230; Venetoulis et al. 2004: 8; Wackernagel et al. 2002: 9268).

Ecological footprint analysis is merely a rough measure of how much land is required for particular populations, based on current management and production practices and levels of consumption, to:

- grow crops for food, animal feed, fibre, oil, and rubber;
- graze animals for meat, hides, wool and milk;
- harvest timber for wood, fibre and fuel;
- fish for food;
- accommodate infrastructure for housing, transportation, industrial production and hydro-electric power;
- absorb carbon dioxide from burning fossil fuels (Wackernagel et al. 2002: 9267).

Analysis at the national level 'uses UN data on agricultural production, forest production, area of built land and trade' and trade data to take account of what is imported and exported (ECOTEC – UK 2001: 17–8). Analysts Mathis Wackernagel and his colleagues (2002: 9266) admit:

> We recognize that reducing the complexity of humanity's impact on nature to appropriated biomass offers only a partial assessment of global sustainability. It is a necessary, but not sufficient, requirement that human demand does not exceed the globe's biological capacity as measured by our accounts.

Advocates also recognise that the measure 'provides a utilitarian view of nature – nature as a big bucket filled with resources – and measures who gets what' (Chambers et al. 2000: 31–2). In addition, ecological footprint analysis is based on current actual use of technology rather than potential use of technology. Its advocates state:

> While some technologies exist to reduce human impact, most technology has been used to gain access to limited resources at a faster rate and with more ease. In other words, while we have the technological capacity for a sustainable world, we seem to choose technologies that increase our overall footprint and increase human overshoot. (Chambers et al. 2000: 115)

The estimates of footprints for particular nations, done by different experts, vary quite considerably, although not by whole orders of magnitude. Nevertheless the simplicity of the concept enables people to easily understand it, and analysts are generally open about their assumptions and omissions. It is based on publicly available government information. As such it provides an alternative measure of human progress to economic measures such as GDP, and emphasises the principle of ecological sustainability (ECOTEC–UK 2001: 30; Wackernagel et al. 2002: 9267).

The concept of ecological footprint has been criticised for reducing the value of land, and therefore ecosystems, down to productive capacity alone, and ignoring other environmental values such as diversity and beauty. It has also been criticised for implying that environmental protection is an individual responsibility; that each person is to blame for their own footprint and can reduce it by consuming less:

> This obscures the institutional and economic factors that constrain our choices, and that make it difficult to cut our own footprint down to size, even if we wish to. The problem is perpetuated in footprint analyses of nations, provinces and cities because the products of such analyses are usually interpreted in terms of the aggregated consumption behaviour of individuals. (Bocking 2004)

Rees (2002: 276) notes in response to criticisms that it would be unrealistic to expect any single measure to 'represent the total human impact on the ecosphere'. Nevertheless, ecological footprint analysis 'is comprehensive enough to show, unambiguously, that the human eco-footprint on Earth is steadily increasing'.

Fair share

Ecological footprint analysis enables the resource use of different populations to be compared and for those that are clearly unsustainable to be identified, that is, those that use more land than they own or more than their fair share of land. By considering the footprint of each nation, the disparities between nations become evident. The USA has the largest footprint per person of all nations (9.57 hectares) and various European nations and Australia are in the top ten (see table 1.2). These figures compare with the footprints of the poorest countries at 0.5 to 1 hectare per person, an average of around 2.2 hectares per person, and a sustainable footprint of 1.7 hectares per person, a figure most nations exceed (Venetoulis et al. 2004: 12; Wackernagel et al. 1997).

Table 1.2 Ecological footprint of ten heaviest nations

Country	Footprint (global hectares per capita)
USA	9.57
United Arab Emirates	8.97
Canada	8.56
Norway	8.17
New Zealand	8.13
Kuwait	8.01
Sweden	7.95
Australia	7.09
Finland	7.00
France	5.74

Source (Venetoulis et al. 2004: 12)

Although the United Kingdom does not make the top ten, London's ecological footprint, at 5.8 global hectares per person, is amongst the highest, and means that an area twice the size of Great Britain is required to support the city (*Edie News* 2005). This is the case for all large cities: 'However brilliant its economic star, every city is an entropic black hole drawing on the concentrated material resources and low-entropy production of a vast and scattered hinterland many times the size of the city itself' (Wackernagel quoted in ISEE 1994).

Through such analysis of national ecological footprints, it becomes obvious that some countries are using more than their fair share of resources. Rees (1996) concludes that since affluent nations would need to use even more of their fair share of ecological space to achieve economic growth, to do so 'is both ecologically dangerous and morally questionable. To the extent we can create room for growth, it should be allocated to the third world'.

Other measures of human impact on the environment have been developed. One index, for example, measures the proportion of the planet's net primary production devoted to human use, where net primary production is:

> [the] net amount of solar energy converted to plant organic matter through photosynthesis ... Human appropriation of net primary production, apart from leaving less for other species to use, alters the composition of the atmosphere, levels of biodiversity, energy flows within food webs and the provision of important ecosystem services. (Imhoff et al. 2004: 870)

This and other indexes also show that humans, particularly those in affluent countries, are overshooting the carrying capacity of the planet.

Consequences of overshoot

The consequences of overshoot, that is, the way humans are exceeding the capacity of the environment to sustain their impact, are evident in the UN's *Millennium Ecosystem Assessment* (Reid et al. 2005), written by some 1360 scientists from 95 countries. The Assessment found that not only are humans already consuming ecosystems at an unsustainable rate and therefore degrading them, but that consumption is likely to increase by 3 to 6 times by 2050:

> First, approximately 60% (15 out of 24) of the ecosystem services examined during the Millennium Ecosystem Assessment are being degraded or used unsustainably, including fresh water, capture fisheries, air and water purification, and the regulation of regional and local climate, natural hazards, and pests …
>
> Second, there is established but incomplete evidence that changes being made in ecosystems are increasing the likelihood of nonlinear changes in ecosystems (including accelerating, abrupt, and potentially irreversible changes) that have important consequences for human well-being.

CONTINUING DEBATE

The optimism of the 1980s that ecological limits could be overcome is as easy to refute as the predictions of imminent catastrophe of the 1970s. It is becoming increasingly clear that the environment is deteriorating and that rather than depletion of resources providing the limits to growth, it is the pollution and environmental degradation resulting from ever-increasing production and consumption that is the real threat to the planet's future.

In 1996, respected economist Robert U Ayres (1996: 117) said, 'I have changed my view radically … Today I have deep misgivings about economic growth per se.' His reasoning was as follows:

> [E]vidence is growing that economic growth (such as it is) in the western world today is benefiting only the richest people alive now, at the expense of nearly everybody else, especially the poor and the powerless in this and future generations. To those who follow us we

are bequeathing a more and more potent technology and significant investment in productive machinery and equipment and infrastructure. But these benefits may not compensate for a depleted natural resource base, a gravely damaged environment and a broken social contract.

It is theoretically possible that economic growth could be achieved without additional impacts on the environment, but this would mean many activities that might otherwise provide economic growth would have to be forgone – which will not happen while priority is given to achieving economic growth. Whether they believe economic growth and environmental protection are compatible, almost everyone agrees that there will inevitably be situations in which the goals of economic growth and environmental protection are irreconcilable and choices will have to be made.

Also, as Paul Ekins (1992: 280–1) noted in his review of the shift from limits to growth to sustainable development, whether one is a technological optimist or pessimist, the technological changes that are necessary require 'adoption of ecological sustainability as the principle economic objective in place of economic growth'.

Further Reading

Chambers, N, C Simmons & M Wackernagel (2000) *Sharing Nature's Interest: Ecological Footprints as an Indicator of Sustainability*, Earthscan, London.

Ekins, P (1992) 'Limits to growth' and 'sustainable development': grappling with ecological realities, *Ecological Economics*, 8: 269–88.

Hardin, Garrett (1986) *Cultural carrying capacity: a biological approach to human problems*, Die Off Web Site, viewed 15 March 2006, <http://dieoff.org/page46.htm>

Meadows, DH, DL Meadows, J Randers & WW Behrens (1972) *The Limits to Growth: A Report for the Club of Rome's Project on the Predicament of Mankind*, Pan, London.

Rees, WE (1996) Revisiting carrying capacity: area-based indicators of sustainability, *Population and Environment*, 17(3).

Reid, WV et al. Millennium Ecosystem Assessment (2005) *Ecosystems and Human Well-being: Synthesis*, Island Press, Washington DC.

Wackernagel, M, NB Schulz, D Deumling, A Callejas Linares, M Jenkins, V Kapos, C Monfreda, J Loh, N Myers, R Norgaard, & J Randers (2002) Tracking the ecological overshoot of the human economy, *PNAS*, 99(14): 9266–71.

2

THE POLLUTER PAYS PRINCIPLE

In the past, companies which have polluted have not paid the cost of that pollution. They have been allowed to discharge pollutants into the air and water while others bear the consequences. 'When companies are allowed to pollute, or to use natural resources without paying their full price, they are in effect appropriating natural capital – land, air, and water – without compensation to society at large' (Templet 2001: 2). The resulting pollution or resource depletion is called an 'externality' by economists because it is a cost that is external to the company's accounts and external to the market transactions the company is involved in.

The polluter pays principle (PPP) seeks to change this, so that a company has to either pay to prevent the pollution or pay for the damage (or for remediating the damage) that it causes. This does not mean that the polluter necessarily has to pay money to the government or to others, merely that they should pay for the appropriate pollution control measures to prevent pollution or for the clean-up if they fail to do so (JWPTE 2002: 9). Governments can ensure that the polluter pays by:

- regulating what polluters are able to discharge into the environment, so that they have to install their own pollution control equipment;
- charging polluters taxes and levies to cover government costs of protecting the environment, including the cost of sewage treatment facilities;
- making polluters liable for the damage they cause.

Organisation for Economic Cooperation and Development

The 1972 OECD Council recommendation on guiding principles for economic aspects of environmental policies stated:

> The principle to be used for allocating costs of pollution prevention and control measures to encourage rational use of scarce environmental recourses and to avoid distortions in international trade and investment is the so-called 'Polluter-Pays Principle'. This principle means that the polluter should bear the expenses of carrying out the above-mentioned measures decided by public authorities to ensure that the environment is in an acceptable state. In other words, the cost of these measures should be reflected in the cost of goods and services which cause pollution in production and/or consumption. Such measures should not be accompanied by subsidies that would create significant distortions in international trade and investment. (quoted in JWPTE 2002: 9)

The PPP was never supposed to be a way for polluters to pay to be allowed to pollute; the OECD intended it as a way to get the polluter to both 'limit their pollution *and* bear the cost of measures taken to that end' (JWPTE 2002: 12).

OECD guidelines allowed exceptions to the PPP in the form of government subsidies for the research and development of new pollution control technologies and for pollution control infrastructure for regions or industries experiencing severe difficulties. The OECD Recommendation on the Polluter-Pays Principle (OECD 1974) also allowed that:

> In exceptional circumstances, such as the rapid implementation of a compelling and especially stringent pollution control regime, socio-economic problems may develop of such significance as to justify consideration of the granting of government assistance, if the environmental policy objectives of a Member country are to be realised within a prescribed and specific time.

In each case the subsidies had to be selectively applied, temporary, and 'not create significant distortions in international trade and development'. The OECD noted that financial incentives (payments made to induce polluters to reduce their emissions) were not compatible with the PPP (JWPTE 2002: 17).

Towards the end of the 1980s the PPP was extended to include accidental pollution, not just routine pollution. In 1989 the OECD (1989b) published a Recommendation on the Application of the Polluter-Pays Principle to Accidental Pollution. The recommendation covers both the cost of specific measures associated with particular hazardous installations and general costs associated with accidental pollution which would be covered by fees and taxes on hazardous installations, including 'reasonable measures' taken by government authorities to prevent, prepare for and deal with accidents. These measures include:

- improving the safety of hazardous installations and accident preparedness;
- developing emergency plans;
- protecting human health and the environment following an accident;
- cleaning up and minimising ecological damage following an accident.

International acceptance

The PPP is now an accepted principle underlying the environmental policies of many countries including OECD countries. In Canada the polluter pays principle is 'enshrined in the preamble to the Canadian Environmental Protection Act, 1999' and is 'firmly entrenched' in its environmental laws at both federal and provincial levels (Canadian Supreme Court quoted in Buttigieg & Fernando 2003: 2).

The PPP was first included in European agreements in 1973 as part of the European Community Action Programme on the Environment, which stated that the 'cost of preventing and eliminating nuisances must in principle be borne by the polluter'. It was incorporated into the Treaty Establishing the European Community in 1987 and the Maastricht Treaty. In its latest Environmental Action Programme, *Environment 2010: Our Future, Our Choice*, the EC commits to the PPP (Coffey & Newcombe 2001: 1–4).

The PPP has also been incorporated into the Rio Declaration, Agenda 21 and the 2002 World Summit on Sustainable Development Plan of Implementation, as well as various international agreements including:

- 1985 ASEAN Agreement on the Conservation of Nature and Natural Resources
- 1990 Convention on Oil Pollution Preparedness, Response and Cooperation (OPRC)
- 1992 Helsinki Convention on the Transboundary Effects of Industrial Accidents
- 1996 London Protocol to the Convention on the Prevention of Marine Pollution by Dumping of Wastes and Other Matter
- 2001 Stockholm Convention on Persistent Organic Pollutants.

Some agreements, including the OECD agreements, are non-binding but others, including the Porto Agreement creating a European Economic Area and the Oslo and Paris Conventions on marine pollution, make implementation of the PPP compulsory for all nations which are party to the agreements (Smets 1994: 132).

It was observed in the 1990s that there was no evidence that the implementation of the PPP over its first 20 years had had any negative impact on economic growth, inflation, international trade or balance of payments.

In fact, 'in countries with strict environmental standards, low subsidies and a high degree of dependence on international trade, technological progress in pollution control was rapid and profitable', as could be seen in the case of the Japanese motor vehicle industry (Juhasz 1993: 42–3).

Defining pollution

During the 1970s, pollution in the context of the PPP referred to waste products that were put into the air and water, but by 2002 the OECD (quoted in JWPTE 2002: 11) had expanded the definition of pollution to:

> the introduction by man, directly or indirectly, of substances or energy into the environment resulting in deleterious effects of such a nature as to endanger human health, harm living resources and ecosystems, and impair or interfere with amenities and other legitimate uses of the environment.

The definition of pollution was later broadened to cover many types of environmental damage, not just those caused by the discharge of contaminants. The EC (2004: 59) defines 'environmental damage' as:

> (a) damage to protected species and natural habitats, which is any damage that has significant adverse effects on reaching or maintaining the favourable conservation status of such habitats or species ...
>
> (b) water damage, which is any damage that significantly adversely affects the ecological, chemical and/or quantitative status and/or ecological potential ... of the waters concerned ...
>
> (c) land damage, which is any land contamination that creates a significant risk of human health being adversely affected as a result of the direct or indirect introduction, in, on or under and, of substances, preparations, organisms or microorganisms.

The EC and the OECD define pollution by its impact on the environment and human health, rather than in terms of compliance with government regulations. This raises the question of whether a company that complies with environmental regulations and standards set by government authorities should bear the costs of its pollution.

Nicolas de Sadeleer (2002: 40) argues that the definition of pollution should be independent of what may or may not be legal. He argues that this is a fair approach because polluters are responsible for their discharges, even if a government body authorises them, otherwise the public would have to bear the costs of clean-up when government regulations are inadequate. Given that companies have a direct influence on the limits and standards which governments set or don't set, when government regulation allows too much pollution it is often because of industry pressure.

Defining pollution by its impact rather than by government-set standards is also appropriate, according to de Sadeleer, because it provides polluters with an incentive to do better than government-set standards. It is legally coherent because it fits with civil liability, which requires pollution to be 'evaluated from the perspective of the requirement of duty of care owed by the liable party, whether or not he respected the standards incumbent upon him'. Being allowed to pollute by the government should not absolve a polluter from liability.

The issue of what environmental impacts are deleterious or impair and interfere (as in the OECD definition of damage), and how deleterious an impact should be before it has to be paid for or prevented, is not defined by the PPP and remains both a scientific and a political question. However, some legislation does attempt to define significant damage, and the EC has developed criteria for deciding if damage is significant (EC 2004).

Defining the polluter

As the definition of pollution was broadened, so the definition of polluter became 'someone who directly or indirectly damages the environment or who creates conditions leading to such damage' (quoted in JWPTE 2002: 11). In 1989, when the PPP was extended to cover accidental pollution, the polluter became someone who might cause pollution in the future rather than being limited to someone who was already polluting or had done so in the past (de Sadeleer 2002: 41).

However, the question of responsibility for environmental damage is not always so clear cut. Is the polluter the person who disposes of waste in the environment or the person who creates the waste or the person who produces the product that will become waste after use? 'The person in charge of the installation, the manufacturer of the defective plant, and the licence-holder or his representatives may all be liable for pollution.' And what about situations where there are multiple sources of pollution? In this case the regulatory authority might prefer to apply the PPP 'at the point where the number of economic operators is least and control is easiest'. For example, where agricultural chemicals are polluting an area, the authority may target the manufacturer of the chemicals rather than every farmer who has used them (de Sadeleer 2002: 41–2).

FUNCTIONS OF THE POLLUTER PAYS PRINCIPLE

The PPP is merely a means of allocating costs, and on its own does not necessarily result in reduced pollution – although this may occur. Although the PPP was originally formulated to combat trade distortions, it also became a means of distributing some of the profits made from products which caused pollution back to the government authorities and regulatory agencies whose job it was to control and prevent pollution. The charges covered the cost of monitoring and inspecting and regulating pollution.

PPP in the strict sense

At first the polluter pays principle was only applied to the costs of pollution prevention and control, as required by government regulation. This was PPP 'in a strict sense' or 'standard' PPP. The polluter pays principle 'in a strict sense' includes costs of pollution control equipment, the cost of government provision of pollution removal infrastructure and services and, in some cases, the administrative costs of government in overseeing pollution control ('measurement, surveillance, supervision, inspection etc.'). PPP 'in a strict sense' sometimes covers the cost of clean-up as well, including cleaning up after an accidental spill or long-term routine pollution (JWPTE 2002: 12).

Such payments could be seen by some polluters as legitimising the pollution, in other words, that they were paying to be allowed to pollute. Government charges were not much of a disincentive when they were viewed as just another tax on the production process and simply incorporated into the cost of the final goods. So PPP charges had to be accompanied by standards and regulations that limited allowable discharges.

Nations can have differing environmental standards and thus the amount that a firm has to pay to keep pollution within those standards will vary. Within the OECD, for example, it is accepted that national standards will differ according to different social objectives, differing assumptions about local assimilative capacity, differing population densities, and how industrialised a region is (Juhasz 1993: 38).

Under these conditions, lower environmental standards became essentially a form of subsidy, provided at the expense of the local environment, to local firms in a competitive international market, since those firms didn't have to pay to keep their pollution within the higher standards expected in other countries. In general, polluters paid only part of the costs of pollution, as regulations never required all pollution to be prevented, just that a specified environmental standard be met. Environmental damage continued to occur despite the standards and charges.

PPP in the broad sense

During the 1990s, the idea of putting limits on discharges fell out of favour. Under pressure from industry, many governments began to adopt an approach whereby pollution would be controlled, not by government-imposed limits, but by charges and fees that would provide an incentive for companies to voluntarily reduce their emissions. It was believed that it would be more efficient if environmental goals were met by internalising the full costs of pollution, thereby providing incentives for polluters to reduce their pollution in the most efficient way and for consumers to use the products more efficiently because they cost more: 'Prices which fail to incorporate costs resulting from environmental damage may lead to inefficient use, often in the form of excessive consumption of natural resources' (JWPTE 2002: 9).

The 1991 OECD Recommendation on the Use of Economic Instruments in Environmental Policy called for the costs of environmental damage caused by polluters, as well as the costs of preventing and controlling pollution, to be covered by the PPP (cited in de Sadeleer 2002: 37). Subsequent EC documents have made polluters liable for damage done (see next section). In this way the PPP can be used to ensure that the costs of repairing damage caused by pollution, or compensation payments, are paid by the polluters.

This broadening of the PPP is aimed at pollution prevention. 'If polluters have to pay for damage caused, they will cut back pollution' if the costs of pollution control are less than the compensation or reparation they might otherwise have to pay. It is also aimed at internalising more fully the costs of environmental damage and is referred to as PPP 'in a broad sense' or 'extended' PPP (EC 2000b: 14; JWPTE 2002: 12).

Principle 16 of the Rio Declaration on Environment and Development promotes the idea of PPP in the broad sense:

> National authorities should endeavour to promote the internalisation of environmental costs and the use of economic instruments, taking into account the approach that the polluter should, in principle, bear the cost of pollution, with due regard to the public interest and without distorting international trade and investment.

Despite its reference to internalisation of environmental costs, this particular version of the principle is fairly weak since it refers only to national regulation, not international; does not require the application of PPP, only an effort towards it; and maintains international trade and investment as a more important goal (de Sadeleer 2002: 25). The internalisation of all environmental costs is more of an ideal than a prescription, as is the case with the PPP in the strict sense. Once it has been expanded to include all costs, it is too difficult to make the PPP mandatory.

In its latest Environmental Action Programme, *Environment 2010: Our Future, Our Choice*, the EC (quoted in Coffey & Newcombe 2001: 4) also seeks: 'To promote the polluter pays principle ... to internalise the negative as well as the positive impacts on the environment' (Article 3(3)).

The PPP therefore seeks to achieve various functions, some of which can at times be contradictory:

- to ensure fairness in international trade
- to achieve economic integration – internalising costs
- to provide more equitable redistribution of costs
- to prevent pollution
- to provide compensation and reparation (de Sadeleer 2002: 33–4).

The ideal of polluters paying the full cost of their pollution and environmental impact so that external costs of economic activities are internalised into company decision making is not only politically difficult, because companies argue that they cannot afford such costs, but also practically difficult, because the value of environmental damage is very hard to quantify, particularly in the case of irreversible or irreparable damage. Some say that such damage is beyond costing (see chapter 8). One way of dealing with this problem is to ensure that polluters are truly liable for the cost of repairing or cleaning up the environmental damage they cause.

LIABILITY

USA: Superfund

A wave of publicity about hazardous waste contamination of residential areas in the 1970s, including Love Canal in New York State and Times Beach in Missouri, raised the issue of contaminated sites in the USA. The legislation that followed from this public concern included the 1980 Comprehensive Environmental Response, Compensation and Liability Act (CERCLA) otherwise known as Superfund. The Superfund legislation was based on the idea that the polluter should pay, and required that those associated with the contamination of sites (including site owners, banks, insurers and hauliers) be identified and liable for their clean-up. If they would not clean up the sites themselves the EPA would do the work and then charge the polluter the costs of clean-up plus penalties (Haggerty & Welcomer 2003).

In addition, the chemical and oil industries, as industries likely to cause contamination, were charged a tax to fund the clean-up of sites where the parties who were liable could not be directly identified (about 30 per cent of sites). This tax was later supplemented by a corporate environmental income tax. The total industry contribution was running at around $2 billion per year in the early 1990s. From 1995, however, Congress refused to authorise these taxes, so that increasingly the clean-up of contaminated sites has been funded by general taxpayers. Inevitably, the rate of clean-up has slowed right down. Holdings in the Superfund trust fund declined from $3 billion in 1995 to $25 million in 2003 (Haggerty & Welcomer 2003).

Without those funds, the EPA is no longer able to clean up more than a few sites, or to force polluters to pay. Moreover, the community rather than the responsible industry is being forced to pay for the clean-up of sites where individual polluters cannot be identified. Consequently, the community is paying for the cost of pollution, particularly those who live near the contaminated sites that are not being cleaned up. About one in four people in the USA now lives within a mile of a Superfund site. Forty-five per cent of those sites are thought to have a high risk associated with them; only 25 per cent are thought to be low risk. One of the major risks is to groundwater, and about half of all Americans rely on groundwater for drinking water (Haggerty & Welcomer 2003).

The discontinuance of the tax is the result of industry lobbying, industry spokespersons having justified the shift of the burden to the general community by arguing that everyone is a polluter: 'We're all polluters to some extent. I mean, anyone who's ever thrown paint in the garbage can or pesticides in the garbage can or used oil or whatever, not to mention some of the cities have not done a good job on their landfills' (quoted in Haggerty & Welcomer 2003). Such reasoning runs counter to the whole rationale of the PPP, which seeks to identify those directly responsible for particular instances of environmental damage and make them liable in order to ensure fairness and promote prevention.

Europe

While the USA has been moving away from the PPP, it is being given greater emphasis in other parts of the world. In 1993 the EC adopted a strict liability regime for waste as a way of further enforcing the PPP. Many countries also adopted liability laws to deal with damage to property and human health.

In 2004 the EC issued a directive on environmental liability (EC 2004) that extends the notion of liability to cover damage to natural resources. Like Superfund, it was aimed at repairing environmental damage rather than the mere collection of money from polluters, but its application was far wider than contaminated sites. It specifically covered damage to protected natural habitats and wild flora and fauna, including wild birds, and also water contamination and air pollution that damaged water, land, natural habitats or protected species.

The directive was aimed at making 'the causer of environmental damage (the polluter) pay for remedying the damage that he has caused' (EC 2000b). It was thought that this would prove a greater deterrent to polluters than mere charges and fines, and encourage them to adopt prevention and control measures. Under the directive, liability can only be applied if: the polluters can be identified; the damage is tangible and can be quantified; and a causal link between the polluter and the damage can be established. This means that it is not designed to be applied where pollution is widespread and diffuse, such as carbon dioxide emissions, acid rain or urban smog. A party who is found liable for environmental damage is required to pay:

- administrative, legal and enforcement costs;
- the costs of data collection and other general costs;
- measures to control and contain the damage and prevent further damage;
- the costs of assessment of actual damage, imminent threats of damage, remediation options;
- remedial measures including 'mitigating or interim measures to restore, rehabilitate or replace damaged natural resources and/or impaired services, or to provide an equivalent alternative to those resources or services' (EC 2004: 58–60).

The EC notes that for the PPP to be fully and properly implemented, environmental damage should be repaired whenever there is an identifiable polluter who can pay for the repair, rather than fining the polluter and using the money for something else. Where several parties are responsible for the damage, the allocation of costs should be decided according to national laws.

Strict liability

The idea of strict liability, that is, making polluters liable for damage whether or not it can be proven that they were at fault or negligent, has often been adopted in the case of environmental liability because it is more effective in protecting the environment. This is because fault can be difficult to prove in the case of environmental damage. Moreover, it is thought to be only fair that someone undertaking an activity which is recognised to be dangerous should bear the risk of the damage it might cause, rather than those who suffer the damage or the wider community (EC 2000b: 18). That said, polluters will not be liable under the directive if the damage was the result of events beyond their control.

The EC Directive (EC 2004) lists the following activities as subject to strict liability:

- waste management operations
- all discharges into inland surface water
- discharges into groundwater that require permits, authorisation or registration
- discharges into surface water that require permits, authorisation or registration
- water abstraction and impoundment
- manufacture, use, storage, processing, filling, release into the environment and onsite transport of:
  - dangerous substances
  - dangerous preparations
  - plant protection products
  - biocidal products
- all transport of dangerous or polluting goods
- operation of installations subject to authorisation
- use, release, sale and transport of genetically modified micro-organisms
- transboundary shipment of waste.

Environmental groups have criticised this list for leaving out many dangerous activities, including the activities of small installations, mining activities and oil and gas drilling and transport. They have also criticised the directive for only covering protected habitats and species rather than all habitats and endangered species (BirdLife International et al. 2001).

Activities not included in the list – apart from armed conflict, civil war, national defence and international security, and natural disaster, which are not covered by the directive – incur liability only if the operator is at fault or negligent; this is 'fault-based liability'. Moreover, the Directive (EC 2004: 58–61) allows national governments to exempt polluters who have not been negligent, provided their discharges were authorised by the government and they could not have known the damage those discharges would cause.

Court cases

Environmental liability has been enforced by the courts in Canada as a way of upholding the polluter pays principle. The Supreme Court of Canada ruled in 2005 that BC Hydro was liable to clean up a severely contaminated site where, as the BC Electric Corporation, it had disposed of toxic coal tar for 37 years (FOE Canada 2005).

Similarly, the Canadian Supreme Court reinforced the PPP when it dismissed an appeal by Imperial Oil in 2003. Imperial Oil had contaminated a site where it had a petroleum depot some 25 years earlier. It had sold the site six years later, and the new owners had partially remediated the area in order to develop it for residential housing, with the approval of the Quebec government. When high levels of hydrocarbon contamination were later found there, the residents sued the developer, the city and the Quebec Ministry of the Environment. In turn, the Minister for the Environment ordered Imperial Oil to do a full assessment of the site and clean-up options. Quebec's environmental legislation incorporates the PPP and allows it to be applied retrospectively, and the court duly found that Imperial Oil had to comply with the order, despite its pollution having predated the legislation and even though it had no say in the decision to build residences on the site (Buttigieg & Fernando 2003; Ferrara & Mesquita 2003).

In Ireland, the High Court found that individual directors of a company that was responsible for dumping 8000 tonnes of waste – including hazardous waste – were personally liable despite the limited liability that directors of corporations are afforded. The Court argued that unless the liability flowed on to directors, the PPP could not be fully implemented if a company was unable to pay its liability costs (Linehan 2003).

Australasia

The Australian and New Zealand Environment and Conservation Council (ANZECC), which is made up of environment ministers in state and national governments, published a paper on liability for contaminated sites in 1994. The recommendations in that paper (Environment Australia 1999) were adopted in each state. These included:

- Governments should ensure that the polluter, when solvent and identifiable, ultimately bears the cost of any necessary remediation.
- When the polluter is insolvent or unidentifiable, the person(s) in control of the site, irrespective of whether that person is the owner or the current occupier, should be liable, as a general rule, for any necessary remediation costs.
- If a site is a risk to human health and/or the environment, governments should be empowered to intervene to direct remedial action to minimise risk (and to recover costs as above).
- The polluter is responsible for bearing the cost of any offsite remedial works, as a result of contamination from their site.
- When ownership of a non-risk site is transferred, the level of cleanup prior to transfer is a matter for commercial agreement between the parties. This would apply to most land transfers in the mining industry in the form of a mining lease.

However, unlike the US and EU legislation, the ANZECC approach was to clean up sites only to suit their proposed use. Thus a site to be used for housing would require a higher standard of clean-up than a site to be used for a factory, and other sites might remain contaminated but still be judged non-risk until such time as their use changed. In the latter case, as long as environmental contamination remains confined to the site, it is not considered a problem. If a later owner wishes to use the site differently, it is then their responsibility to clean it to the required standards. In buying a potentially contaminated site it is up to buyers to inform themselves about its state; in other words, 'buyer beware' (Schulz 1994: 442).

In the case of a site that poses a health risk or environmental risk due to migration of pollution, government can direct the owner to remediate the site, but the polluter is strictly liable. Owners or government authorities that undertake such remediation have 'a statutory entitlement to recover costs incurred from the polluters'. Where the polluter cannot be identified, however, it is government's responsibility. The Superfund approach of an industry levy or tax was rejected in Australia (Schulz 1994: 443).

EXTENDED PRODUCER RESPONSIBILITY

Extended producer responsibility (EPR) is based on the polluter pays principle but goes beyond a manufacturer's responsibility for pollution from product manufacture to make the manufacturer responsible for the environmental impact of a product from manufacture to disposal. It was defined in a 1990 report to the Swedish Ministry of Environment (ILSR 2005) as:

> an environmental protection strategy to reach an environmental objective of a decreased total environmental impact from a product, by making the manufacturer of the product responsible for the entire life-cycle of the product and especially for the take-back, recycling and final disposal of the product.

Normally, government authorities take responsibility for disposal of products and thus disposal is paid for by taxpayers. EPR, however, recognises that product design and manufacturing decisions can determine how environmentally damaging a product will be when used and disposed of, and how readily it can be recycled. Because governments have traditionally taken responsibility for waste management, manufacturers have created an excess of throwaway products and packaging without giving thought to the environmental and other costs associated with them. Manufactured goods now make up more than three-quarters of municipal waste (ILSR 2005).

By shifting the responsibility back to the manufacturer, EPR is supposed to provide an incentive to ensure that design, manufacturing and packaging decisions are made with an eye to environmental and disposal costs. There are four facets of EPR:

- Liability – responsibility for proven environmental damage caused by products
- Economic responsibility – responsibility for the cost of collection, disposal and/or recycling of products
- Physical responsibility – responsibility for actually collecting and dealing with products at the end of their lives
- Informative responsibility – responsibility to supply information on the potential environmental impacts of a product. (ILSR 2005)

'Product stewardship' is a related idea, in that it is concerned with the environmental impacts of the product throughout its life-cycle. However, product stewardship shares responsibility between all those involved in a product's life-cycle – including designers, suppliers, manufacturers, distributors, retailers and consumers – rather than shifting it to the manufacturer.

EPR was adopted during the 1990s by various OECD countries. The Swedish eco-cycle legislation embraces EPR. In Germany, the Netherlands, Austria, Switzerland and France manufacturers have legal responsibility for taking back packaging and recycling their products; these countries also have 'end-of-life legislation and voluntary agreements concerning a number of complex products' such as cars and batteries (IIIEE 1998).

EU directive on waste electrical and electronic equipment

The EU's directive on waste electrical and electronic equipment (WEEE) is an example of EPR. Electrical and electronic products, ranging from washing machines to television sets and mobile phones, are responsible for a rapidly growing waste stream that is estimated to be increasing at 3–5 per cent per year and will reach 12 million tonnes per year in Europe by 2010. Much of this waste stream currently goes to landfill but it contains hazardous materials and poses environmental risks (Waste Not 2002).

In 2001 the EU environment ministers proposed extending the polluter pays principle to cover disposal of products at the end of their useful life. In this case they defined the polluter not as the consumer but as the manufacturer of the electrical and electronic equipment. They reasoned that manufacturers should be responsible for the disposal and recycling of these products after consumers had finished with them.

The 2003 WEEE Directive (EC 2003) aimed at 'as a first priority, the prevention of waste electrical and electronic equipment, and in addition, the reuse, recycling and other forms of recovery of such wastes so as to reduce the disposal of waste'. It was therefore designed to encourage manufacturers to design products to enhance their potential for reuse, recovery and recycling: 'Member States shall encourage the design and production of electrical and electronic equipment which take into account and facilitate dismantling and recovery, in particular the reuse and recycling of WEEE, their components and materials' (Waste Not 2002).

The equipment covered includes:

- Large household appliances
- Small household appliances
- IT and telecommunications equipment
- Consumer equipment
- Lighting equipment
- Electrical and electronic tools (with the exception of large-scale stationary industrial tools)
- Toys, leisure and sports equipment
- Medical devices (with the exception of all implanted and infected products)
- Monitoring and control instruments
- Automatic dispensers.

The directive, which took effect in 2005, requires that consumers be able to return their used equipment free of charge, and that governments ensure collection facilities are made available. The final treatment of the collected equipment should use the 'best available treatment, recovery and recycling techniques'.

Further Reading

Dommen, Edward (ed.) (1993) *Fair Principles for Sustainable Development*, Edward Elgar, Aldershot, Hants, UK.

Coffey, C & J Newcombe (2001) *The Polluter Pays Principle and Fisheries: The Role of Taxes and Charges*, Institute for European Environmental Policy, London, <http://www.jncc.gov.uk/pdf/Thepollute2.pdf>

IIIEE (1998) *Extended Producer Responsibility as a Policy Instrument*, International Institute for Industrial Environmental Economics, 1998, <http://www.lu.se/IIIEE/research/products/epr/epr_1998.html>

JWPTE: Joint Working Party on Trade and Environment (2002) *The Polluter-Pays Principle as It Relates to International Trade*, OECD, Paris, 23 December.

<http://www.olis.oecd.org/olis/2001doc.nsf/43bb6130e5e86e5fc12569fa005d004c/988d25625e791068c1256c98003a2fcb/$FILE/JT00137174.PDF>

Recommendation of the Council Concerning the Application of the Polluter-Pays Principle to Accidental Pollution (1989) OECD, Paris, 7 July.

de Sadeleer, Nicolas (2002) *Environmental Principles: From Political Slogans to Legal Rules*, Oxford University Press, Oxford.

White Paper on Environmental Liability (2000) European Commission, Luxembourg, 9 February, <http://europa.eu.int/scadplus/printversion/en/lvb/128107.htm>

3

THE PRECAUTIONARY PRINCIPLE

Although uncertainties about the consequences of human behaviour have always existed, they have become more significant in recent times because of the growing scope, complexity and hazardous consequences of human activities. This means it is becoming ever more vital to prevent the harm these activities might do, even without being sure what that harm might be.

While modern environmental regulations are anticipatory and preventive they are not necessarily precautionary. They generally aim to prevent known risks rather than anticipate and prevent uncertain potential harm. This is where the precautionary principle comes in.

Risk 'is usually defined as the amalgam of the probability of an event occurring and the seriousness of the consequences should it occur' (Cameron 1999: 37). For example, the risk of a major nuclear power accident is the combination of a low probability of such an accident, which engineers claim can be calculated, multiplied by the serious damage that would occur as a result of the spread of nuclear radiation, including thousands of deaths, cancers, birth defects. If the risk of an accident is considered too high then a nuclear power plant will not be granted approval and thus the risk is prevented.

If one accepts that the risk of a nuclear accident can be calculated with some degree of accuracy, the precautionary principle does not apply. If, however, one believes that engineers are unable to calculate the probability of a major nuclear accident with any reasonable certainty or accuracy, then the precautionary principle does apply.

If an activity or product poses a known high risk then preventive action is called for rather than precautionary action. It is only when the risk is uncertain because either the probability of damage is uncertain and/or the extent of damage is uncertain that the precautionary principle applies.

Box 3.1 Definition of the precautionary principle

When human activities may lead to morally unacceptable harm that is scientifically plausible but uncertain, actions shall be taken to avoid or diminish that harm.

Morally unacceptable harm refers to harm to humans or the environment that is

- threatening to human life or health, or
- serious and effectively irreversible, or
- inequitable to present or future generations, or
- imposed without adequate consideration of the human rights of those affected.

The judgment of *plausibility* should be grounded in scientific analysis. Analysis should be ongoing so that chosen actions are subject to review.

Uncertainty may apply to, but need not be limited to, causality or the bounds of the possible harm.

Actions are interventions that are undertaken before harm occurs that seek to avoid or diminish the harm. Actions should be chosen that are proportional to the seriousness of the potential harm, with consideration of their positive and negative consequences, and with an assessment of the moral implications of both action and inaction. The choice of action should be the result of a participatory process.

Source (COMEST 2005: 14)

SHIFTING THE BURDEN OF PROOF

In the past many products and processes have been marketed without prior approval or any requirement that the manufacturer show evidence that they will not harm human health or the environment. Similarly, many activities and developments have been undertaken without the need for developers to show they will not have an adverse environmental impact. Traditionally it has been up to consumers, environmentalists or government authorities to make a convincing scientific case that such activities or products were harmful before they could be regulated. The thinking was that regulations constrained economic activity and would only be justified if there were undisputed scientific evidence that such activity would cause harm. This is a 'wait and see' approach where the burden of proof is on those asserting damage is being or will be done.

Should a chemical be assumed safe until proven dangerous, or should the chemical not be used until it has been proven to be relatively harmless? Normally, people are innocent until proven guilty. But should the same rule apply to chemicals? Like many environmentalists and regulators, Steven Jellinek of the US EPA argues that granting civil rights to toxic substances does not make sense, and that the burden of proof should be on those wanting to use or dispose of the chemicals to demonstrate they are safe before releasing them. 'Rarely will there be overwhelming evidence of a hazard – the smoking gun or dead bodies – but the most obvious implication of this sort of proof is that we have waited too long to take precautionary action' (Jellinek 1980: 8–9).

In the 1970s the US EPA imposed limits on lead in petrol based on scientific evidence that it was causing problems but without proof that it had actually harmed particular people. The oil industry opposed the regulations in the courts but the EPA won. 'The case is considered a landmark in U.S. environmental law because it established that EPA could act in a precautionary fashion rather than wait for scientific certainty about the harmfulness of a substance before acting' (Ackerman & Heinzerling 2004: 4).

These days certain activities require developers to prepare environmental impact statements or assessments and some products, such as pharmaceutical drugs, pesticides and food additives, must gain approval before they can be marketed. In these cases it is initially assumed that the activity in question or the product may be hazardous or environmentally damaging, and the burden of proof has been shifted to the developer or manufacturer, who needs to produce scientific evidence that the activity or product is safe in order to get approval (see table 3.1). Although we say the burden of 'proof' has been shifted, proof is not actually required, just a convincing case – supported by scientific evidence – that the activity or product is safe.

Table 3.1 Shifting burden of proof

Before precautionary principle	Precautionary principle
People exposed to risky actions must bear the risks of such actions until it can be demonstrated that they cause harm to health or the environment.	People exposed to risk can ask for precautionary actions to be taken before risky actions can be proven to cause harm.
The people exposed to risk bear the responsibility for demonstrating that actions caused harm.	Once some preliminary basis for taking precautionary action exists, risk creators bear the responsibility of showing that actions are safe, or at least acceptably risky.

Adapted from (CPR 2005b)

This shifting of the burden of proof from one party to another, for example from the regulatory authority to the polluter, is only one element of the precautionary principle. However, the fact that those proposing an activity have to show it is safe before it is approved – rather than the government needing to show it is unsafe before it can be restricted – is an important aspect of the precautionary principle.

In practice, the burden of proof has been shifted for new products and activities only where there is a long history of harm arising from like products and activities. Existing products are generally 'presumed safe'. This bias is based partly on the assumption that it is cheaper and more politically acceptable to prevent new products being manufactured than it is to ban existing products, and partly on the assumption that it is easier to prevent new developments than dismantle existing ones. Similarly, synthetic substances may require licences but natural substances are assumed safe, even if they are added in unnatural quantities to the environment (Bodansky 1994: 212–3).

Those proposing new environmental regulations often still have the burden of making a watertight scientific case that the regulations are necessary to protect human health or the environment. This gives opponents the opportunity to undermine the justification for such regulations by emphasising the uncertainties in their scientific evidence.

What the precautionary principle does is ease the standard of proof, so that scientific evidence of *possible* harm is sufficient to prompt regulatory action. The assumption that an activity or product is safe until proven harmful shifts, so that it can be considered harmful before that proof is available. It is no longer sufficient to raise doubts about whether the harm will happen to prevent an activity or product from being regulated. In this way the balance between environment and economic development is shifted a little more towards environmental protection: 'previously the polluter benefited from scientific doubt; henceforth doubt will work to the benefit of the environment' (de Sadeleer 2002: 203).

NATURE OF THE PRECAUTIONARY PRINCIPLE

Wisdom

Roberto Andorno (2004: 11–12) points out that the precautionary principle is based on the classical virtue of prudence, where prudence means the 'ability to discern the most suitable course of action'. Prudence therefore represents 'practical wisdom' rather than risk aversion or lack of courage. It embraces the folk wisdom of 'better safe than sorry', 'look before you leap', 'a stitch in time saves nine', and the commonsense idea that if you are about to try something new, it is best to consider whether it is safe and not to go ahead until you can be reasonably confident that it is, particularly if the consequences of the action could conceivably lead to some disastrous outcome.

In the case of the precautionary principle, it is not only a matter of considering consequences for the individual or the action taker, but considering also the broader consequences for the planet and for future generations. It says that if the environmental consequences could be serious we should be cautious. In this way the precautionary principle is a form of 'planetary wisdom'. It is antithetical to a 'wait and see' approach, where policy makers wait till they have more information before acting.

Merits of postponement

Economists argue that in some circumstances it may be preferable to postpone acting on a problem, and incur the costs of fixing it up later, because:

- future costs are perceived to be less burdensome than current costs.
- if good scientific research accompanies the delay, the extra information might enable the problem to be solved in a cheaper and more effective way (Pearce et al. 1989).

Postponing action might not be the best decision, however, because it may cost considerably more to solve a problem in the future than it does to solve it now. In fact, if the damage done in the ensuing time is irreversible, the problem may not be able to be solved at all. Moreover, it is not fair (morally justifiable) to pass environmental risks on to future generations with the assumption that they will have the knowledge and/or technology to deal with them.

Thus, while the cost of precaution may be high and it may be possible to come up with more cost-effective solutions later, 'a society committed to sustainable development will shift the focus of its environmental policy towards an anticipatory stance, especially as reactive policy risks shifting the burden of environmental risks to future generations' (Pearce et al. 1989: 19).

Critics

The precautionary principle remains controversial in the USA, where corporate interests have succeeded in spreading confusion about what it means and what it implies. Opponents argue that the precautionary principle is unscientific; that it can be triggered by irrational concerns; that it aims at an unrealistic goal of zero risk; and that it will result in the banning of useful chemicals and the prevention of technological innovation. Excessive caution, it is argued, leads to paralysis and stagnation.

In fact, as this chapter will show, the precautionary principle cannot be applied without scientific evidence of harm. The Canadian government (Environment Canada 2001) points out that 'sound scientific information and its evaluation must be the basis' for applying the precautionary principle and that, in deciding whether scientific evidence is sound, 'decision makers should give particular weight ... to peer-reviewed science'.

Nor does the precautionary principle aim to reduce risk to zero – it aims to avoid or mitigate likely harm. The measures to be adopted to achieve this are not dictated by the precautionary principle and there is no requirement on the part of the precautionary principle to ban anything, although decision makers may conclude that a ban is appropriate in certain circumstances. The precautionary principle is not a 'decision-making algorithm' telling managers how to choose between pre-existing solutions, it is a guide as to when precaution needs to be exercised and to the criteria that should be used to evaluate measures adopted (Andorno 2004: 16).

The precautionary principle does not conflict with technological innovation, but requires a new approach – an approach that 'encourages the exploration of *alternative modes of development* that are compatible with a good quality of life for present and future generations'. It calls for 'greater imaginative effort in the development of safer and cleaner technologies'. What the precautionary principle does do is redirect innovation in more humane and environmentally sound directions (Andorno 2004: 16).

How it works

The precautionary principle has two parts:

(i) The political decision whether to act, which requires:
- identification of potential adverse effects that threaten the desired level of protection now or in the future, when
- these adverse effects are caused or exacerbated by human activity, and
- scientific evaluation of such effects shows they are plausible and highly probable, and
- the exact risk cannot be determined because of scientific uncertainty, and
- postponing action will make effective action more difficult later on.

(ii) The measures to be taken if action is decided upon.

THREAT TO DESIRED LEVEL OF PROTECTION

Political judgment

All human activity has some impact on the environment. The question is: What is an acceptable impact and what impacts need to be prevented or mitigated? Clearly this is a political question that requires broad community participation rather than a scientific question, given that the scientific evidence is inconclusive and the question of acceptability is a value judgment.

Definitions of the precautionary principle restrict precautionary measures to situations where the potential harm is 'serious and irreversible' or 'unacceptable' or 'transgenerational' or 'global' or 'significant', as in 'significant reduction in biological diversity'. But most of these terms cannot be quantified scientifically or economically (de Sadeleer 2002: 163–5). For this reason the judgment should be made by a wide cross-section of the community, not by just a few experts.

'Judging what is an "acceptable" level of risk for society is an eminently political responsibility' (EC 2000a: 4). This is recognised by the EC (2000a: 8) definition of the precautionary principle, which states:

> The precautionary principle applies where scientific evidence is insufficient, inconclusive or uncertain and preliminary scientific evaluation indicates that there are reasonable grounds for concern that the potentially dangerous effects on the environment, human, animal or plant health may be inconsistent with the high level of protection *chosen by the EU* [emphasis added].

According to the World Trade Organization (WTO), each nation should be able to decide for itself the level of environmental and health protection which is appropriate, even if this means that in applying the precautionary principle it adopts a level of protection that is higher than required by international standards and guidelines (cited in EC 2000a: 11).

Threats not only to present generations but to future generations must be considered:

> It is not the existence of risk in itself that is the challenge, but the distribution of risk and control of it. The fact that a society accepts certain risks, is not the same as accepting all sorts of risk. The risk must be within certain ethically acceptable limits, and these must be the objects of political processes of decision. The risk should be distributed equitably without reinforcing already existing dissimilarities in a society. (NENT 1998: 12)

Scientific judgments

Uncertainty may not only relate to the probability of a serious event occurring; it may also relate to how serious the consequences might be. For example, there is a general scientific consensus that global warming will occur if greenhouse gas emissions are not reduced, but the consequences of this are uncertain. There is no scientific consensus about the scope or rapidity of sea level rise or its consequences. There is even less consensus about the impacts in particular parts of the world (de Sadeleer 2002: 162).

Even if the potential consequences could be determined, their significance will vary from person to person depending on, amongst other things, how they themselves will be affected; how resilient they believe nature to be; and how important environmental values are to them. Judgments about whether potential harm will be serious and irreversible will also vary between scientists, because such judgments include issues of the value of the area or species under threat, and of the time-span for reversibility to be considered feasible.

The impact of a particular activity or product may be small on its own but the impact of many such products and activities has also to be considered, both in terms of their cumulative impact and also the way various impacts interrelate. What may begin as a small impact may contribute to a major disturbance:

> Economists call this phenomenon the 'tyranny of small decisions' because of the perverse effects that may result from a large number of micro-decisions that individually have no importance for environmental protection but which, taken together, give rise to considerable damage. (de Sadeleer 2002: 164)

Guidelines

Adrian Deville and Ronnie Harding (1997: 26) suggest the following types of threats are widely regarded as serious or undesirable:

- Loss of species
- Loss of biodiversity (including species, genetic and ecosystem diversity)
- Damage to ecological processes
- Contamination of soils, water bodies and food chains
- Introduction of 'exotic' organisms to ecosystems
- Releases of 'new' chemicals.

'Irreversibility' is another term often used to decide if the precautionary principle should be triggered. It 'is usually defined as involving environmental resources that cannot be replaced, or which could be restored, but only in the long term or at great expense' (Dovers & Handmer 1999: 172). Whether the potential harm is reversible or not may be uncertain or disputed, and the issue of whether it can be reversed in the short term at a reasonable cost is a value-laden judgment.

Irreversibility may not be seen as a bad thing if that which cannot be reversed is not thought to be important. The loss of a particular insect, although irreversible, may not seem to be particularly serious, particularly if the activity that will result in its loss brings many benefits with it. For this reason many definitions specify that damage should be 'serious *and* irreversible' to trigger the precautionary principle. However, serious damage, such as an oil spill, may be reversible, but not before a great deal of harm is done, so some definitions specify that harm should be either 'serious *or* irreversible'.

One thing that should be noted is the lopsided nature of reversibility with respect to policy decisions. The decision to conserve an area and not go ahead with a development can usually be reversed at a later date. However, the decision to go ahead with a development is usually irreversible once the development takes place.

The Louisville Charter for Safer Chemicals (Myers et al. 2005: 4) outlines conditions for application of the precautionary principle with respect to chemicals:

1. Credible evidence that a synthetic chemical can cause biological changes that are known to result in unintended harmful outcomes in some cases.

2. The presence of such a chemical where it does not belong and where it can cause damage to biological systems (such as human bodies).

SCIENTIFIC UNCERTAINTY

If the impact of a particular activity is well known, that is, there is widespread scientific agreement about it, and the likelihood of its occurring is known with some confidence, the precautionary principle is not relevant. However, preventative measures may still be necessary. 'The more uncertain the threat, the greater the degree of precaution required' (Deville & Harding 1997: 34–7).

In the area of environmental policy, decisions often have to be made before scientific experts are 'able to present unambiguous and scientifically well-founded recommendations' (NENT 1998: 59). Scientists are usually unable to tell policy makers exactly where and how far a pollutant will spread, how it will interact with other pollutants, and how it will affect the health of people and the functioning of ecosystems.

Types of uncertainty

Steven Yearley (1991: 129–31), a British social scientist, identifies four different reasons why scientists face uncertainties when dealing with environmental problems.

Pragmatic uncertainty

Scientists are often asked to make recommendations when they do not have enough time or funds to investigate the answers fully. The available research may be of poor quality or not immediately applicable to the situation at hand. Pragmatic uncertainty arises from:

- Lack of data
- Doubts about accuracy of data
- Doubts about relevance of data.

Theoretical uncertainty

Ecological science is less developed than other sciences; consequently, there is less agreement than in other scientific disciplines, and more variety of interpretations of data and findings. Theoretical uncertainty arises from:

- Disagreements over interpretation of data
- Disagreements over scientific methodology
- Lack of knowledge about causal connections
- Doubts over knowledge framework – epistemological uncertainty.

Complexity in open systems

Uncertainty arises from 'the sheer complexity of large-scale phenomena taking place in open systems'. Nature is less knowable and less predictable than complex systems, such as nuclear power plants, that are created and controlled by humans. Complexity arises from:

- Variability of ecological processes
- Indeterminacy (explained on the next page).

Intangible damage

Environmental damage may not be easily observable and therefore may be difficult to monitor and understand. For example, depletion of the ozone layer can only be measured by high-technology equipment and would previously have been extremely difficult to predict.

A lack of data can result from a lack of past studies. Thousands of chemicals used commercially have not been tested for their ability to bioaccumulate in the food chain or for their toxicity to a whole variety of organisms because the cost seems to be prohibitive. Scientists try to fill gaps in knowledge by extrapolating from what they do know and estimating probabilities based on past experiences and observations (MacGarvin 1994). This can be done with computer modelling.

However, where processes are not known or understood, computer modelling may not be of much use because the relationships between various parameters, such as what happens to plankton when surface temperatures change, is unknown and may not change in a linear or predictable fashion (O'Riordan & Cameron 1994: 64). Even if the impacts of individual chemicals were known, their synergistic impact, that is, the effect of two or more chemicals interacting in the environment, would be difficult to predict.

Moreover, scientists lack full knowledge of the 'ecological interactions that maintain ecosystems'. A particular species may play a key role in maintaining the health of an ecosystem, yet because it appears to play a relatively minor role, remains unstudied. Marine ecologists, for example, study organisms that bioaccumulate contaminants in a way that can be easily measured, and study commercial fish species which need to be monitored for human health reasons. Yet there is no reason to suppose that these are the species that are vital to the ecosystem, or whose health is a good indicator of the health of the ecosystem. This means that it is 'unreasonable to expect that we can predict the effect of human actions upon marine ecosystems with any accuracy' (MacGarvin 1994).

Even when harm is beginning to occur it may not be self-evident because:

- the first signs of damage are not outside the bounds of normal variation in individuals or populations
- the first effects are not recognised to be harmful
- changes may be followed by a long time period before the consequences become evident
- the harm that is caused may be attributed to a number of causes (Myers et al. 2005: 2).

Ignorance and indeterminacy

In a situation where change happens chaotically, or where relationships are unstable and subject to sudden dramatic change, the situation is indeterminate and traditional scientific methods have little to offer in terms of assessment (MacGarvin 1994: 65). 'If we cannot determine the accuracy of the scientific and social assumptions on which our assessment of risk is based, this is referred to as "indeterminacy".' For example, we may not know whether the questions that scientists are asking are the right ones, or be unable to understand the social context of an activity that may impact an environment because of political instability in the region (Deville & Harding 1997: 35).

The idea that more research will resolve uncertainties is not necessarily true. Further research may only serve to increase the uncertainties by raising more issues and questions. The ultimate uncertainty is 'ignorance', where we are completely unaware of possible threats (Deville & Harding 1997: 31). The relationship between uncertainty, indeterminacy and ignorance is shown in figure 3.1.

Figure 3.1 Levels of uncertainty

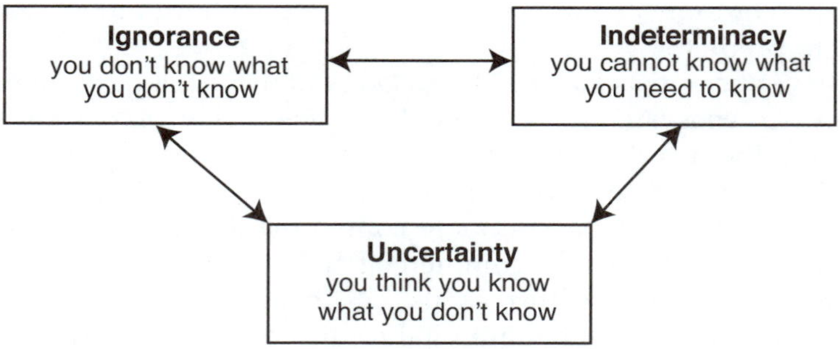

Source (Deville & Harding 1997: 34)

Jerry Ravetz (1986) argues that in dealing with environmental problems, policies must be made, despite uncertain facts and disputed values, on issues for which the stakes are high and about which decisions are urgently needed. In other areas, researchers are able to choose problems that are likely to be solvable, but in policy-related areas they are faced with problems that are imposed by external forces, such as public need. Because of this, researchers are often forced to work in areas of knowledge that are poorly developed, and for which they lack adequate information. The reduction of uncertainties can be extremely difficult. Ravetz argues that in such situations it can be disastrous not to be aware of our ignorance. Decisions need to be iterative and closely monitored so that they can be altered as new information comes to hand.

Alvin Weinberg (1986) also addresses the problem that policy makers face given such substantial uncertainties. He points out that science is best able to make predictions when it is dealing with things that happen regularly or often. When something is rare, or a one-off event, science loses its predictive power; it can only hope to explain what happened after the event. Policy makers have to deal with two types of non-routine events: one is the accident, and the other is the discovery of a chronic, low-level exposure to a chemical or radiation that might affect a few individuals in every thousand or one hundred thousand. Attempting to make predictions in such situations is labelled by Weinberg as 'trans-science'. He says that 'regulators, instead of asking science for answers to unanswerable questions, ought to be content with less far-reaching answers'.

Political uses of uncertainty

Scientific uncertainty is used by both sides in any environmental controversy as an opportunity to 'win'. Scientific uncertainties seem to increase with the increasing relevance of the science to the policy decision, because those with vested interests in the outcomes of the decision-making frequently seek an advantage by highlighting those uncertainties.

In a study of the politics of regulation in Europe and the USA, for example, Ronald Brickman and his colleagues (1985: 187) concluded that scientific uncertainties 'make it possible for proponents and opponents of regulation to interpret the scientific basis for cancer risk assessment in ways that advance their particular policy objectives'. There is no scientific way to *know* whether a substance will cause cancer in humans without testing it on humans – which would be unethical. Scientists disagree over how chemicals should be tested and how the results of those tests should be interpreted. The tests that are used include short-term tests for mutagenic (cell-mutating) activity; high-dose tests on animals such as mice; and studies of humans who have been accidentally exposed to the substances.

Brickman and his colleagues (1985: 197) found that the consequences that should follow from a positive test were disputed:

> Some environmentalists resolutely maintained that positive evidence from one or more short-term tests should trigger regulation, even without convincing support from other sources. At the other extreme, some witnesses for industry argued that no significance should be attached to these tests until they are more thoroughly validated.

Using animal tests to determine whether a substance is carcinogenic (cancer causing) in humans is equally controversial, and not only for ethical reasons. There are also disagreements over such things as how experiments should be designed and whether tumours induced at high doses in animals are relevant to the exposure of humans to low doses of the same chemical.

The regulator is forced to make a decision even though there is scientific uncertainty and debate. He or she is often faced with the situation that a product which has high social or economic benefits has shown some indications of being carcinogenic. On the other hand, the costs of not limiting a chemical might be even greater in terms of human health and environmental damage than the benefits of leaving it freely on the market. A regulator generally does not have the luxury of waiting around until more compelling evidence comes in. Not acting on the given information is just as much a decision as acting.

National differences

Regulators react to this dilemma differently in different countries. In the USA in the past, the EPA has been far more ready to regulate on the basis of experiments done in the laboratory than are the equivalent authorities in France and Germany. German regulators do not automatically view substances that cause cancer in animals as being a threat to humans. British regulators also require much more 'proof' than do US regulators. An example is the case of the pesticides aldrin and dieldrin, which were banned in the USA but not in Britain or Australia, although the same data was available to regulators in all three countries (Gillespie et al. 1982).

The US regulators have also taken a more precautionary approach when it comes to the question of threshold effects. US regulators do not assume that there is a certain level – a threshold – below which a chemical has no effect. Australian and British regulators are far more willing to accept the idea of threshold levels. A US interagency agreement states that because threshold doses that cause cancer have not been established, 'a prudent approach from a safety standpoint is to assume that any dose may induce or promote carcinogenesis'. This stance was condemned by industry, the courts and sections of the public as being 'unduly restrictive and insensitive to socioeconomic costs' (quoted in Brickman et al. 1985: 208–10). In contrast, the British insistence that scientific evidence must support the existence of thresholds has been met with fierce union opposition in the area of occupational health and safety.

Even in the USA, laboratory evidence that a chemical causes cancer is not always enough to result in the banning of that chemical. For example, 2,4,5-T (the active chemical in some herbicides) received only a partial ban after there was evidence that human foetuses had been adversely affected by it.

How much evidence?

Where, between the extremes of speculation and the unattainable full scientific certainty, is the point where there is sufficient knowledge to act? How much evidence does there need to be before the precautionary principle is triggered? If no evidence were required, then any non-scientific speculation or irrational fear would be enough to require precautionary measures and the principle would become impractical. On the other hand, scientific proof would render the precautionary principle unnecessary.

Most definitions of the precautionary principle try to define the level of evidence in terms of 'reasonable grounds for concern' or 'reasonable scientific plausibility' or 'scientific credibility' or require decisions to be made 'on the basis of available pertinent information' (de Sadeleer 2002: 159–60).

David Resnik (2003: 329–44) has summarised a number of criteria that could be used to assess the scientific plausibility of a hypothesis:

> *Coherence.* The hypothesis should be consistent with and supported by our background knowledge and theories. If a hypothesis requires us to reject widely accepted scientific theories and facts, then it is not plausible.
>
> *Explanatory power.* The hypothesis should be able to explain important facts and phenomena. Hypotheses that have no explanatory power are less plausible.
>
> *Analogy.* The hypothesis should posit causal mechanisms or processes that are similar to other well-understood mechanisms and processes. A hypothesis that posits radically new and unfamiliar mechanisms and processes lacks plausibility.
>
> *Precedence.* Events posited by the hypothesis should be similar to previously observed events, which set an historical precedent for the hypothesis.
>
> *Precision.* The hypothesis should be reasonably precise. Although there are limits to precision in science, a hopelessly vague hypothesis should not be regarded as plausible.
>
> *Simplicity.* The hypothesis should be parsimonious. Recondite and complex hypotheses are not as plausible as parsimonious ones.

However, this leaves aside the question of ignorance. If the impacts of a new chemical, for example, are unknown and there is no reasonable scientifically credible case to say whether or not it will cause harm, should the chemical be approved for release? Policy makers have to deal with situations of ignorance as well as uncertainty.

MEASURES TO BE TAKEN

Weak version

Measures to be taken in response to the precautionary principle being triggered are not dictated by the precautionary principle. Some definitions of the precautionary principle do not stipulate the need for any measures to be taken at all. For example, the Rio Declaration's definition states that 'lack of full scientific certainty shall not be used as a reason for postponing cost-effective measures to prevent environmental degradation'. This does not preclude other reasons for postponing or avoiding such measures:

> There is nothing in this version of the precautionary principle which requires decision-makers to give overriding, primary, or even substantial weight to loss of biodiversity, as compared to social and economic factors, when deciding how to proceed. (Farrier 1999: 108)

The view that action should be avoided if the benefits of inaction are greater than the costs assumes, firstly, that costs can be measured despite the uncertainty surrounding them, and secondly, that there is only one way of achieving the benefits and that environmental sacrifices are necessary to achieve them. This is the view economists often take. For example, David Pearce (1994: 144–5) says:

> Put another way, no significant deterioration of the environment should occur unless the benefits associated with that deterioration heavily outweigh the costs of the deterioration ... Clearly, the adoption of the precautionary principle can be expensive. If the benefits foregone are substantial and new information reveals that the measure turns out not to have been warranted, then there will be a high net cost to precaution ... This suggests that some balancing of costs and benefits still must play a role even in contexts where the precautionary principle is thought to apply.

Strong version

A stronger version of the precautionary principle dictates that positive action must be taken to avoid or mitigate the potential harm. In this view, if the harm is judged unacceptable or serious and irreversible, then inaction is not precautionary and is not compatible with the precautionary principle. 'Interventions are required before possible harm occurs, or before certainty about such harm can be achieved' (COMEST 2005: 8).

Monitoring impacts or undertaking further research is merely a way of delaying intervention until more is known (in other words, 'wait and see') and thus is not a precautionary approach.

The Wingspread Statement on the Precautionary Principle (1998) clearly mandates precautionary measures and is therefore a strong version of the precautionary principle: 'When an activity raises threats of harm to human health or the environment, precautionary measures should be taken even if cause and effect relationships are not fully established scientifically ...'

The strong approach assumes that environmental protection is a priority and that other less environmentally damaging ways can be found to achieve the economic benefits which the proposed action would have brought. Nevertheless, even in the stronger version of the precautionary principle, the action that should be taken is not determined by the principle. In only a few rare cases is the precautionary principle defined in a way that dictates measures. For example, the Oslo Commission of 1989 agreed that the dumping of industrial wastes, 'except for inert materials of natural origin', into the North Sea should cease; that it should be allowed only where it could be shown that there were no practical alternatives and it would cause no harm to the marine environment (cited in Harding & Fisher 1999: 305).

Criteria for measures

In most cases, however, the measures to be taken have to be decided and again this is a political decision that should involve the broad community. Measures can either 'constrain the possibility of the harm' or 'contain the harm', should it occur, by limiting its scope or controlling it (COMEST 2005: 8).

According to the EC (2000a: 18–20), measures taken in response to the precautionary principle should be proportional, non-discriminatory, consistent, beneficial, and provisional.

Proportional

Proportionality means that measures adopted should be proportionate to the level of protection required and that aiming at zero risk is not only unfeasible but an overreaction. Similarly, a total ban on a product or process may be more than is required in the situation. It may be that mitigating or reducing the potential harm through reducing exposure pathways or limiting the use of a product may be sufficient to ensure that adequate protection levels are maintained.

Trying to reduce the last 4 per cent of pollution may be excessively expensive and the costs out of proportion to the harm that this last 4 per cent poses. The money might be better spent on other areas of environmental improvement.

Non-discriminatory

Measures should not differ according to the geographical origin of a product or any other extraneous factors. Comparable products or processes should be subject to similar measures.

Consistent

Measures taken should be consistent with, and utilise a similar approach to, measures taken in similar circumstances in the past. In particular, measures taken in response to the precautionary principle should be consistent with measures taken where products or processes have a similar level of harm but where there is less uncertainty.

Beneficial

When deciding measures to be taken the advantages and disadvantages of the measures to be taken should be considered, and compared with the advantages and disadvantages of not taking action, to ensure that some net benefit will result. Advantages and disadvantages include, but are not reduced to, economic costs and benefits.

Provisional

The measures taken should be reviewed periodically so that consideration can be given to relevant new scientific information which may change the assessment of potential harm. There should also be ongoing scientific studies aimed at reducing the uncertainties involved.

LEGISLATION

The use of precaution has a long history. One can argue that John Snow was exercising precaution when he removed the handle from a London water pump in 1854 because he suspected that the water was causing people to be infected with cholera. The causal link between cholera and contaminated water was not understood at that time but the measure succeeded in saving many lives (Harramoës et al. 2001).

International agreements

The precautionary principle achieved widespread recognition after it was incorporated into the Declaration on Environment and Development decided at the 1992 UN Conference on Environment and Development (UNCED) in Rio de Janeiro. The Rio Declaration states, in principle 15:

> In order to protect the environment, the precautionary approach shall be widely applied by States according to their capability. Where there are threats of serious or irreversible damage, lack of full scientific certainty shall not be used as a reason for postponing cost-effective measures to prevent environmental degradation.

In 1993 the Treaty of Maastricht required European Community countries and the European Commission to base environmental policy on the precautionary principle. In 1999 the Council of the European Commission (EC 2000a: 8, 13) urged the Commission to ensure that future legislation and policies were guided by the precautionary principle so that the principle becomes 'a central plank of Community policy'.

The precautionary principle has been incorporated into many international laws and almost all recent international treaties that aim to protect the environment. These include:

- 1992 UN Framework Convention on Climate Change
- 1987 Montreal Protocol on Substances that Deplete the Ozone Layer
- 1992 UN Convention on Biological Diversity
- 2001 Stockholm Convention on Persistent Organic Pollutants (POPs).

In this way, according to the EC (2000a: 11), 'it has become a full-fledged and general principle of international law'. While international courts are still reluctant to accept it as a legal or a general principle, it is, however, widely accepted as a principle with similar standing to that of sustainable development (Andorno 2004: 15–6; Cameron 1999: 30; de Sadeleer 2002: 100).

National legislation

The precautionary principle has been incorporated into national laws in several countries, including Germany, Belgium and Sweden, and has influenced several court judgments. In France it has even been included in the nation's constitution, as part of an environmental charter (see chapter 5). This gives the principle priority over other legislation (Case 2005; de Sadeleer 2002: 124–37).

The legal system in English-speaking countries is less conducive to the incorporation of broad principles as it tends to be based on specific rules and regulations. In the United Kingdom, for example, the precautionary principle is not included in statutory law, nor has it made much headway in the courts. It has been included in a weak form in discussion papers and government policy statements such as the 1990 White Paper *This Common Inheritance* and the 1999 *A Better Quality of Life* (de Sadeleer 2002: 138; Sustainable Development Unit 1999). The updated UK sustainable development strategy published in 2005, *Securing the Future* (2005: 101), states:

> There are, however, still instances where decisions on managing natural resources will have to be taken on the basis of partial information. In these instances, and where, firstly, there is a risk of significant adverse environmental effects occurring and secondly, any

> possible mitigation measures seem unlikely to safeguard against these effects, the precautionary principle will be adopted. Where evidence exists of likely harm to ecosystems or biodiversity, we will adopt practices that avoid irreversible damage.

In the USA the term 'precautionary approach' is preferred but there, as in the United Kingdom, broad statements of principle are not generally found in environmental law. It has been argued that although US environmental and health laws do not refer to the precautionary principle or approach by name, some of the earlier environmental legislation nevertheless adopted it. This has changed in recent years as politicians, under pressure from corporate donors, have demanded all environmental legislation be grounded in scientific rigour and subjected to cost–benefit analysis and risk assessment (Bodansky 1994; de Sadeleer 2002: 139–47).

During the 1970s various court decisions supported the need for the US EPA to take action to prevent harm when cause and effect was unproven and therefore harm was uncertain. For example:

- In 1978 the Minnesota Supreme Court ruled that the EPA could apply standards under the Clean Water Act (CWA) that assumed asbestos in drinking water was harmful, even though they did not have scientific evidence to demonstrate it was.
- In another court case, the EPA was allowed to set tough air emission standards for some chemicals under the Clean Air Act (CAA) based on extrapolation from other chemicals about which more was known.
- In 1978 the Supreme Court found that action that threatened an endangered species should be prohibited, under the Endangered Species Act (ESA), even though the long-term value of that species was unknown (de Sadeleer 2002: 141–45).

In the 1980s, when ozone depletion was put forward as an unproven scientific theory, the United Kingdom decided not to regulate until the theory had been validated but the US government took a precautionary approach and restricted chlorofluorocarbons (CFCs) which were thought to cause ozone depletion (de Sadeleer 2002: 154).

In Australia, the precautionary principle was incorporated in the Intergovernmental Agreement on the Environment (IGAE) in 1992 as one of four guiding principles. The agreement does not have the force of law but provides guidelines for environmental policy-making at the various levels of government throughout Australia. The precautionary principle was also included in the National Strategy for Ecologically Sustainable Development in 1992 (Deville & Harding 1997: 17; Fisher 1999: 83). It has been incorporated in more than 18 laws as well, including:

- *Protection of the Environment Administration Act* 1991 (NSW)
- *Environmental Protection Act* 1993 (SA)
- *National Environmental Protection Council Act* 1994 (Commonwealth)
- *Environmental Protection Act* 1994 (Qld)
- *Environmental Management and Pollution Control Act* 1994 (Tas)

Several Australian court cases have also considered the precautionary principle, defining it as a 'duty to be cautious' (Fisher 1999: 83).

Further Reading

Andorno, Roberto (2004) The precautionary principle: a new legal standard for the technological age, *Journal of International Biotechnology Law* (1), pp 11–19.

COMEST (2005) The precautionary principle, World Commission on the Ethics of Scientific Knowledge and Technology, UNESCO, Paris, March, <unesdoc.unesco.org/images/0013/001395/139578e.pdf>

Deville, Adrian & Ronnie Harding (1997) *Applying the Precautionary Principle*, The Federation Press, Sydney.

Harding, Ronnie & Elizabeth Fisher (eds) (1999) *Perspectives on the Precautionary Principle*, The Federation Press, Sydney.

O'Riordan, T & J Cameron (eds) (1994) *Interpreting the Precautionary Principle*, Earthscan, London.

de Sadeleer, Nicolas (2002) *Environmental Principles: From Political Slogans to Legal Rules*, Oxford University Press, Oxford.

PART II

SOCIAL PRINCIPLES AND ENVIRONMENTAL PROTECTION

4

THE EQUITY PRINCIPLE

Equity implies a need for fairness in the distribution of gains and losses, and the entitlement of everyone to an acceptable quality and standard of living. Equity is not the same as equality, for there may be good reasons for people to have different rewards and burdens or to be treated differently. Equity requires, however, that these reasons be morally relevant, that is, that they be just, fair and impartial. Impartiality means that factors such as race, religion, colour, gender or nationality are not relevant. Justice is about how rewards and burdens are distributed.

Equity can have three aspects:

- People have certain rights that must be respected.
- People get what they deserve – fairness.
- People's needs should be met and their contribution to meeting such needs is based on their ability to do so (Low & Gleeson 1998: 49).

This means that the distribution of rewards and burdens may be deserved on the basis of a person's efforts, choices and abilities, but those rewards and burdens should not be out of proportion to the actions or qualities of that person. It also means that there should be limits to the burdens that individuals are subject to and that their basic needs should be met no matter what their abilities. Each person has a right to life, health and the basic conditions of subsistence, as well as certain political and social rights (which are covered in chapter 5).

Jim Falk and his colleagues (1993: 2) describe equity this way:

> Equity derives from a concept of social justice. It represents a belief that there are some things which people should have, that there are basic needs that should be fulfilled, that burdens and rewards should

> not be spread too divergently across the community, and that policy should be directed with impartiality, fairness and justice towards these ends.

In its narrowest terms, equity means that there should be a minimum level of income and environmental quality below which nobody falls. Within a community it usually also means that everyone should have equal access to community resources and opportunities, and that no individuals or groups of people should be asked to carry a greater environmental burden than the rest of the community as a result of government or business actions.

Equity as a concept is fundamental to sustainable development. The Brundtland Commission's definition of sustainable development is based on intergenerational equity: 'development that meets the needs of the present without compromising the ability of future generations to meet their own needs' (WCED 1990: 87). Equity can be applied across communities and nations, and across generations. The Commission insisted not only on intergenerational equity but also on equity within existing generations. It argued:

> Poverty is not only an evil in itself, but sustainable development requires meeting the basic needs of all and extending to all the opportunity to fulfil their aspirations for a better life ... Meeting essential needs requires not only a new era of economic growth for nations in which the majority are poor, but an assurance that those poor get their fair share of the resources required to sustain that growth (WCED 1990: 8).

INTRAGENERATIONAL EQUITY

Intragenerational equity is concerned with equity between people of the same generation. It covers justice and the distribution of resources between nations. It also includes considerations of what is fair for people within any one nation.

Proximity to existing environmental problems

Worldwide, people living in cities tend to be most affected by pollution, noise and the threats of chemical contamination and accident, although pollution and exposure to agricultural pesticides can be a problem in some rural areas. Urban problems arise from the concentration of industries, people and cars, and the lack of open green spaces.

The impacts of environmental problems are not evenly distributed within cities. They are often determined by where people live. People living near or in industrial areas are more likely to suffer from air or water pollution. People living under a flight path or near a main road are more likely to suffer from noise. People in the inner city are more likely to suffer from urban decay and traffic problems. People living in the outer suburbs are more likely to suffer from lack of provision of urban infrastructure and community facilities.

Poverty

Poorer people tend to suffer the burden of existing environmental problems more than others do. This is because more affluent people have greater choice about where they live: they can afford to pay more to live in areas where the environment has not been degraded. Wealthy areas are more likely to have access to environmental amenities such as parks and protected waterways. More affluent people are also better able to fight the imposition of a polluting facility in their neighbourhood because they have better access to financial resources, education, skills and the decision-making structures.

This is particularly obvious in some countries where shantytowns are found. These are generally located in areas where the better off do not want to live – near garbage dumps or hazardous industrial facilities or in areas prone to flooding, landslips and other dangers. This situation is not confined to low-income countries, however. In the United Kingdom, too, 'low-income communities are twice as likely to have a polluting factory located nearby' (Bachram et al. 2003: 4). A Friends of the Earth study (McLaren et al. 1999) found:

> Over ninety per cent of London's most polluting factories are located in communities of below average income. London is just the most extreme example. A similar pattern is found throughout England and Wales. Overall, almost two-thirds of the most polluting industrial facilities are to be found in areas of below average income ...
>
> The effects are more severe in areas with multiple factories. At the extreme, Seal Sands on Teesside has 17 of the most polluting factories in one small area. The average income here is just £6,200 (just 45% of the regional average income, or 36% of the national average) and over half its households have annual incomes under £5,000.

Vulnerability

Health impacts from environmental problems can also be determined by factors such as age, gender, income and health status. For example, people with existing respiratory problems may be affected more by air pollution, while the very young or the very old may be more vulnerable to environmental pollution in general. There are places in metropolitan Adelaide in South Australia where deaths from respiratory diseases seem to be correlated with failure to meet air quality standards and where 'overlaying the map of factory emissions onto the distribution of clients of Meals on Wheels [a charity service for frail, aged and disabled people] shows that there is a captive population which cannot easily move away from close proximity to potentially toxic emissions' (Falk et al. 1993: 54).

Often the assessments of what is safe are based on consideration of average people of average health with 'normal' lifestyles. Environmental standards are often based on these averages and norms, which leaves those who vary from the norm more vulnerable. For example, people who eat higher than normal amounts of fish are more vulnerable to the effects of mercury and other fish contaminants. Similarly, those who are less than the average weight, particularly children, are more vulnerable to pesticides and other risks (Ackerman & Heinzerling 2004: 143).

Children are also more vulnerable to exposure to pollution and contamination because of their developmental stage:

> In general, children are more vulnerable to environmental hazards than adults. Infants and children breathe, eat, and drink more than adults per unit of body weight. Their organ systems change and develop rapidly, making them vulnerable to small exposures at crucial windows of development. Children's detoxification mechanisms are underdeveloped in some ways compared with those of adults, making them more susceptible than adults to injury from toxic exposures. Children are disproportionately exposed to some hazards because they engage in normal childhood behaviors such as playing on the ground and putting objects in their mouths. (Massey & Ackerman 2003: 3)

This means that children who are exposed to toxic chemicals may have their ability to grow, learn and play impaired, as well as suffering illnesses and disabilities that may remain with them into adulthood.

Occupation

Workers in certain industries – like mining or mineral processing and the chemical industry – are often exposed to higher health risks than the rest of the community. Large proportions of the workforces in very hazardous industries are often made up of migrants who have fewer choices about their work when they first come to a country. In the USA, 7000–11 000 people die from workplace injuries and accidents annually, and another 62 000–86 000 die from diseases like cancer caused by work-related exposure to chemicals and other pollutants (Shrader-Frechette 2002: 135).

In many countries environmental standards in workplaces are not as high as for the general environment. In developing countries, workplace standards can be almost non-existent. Kristin Shrader-Frechette (2002: 164) cites the example of a US firm that moved its asbestos facilities just across the border into Mexico, where workers are not protected by regulations. In these new facilities asbestos dust levels are not monitored, and the poorly paid workers do not wear respirators and are not told how dangerous asbestos is.

Race

In some countries ethnicity, race and colour seem to be a significant factor in determining who is exposed to environmental burdens. A US EPA study has found that 'black Americans are 79 per cent more likely than whites to live in neighbourhoods where industrial pollution is suspected of posing the greatest health danger'. In 19 states blacks were more than twice as likely to live in such neighbourhoods, and in 12 states Hispanics were more than twice as likely as non-Hispanics to live in such neighbourhoods. The neighbourhoods at risk were also the poorest, with the most unemployment (cited in Pace 2005).

There is some debate about whether minorities are deliberately discriminated against or whether they suffer these environmental burdens because polluting facilities tend to be built in poor neighbourhoods. Either way, the placement of hazardous and unhealthy facilities raises equity issues and the outcome is that minorities have a greater environmental burden. Recent studies show 'that Latinos and blacks are much more likely to develop – and die of – diseases related to pollution, like asthma' (Featherstone 2005).

Valerie Taliman (1992), a member of the Navaho nation, also used the term 'environmental racism' when she described the way that Indian reserves in the USA were being used to dispose of hazardous wastes. She claimed that in just two years more than 50 Indian tribes were approached by waste disposal companies offering millions of dollars in return for allowing hazardous waste facilities to be sited on their land. Indian reserves are not subject to as many environmental regulations as other parts of the nation.

As a result of inequities such as these, an environmental justice movement has sprung up, particularly in the USA. In 1991 various people of colour convened the First National People of Color Environmental Leadership Summit, which formulated a set of Principles of Environmental Justice (1991).

Developing countries

Inequities are also caused by the export of hazardous products and wastes to developing countries. Shrader-Frechette (2002: 10, 164–5) notes that a third of the pesticides manufactured in the USA are banned there but are exported to poor countries. They are often imported into developing countries by US-headquartered transnational companies. Imported pesticides contribute to some half a million poisonings and 40 000 deaths each year.

Similarly, although there is an international convention on trade in hazardous wastes – the Basel Convention – toxic waste from affluent nations is shipped to the Caribbean and West Africa for disposal. Poor nations in these regions are offered money in return for disposing of the waste. Although they agree to take it, there is some question as to whether citizens of those nations have given informed consent to such imports.

A study by the Basel Action Network (cited in Hopkins 2005a) has found that Africa is being used as a dumping ground for electronic waste, much of it containing toxic material. Ostensibly, obsolete televisions, computers, mobile phones and other electronic equipment are shipped there for reuse and recycling, but local experts in Lagos, Nigeria, claim that three-quarters of the equipment is junk that cannot be economically repaired or recycled. It is instead mounting up in garbage tips or being burned, posing risks to the local people.

Additionally, developing countries are often subject to more of the impacts of environmental degradation, more vulnerable to them and less able to respond and protect themselves from them. The populations of many poorer countries are more vulnerable to sea-level rise and other impacts of climate change, for example, even though they are least responsible for causing it, and less able to adapt because of poverty, lack of technology and population pressures: 'those who have been the bystanders are likely to be the victims' (Ott & Sachs 2000: 9).

If sea levels rise, low-lying island and coastal communities will suffer. Those which will probably suffer most are low-income countries. It is these nations that often have the densest populations and are least able to afford mitigation measures such as structures to hold the seawater back, or be able to relocate substantial numbers of people. Even now, the densely populated nation of Bangladesh experiences storm surges as much as 160 kilometres upriver, surges which exact a heavy toll in losses of human lives, livestock and fishing vessels. Along with Bangladesh, the nations of Egypt, Gambia, Indonesia, the Maldives, Mozambique, Pakistan, Senegal, Surinam and Thailand have been identified as being the most vulnerable to a rise in sea level. Paradoxically, these countries have contributed little to the accumulation of greenhouse gases in the atmosphere (Jacobson 1990: 88).

Inequities may cause environmental problems

Poverty contributes to environmental degradation because it deprives people of the choice of whether or not to be environmentally sound in their activities. People who cannot be sure of their next meal are likely to pour all their energies into surviving any way they can. Communities need to have a certain level of security before they will turn their attention to solving environmental problems.

Affluence, of course, also contributes to environmental degradation. High levels of affluence are accompanied by high levels of consumption, which leads to more resource depletion and waste accumulation. This is demonstrated by comparing the ecological footprints of nations (see chapter 2). Many environmental problems – such as global warming and chemical contamination – are the result of affluence rather than poverty.

In the past, environmental degradation and resource depletion in low-income countries have been rationalised as part of the necessary costs of economic growth. Citizens of these countries have been told that they would have to 'grin and bear it' while their countries industrialised. But many in those low-income countries are beginning to question this conventional argument. They argue that development does not need to be accompanied by environmental degradation. Development results in environmental degradation because of other inequities, including low prices for commodities and natural resources, trade barriers in high-income countries, a resulting reliance on resource extraction for development, and the adoption of western ways, products and technologies (Beder 1996: ch 16).

The impacts of measures to protect the environment

Measures to improve environmental problems may impact more on some sectors of the community than others.

Loss of competitiveness

Measures to protect the environment can affect the competitiveness of national industries in the international market when such actions are undertaken unilaterally, that is, without other nations also undertaking them. Loss of industry competitiveness can reduce a nation's gross national product, increase its balance of trade deficit and increase national debt. Particular groups of people may suffer more than others from loss of competitiveness, including individual firms and their workers.

The idea that environmental measures generally affect a company's competitiveness is debated, however. 'The consensus in the economics profession,' concludes Eban Goodstein, 'is that environmental regulation has had no reliably measurable negative impact on the competitiveness of U.S. firms.' In fact, the extra cost to firms of complying with environmental regulations is rarely more than 2 per cent of total sales income. Goodstein's analysis shows that in the USA at least, 'in terms of import competition from developed countries in the 1980s, firms facing higher levels of regulation fared better than those without it' (Ackerman & Massey 2002: 4; Goodstein 1997: 15; 1999: 3–4).

Loss of employment

It is often argued that if environmental laws and standards are too tough, the costs of complying will be high – which could lead to a firm having to shed staff or, in an extreme case, having to shut down. But environmental regulations to control pollution may actually create more jobs than are lost. The impact of environmental regulations on employment has been greatly exaggerated by those who oppose those regulations. Environmental regulation shifts jobs but does not tend to reduce the overall level of employment. In the USA, according to Bureau of Labor Statistics, only about 1 per cent of major layoffs have been due to environmental regulations (Ackerman & Massey 2002: 3; Goodstein 1999: 3–4).

Nevertheless, it is true that even if overall employment levels are not reduced by environmental measures, some workers may suffer by losing their jobs; and in times of high unemployment they may find it difficult to find other work. Unions are often concerned that measures taken to protect the environment might lead to a larger pool of unemployed, the downgrading of average wages and conditions and non-wage benefits, and a winding-down of towns and infrastructure in some areas:

> There will be losers as well as winners in any restructuring of our economy, regardless of whether the aggregate outcome is positive or negative. In many instances those affected will also be those with the least options in alternative employment (eg workers without tertiary or adaptable trade qualifications). (ACTU & UMFA 1992: 13)

Halting development

It is argued that important benefits and jobs are lost each time a development is stopped on environmental grounds. People in poor countries claim that demands by people in affluent countries that they conserve their forests as a global resource would require them to slow economic development. They say that affluent nations cut down their own forests as part of their development process, and consume the majority of the produce from timber-felling in developing countries, so it is inequitable to demand that their forests be conserved without offering full compensation.

On the other hand, forestry operations are often carried out at the expense of indigenous people who depend on the forests for their traditional lifestyles. 'Even the possibility of their receiving financial compensation for the destruction of their forests is an unattractive proposition for most indigenous peoples, as money is seen to be destructive of traditional lifestyles every bit as much as deforestation' (Humphreys 1999: 113).

Shrader-Frechette (2002: 31) argues that the problem with using economic development as an argument for environmental degradation is that the supposed benefits of economic development are based on dubious assumptions which are not borne out by past experience:

> One doubtful premise is that economic development, accompanied by unequal environmental standards or protection, actually creates more market value than does environmentally just economic development ... Another doubtful premise is that economic expansion, and its attendant inequitable pollution and development, will lead to greater equality of treatment in the long term.

Costs to disadvantaged groups

Another way in which measures to protect the environment can have an impact on equity is through costs being imposed on a certain section of society whose members may not be able to afford them. Also, if prices are to rise, for example as a result of the application of the polluter pays principle, those who can barely afford such goods now will suffer. Supporters of the polluter pays principle argue that to ensure equity the poor need to be compensated with extra income support rather than subsidies being provided to the polluter to keep the price down. Income support would be more efficient, since the more affluent consumers can afford to pay the higher price, and it would also ensure the price more accurately reflected the real cost of the products (Dommen 1993: 17).

In Delhi, India, which has a population of 14 million people, local groundwater and the Yamuna River have become increasingly contaminated with toxic industrial waste and pesticides. In an effort to deal with this problem the Supreme Court banned the discharge of industrial effluent into the river in 2000. That same year the government passed an act that required industry to pay half the cost of 15 new effluent treatment plants. Polluters include 'thousands of small engineering units, textile industries, detergent makers and auto-component factories', as well as factories carrying out electro-plating, battery recycling and leather tanning. While many of these concerns are operating illegally, stealing electricity and paying no taxes, their supporters claim that the extra costs to pay for the pollution control facilities will cause thousands of workers to lose their jobs (Devraj 2004).

Displacement of local people

The creation of national parks and wilderness areas can also impact unfairly on people who are displaced by those parks or whose access to traditional livelihoods is restricted as a result. In many parts of Africa, for example, national parks have been created by clearing indigenous inhabitants out of the area.

As recently as 2004, '5000 people from the Kore tribe were escorted from their thatched huts in Nechisar [in Ethiopia] and dumped onto distant land owned by other rural communities' without consultation or compensation. Locals will not even be able to walk through the newly created wildlife park to get to a nearby town (Pearce 2005c).

In Kenya, between 10 000 and 50 000 people have been forced out of their homes in an environmentally sensitive forest area on the edge of the Mau Forest. Armed police evicted them at short notice, using teargas and whips, and ignoring their claims to have title deeds to their homes, which were burned down (Cawthorne 2005).

Shifting environmental problems

Environmental measures can also have inequitable effects if environmental problems are shifted from one place to another, or concentrated in one place. A traditional example of this occurs when an area is sewered for the first time and the sewage is discharged into a waterway. The environment of the newly sewered area is certainly improved; but the waterway is degraded, and its users, particularly those who might draw water from it downstream, are disadvantaged.

Another example of this was seen when some European nations made their factory smokestacks higher to avoid localised pollution. This served only to spread the pollution – particularly acid rain – to other countries.

Inequity in decision-making structures

Inequities in power lead to inequities in people's ability to influence decisions affecting their environment. Although there may be just reasons for economic inequality, there is little reason for political inequality. Every person should have the right to be considered in environmental decision making (see chapter 6).

People should only be subjected to increased environmental burdens if they have given their informed consent, that is, if they have consented in full knowledge of the risks they are undertaking. This is a requirement of medical and legal ethics and should also be a requirement of environmental professionals, bureaucrats and politicians. Informed consent requires that:

1. full information about the risks be supplied to potential victims and decision-makers;
2. those being subjected to the risk understand the risk they are taking;
3. those consenting to the risk do so voluntarily without coercion or manipulation;
4. they are competent to give this consent. (Shrader-Frechette 2002: 77)

People who live in areas of high unemployment and low education may not understand the risks of a proposed facility, and may be so desperate for employment opportunities that they are not really making a free choice. Similarly, where workers have to put up with hazardous work conditions in order to keep their jobs, their consent is not voluntary.

Even with informed consent there are limits to what burdens can be morally imposed on people (Shrader-Frechette 2002: 142). In most countries, for example, people are not able to sell their organs, even if they wish to, and testing chemicals on humans is not allowed even if volunteers can be found. The right to life and health is paramount.

In many places around the world, existing decision-making structures do not adequately represent all sectors of society. Robert Bullard (1992) argues that environmental racism in the USA, for example, causes minorities to be excluded from decision-making bodies such as company and government agency management boards, city councils and industrial commissions.

INTERGENERATIONAL EQUITY

Intergenerational equity refers to the need for a just distribution of rewards and burdens between generations, and fair and impartial treatment of future generations. 'Time of birth, in other words, has no more to do with how a person should be valued than do place of birth, tribe, nationality, religion, or gender' (Nolt 2005).

However, unless substantial change occurs, and rapidly, the present generation is unlikely to pass on a healthy and diverse environment to future generations because of three main factors:

> Firstly, the rates of loss of animal and plant species, arable land, water quality, tropical forests and cultural heritage are especially serious. Secondly, and perhaps more widely recognised, is the fact that we will not pass on to future generations the ozone layer or global climate system that the current generation inherited. A third factor that contributes overwhelmingly to the anxieties about the first two is the prospective impact of continuing population growth and the environmental consequences if rising standards of material income around the world produce the same sorts of consumption patterns that are characteristic of the currently industrialised countries. (ESD Working Group Chairs 1992: 10)

Achieving intergenerational equity thus requires significant changes. But why care about the future? As cynics have said, 'What has posterity ever done for me?' After all, the people of the far-off future are strangers, potential people who do not yet exist and may not exist. They will be in no position to reward us for what we do for them, to punish us for our lack of care or responsibility, or to demand compensation. We don't know what their needs, desires or values will be. How can people not yet born demand rights? And if they cannot claim rights do they have any?

Although future generations do not yet exist we can be reasonably sure they will exist. And, like us, they will require clean air and water and other basic physical requirements for life. And although we don't know who the people of the future will be – they are not individually identifiable – they can have rights as a group or class of people, rather than individually, and we can have obligations and duties towards them. What is more, morality is not dependent on identity. The murder of any person is morally wrong, no matter who that person is.

Future people may not be able to claim their rights today, but others can on their behalf, and various national and international laws protect the rights of future generations. Where future generations do not have formal legal representation, people are able to make claims on their behalf using reasoning based on moral principles, such as those outlined below.

Justice

According to philosopher John Rawls (quoted in Visser 't Hooft 1999: 5), justice is about 'the way in which the major social institutions distribute fundamental rights and duties and determine the division of advantages from social cooperation'. According to Hendrik Visser 't Hooft, 'a consensus is clearly emerging in contemporary society that it would be contrary to justice to ignore' the presumed environmental needs of future generations:

> Our moral convictions tell us that we must share the resources of the planet, which have shown themselves to be finite, with our descendents ... Each generation is thus both a beneficiary with a right to use the planet and a trustee with the obligation to care for it. (Visser 't Hooft 1999: 3–5)

This idea of environmental resources being a 'common heritage of mankind' was incorporated in the 1982 UN Treaty on the Law of the Sea. A similar doctrine is that of public trust, which is incorporated into US environmental law and has been reinforced by the courts. It affirms 'a duty of the state to protect the people's common heritage of streams, lakes etc., surrendering the right of protection only in rare cases when the abandonment of that right is consistent with the purposes of the trust'. The idea of a public trust or common heritage across generations means that environmental resources/values should not be destroyed merely because the majority of a current generation decides it has better uses for them (Visser 't Hooft 1999: 35–6).

Responsibility

Responsibility arises from the power and the ability to impact and affect others, and the knowledge that what we do may affect others. A person has moral responsibility for their actions if that person:

> a. has, or is capable of having, *knowledge* of those actions;
> b. has the *capacity* to bring about these consequences;
> c. has the *choice* to do otherwise; and
> d. that these consequences have *value significance* [explained below]. (Partridge 2001: 377)

Increasingly, the activities of modern industrialised nations have impacts that are felt not only globally now, but will be felt well into the future. If we know that our actions may harm future generations, and we have a choice about whether to take those actions, then we are morally responsible for those actions. This is particularly pertinent to the environment, for many environmental impacts, such as radioactive waste disposal, global warming and the spread of chemical toxins, have long-term implications. The fact is that current generations have 'unprecedented power to enhance or diminish the life prospects of our posterity' and this gives us a measure of responsibility for the welfare of future generations (Partridge 1981; 1990).

Criteria for judging the value significance of our actions into the future include 'whether activities have a significant impact, either spatially or over time, whether the effects are irreversible or reversible only with unacceptable costs, and whether the effects will be viewed as significant by a substantial number of people' (Weiss 1990). Inaction can also have consequences. Inaction can be just as irresponsible as any action, particularly if it entails allowing existing trends to continue in the knowledge that these will be harmful.

The fact that the consequences of our actions or inactions will occur some time in the future does not diminish our responsibility:

> And, if a person is duty-bound not to cause deliberate harm during his lifetime, is he any less duty-bound to prevent such injuries that may occur after his death due to neglect *during* his lifetime? If one is both aware of the harm he might cause and capable of preventing it, does it matter if the calamity takes place five years after his death? Five hundred years? Five hundred *thousand* years? (Partridge 1990)

Because a healthy environment is a shared interest that benefits whole communities, and is often threatened by the 'cumulative effects of human enterprise', there is a collective responsibility to protect it.

Individual actions can only offer limited solutions and there is a need for government action, and international cooperation (Visser 't Hooft 1999: 42–3).

Avoiding harm

Some philosophers argue that the more distant future generations are from us the less our obligation is to them, because we cannot know what their needs and wants will be nor what is good for them (Golding 1999: 69). Others argue that even if we do not know what will be *good* for future generations we do know what will be *bad* for them:

> Of course, we don't know what the precise tastes of our remote descendents will be, but they are unlikely to include a desire for skin cancer, soil erosion, or the inundation of all low-lying areas as a result of the melting of the ice-caps. (Barry 1999: 84)

According to Partridge (1990):

> While we may share few of the aesthetic tastes, or even the cultural mores, of our remote successors, we can still surmise much regarding their fundamental needs. They will require just institutions, basic energy and material resources, a functioning atmosphere and flourishing ecosystem, and an unpolluted and unpoisoned environment.

Therefore, while we may not have positive obligations to provide for the future, we do have negative obligations to avoid actions that will harm the future. We can fairly safely assume that future generations will want a safe and diverse environment, and therefore we have an obligation to:

> make certain (a) that there will be future generations – which is a way of reaffirming the value we attribute to our own life; and (b) that the possibility of those generations planning for themselves is not irrevocably destroyed by our failure now to refrain from those acts that could have evil consequences for them; we have no right to preempt their choices. (Callahan 1999: 75)

We cannot just assume that future generations will have better technological and scientific means to solve the problems we leave them. For this reason we should endeavour to pass on the planet to future generations in no worse shape than previous generations passed it on to us.

International agreements

Intergenerational equity has been recognised in various international agreements, including the:

- Convention for the Protection of the World Cultural and Natural Heritage, 1972
- United Nations Framework Convention on Climate Change, 1992
- Convention on Biological Diversity, 1992
- Rio Declaration on Environment and Development, 1992
- Vienna Declaration and Programme of Action, 1993.

These agreements led up to the UNESCO Declaration on the Responsibilities of the Present Generations towards Future Generations (1997). The text of the declaration was adapted from a Bill of Rights for Future Generations presented to the United Nations in 1993 by the Cousteau Society (2005), together with over 9 million signatures of support from people in 106 countries. It had five articles which emphasised rights, responsibility and common heritage, including:

> *Article 1*. Future generations have a right to an uncontaminated and undamaged Earth and to its enjoyment as the ground of human history, of culture, and of the social bonds that make each generation and individual a member of one human family.
>
> *Article 2*. Each generation, sharing in the estate and heritage of the Earth, has a duty as trustee for future generations to prevent irreversible and irreparable harm to life on Earth and to human freedom and dignity.
>
> *Article 3*. It is, therefore, the paramount responsibility of each generation to maintain a constantly vigilant and prudential assessment of technological disturbances and modifications adversely affecting life on Earth, the balance of nature, and the evolution of mankind in order to protect the rights of future generations.

Today the principle of intergenerational equity is a principle of international law. 'It finds explicit support in many international instruments, and it articulates the wider temporal horizon implicit in many forms of international cooperation on the environmental front' (Visser 't Hooft 1999: 26).

A number of national laws and agreements also include intergenerational equity, such as Australia's 1992 Intergovernmental Agreement on the Environment (IGAE) and the US's 1969 National Environmental Protection Act (NEPA). Such sentiments go back as far as 1916, to the National Park Act in the USA, which charges the National Park Service with the duty of protecting the land 'unimpaired for the enjoyment of future generations' (quoted in Partridge 1990). In general the ideals behind national parks in all countries have the same intergenerational goals.

WHAT SHOULD BE SUSTAINED?

Even if it is agreed that we have an obligation to future generations, the nature of that obligation is controversial. Do we need to do more than simply protect those aspects of the environment necessary for survival and health, such as ensuring a minimal standard of clean air and water? And what standard would that be? Which risks from hazardous and radioactive substances do we need to prevent?

The problem is that protecting the interests of the future may conflict with the interests of current generations. How do we balance our obligations to current generations with our obligations to future generations when these conflict? At one extreme is the *preservationist model*, which requires that present generations do not further deplete any resources or destroy or alter any part of the environment. In this case an industrialised lifestyle would become impossible, and the present generations would have to make significant sacrifices, living subsistence lifestyles, to benefit future generations (Weiss 1992).

At the other extreme is the *opulence model*, where present generations consume all they want and assume that future generations will be able to cope with the impoverished environment that remains because they will be technologically better off. Alternatively, advocates of this model assume that future generations will have the technological expertise to find new sources or substitutes for exhausted resources and extinct species (Weiss 1992). This model seems overly optimistic about the ability of wealth and technology to deal with environmental catastrophe and losses.

Weak sustainability

Many economists and businesspeople argue that communities can use up natural resources and degrade the natural environment as long as they compensate for the loss with 'human capital' (skills, knowledge and technology) and 'human-made capital' (buildings, machinery, etc). This is the 'weak sustainability' argument.

Economists often think of the environment in terms of 'natural capital', that is, aspects of nature that are of use to humans including minerals, biological yield potential, and pollution absorption capacity. There is also 'cultivated capital', which includes natural capital that has been transformed or adapted by humans. Examples include domesticated animals and plant varieties (Holland 1999: 50). These economists argue that what needs to be maintained for future generations is 'total capital':

Total Capital = Natural Capital + Cultivated Capital + Human Capital + Human-made Capital

In this formula the actual mix or proportions is not important. The Business Council of Australia (BCA 1991: 4), for example, has argued that:

> The principle of sustainable development does not require that the physical configuration of the environment or the economy's capital stock remains constant. The current generation does not owe future generations a share of particular resources. Rather, it requires that the capacity to generate resources from the total stock of environmental, physical and human capital resources not be diminished.

Advocates of weak sustainability point out that the loss of income from a depleted resource could be compensated for by other investments which generate the same income. If the money obtained from exploiting an exhaustible resource, such as oil, is invested so that it yields a continuous flow of income, this is equivalent to holding the stock of oil constant. They argue that not only is some substitution inevitable when it comes to the commercial exploitation of minerals, but that this is consistent with intergenerational equity, 'provided that the community returns from that exploitation are reinvested to give an equivalent income indefinitely' (ESD Working Group Chairs 1992: 37).

Economist David Pearce (1991: 2–3) says that this means that the Amazon forest can be removed so long as the proceeds from removing it 'are reinvested to build up some other form of capital'. He points out that this principle requires that 'environmental assets be valued in the same way as man-made assets, otherwise we cannot know if we are on a "sustainable development path"'.

Weak sustainability provides a rationale for continuing to use non-renewable resources at ever-increasing rates. 'Inevitably, as we deplete the stock of resources, there are less resources for future generations. While this can cause temporary shortages it is not regarded as a matter of longer-term concern' (ESD Working Groups 1991: 78–9). This is because during times of shortage the prices will go up and new reserves will be found, substitutes discovered and more efficient use encouraged. It is for this reason that Pearce and his colleagues (1989) suggest that what should remain constant is not the stocks of non-renewable resources but the economic value of the stock.

Natural limits

While the economic value of natural resources can be easily replaced, their functions are less easily replaced. Most people, even economists, agree that there are limits on the extent to which natural resources can be replaced without changing some biological processes and putting ecological sustainability at risk. Pearce and his colleagues (1989), for example, argue that the requirement to keep the total amount of capital constant 'is consistent with "running down" natural capital – i.e. with environmental degradation', as long as human-made capital can be substituted for natural capital. He recognises that some environmental assets could not be 'traded-off' because they are essential for life-support systems and as yet they cannot be replaced. In this view, the proportion of natural to human-made capital does matter, as economist David James (1999: 156) notes:

> Community welfare, in the widest sense, is derived from a combination of natural and man-made capital. In achieving an acceptable balance of economic development and resource protection, and in ensuring that excessive risks of damage are minimised, the practical policy issue to be addressed is how to define and achieve an optimal or acceptable mix of both kinds of capital.

Others advise caution with respect to declining natural capital. 'As an economist I would say that loss of natural capital can be compensated for by human made capital but in practice I would advise policy-makers to avoid depletion of natural resources unless there was a good reason' (Harris 1991). In fact, the precautionary principle would prevent us from assuming that natural resources can be replaced without good evidence that they can.

Despite holding that stocks of non-renewable resources need not remain constant, Pearce and his colleagues (1989: ch 2) give the following reasons for maintaining a minimal level of natural capital:

Non-substitutability

There are many types of environmental assets for which there are no substitutes: for example, the ozone layer, the climate-regulating functions of ocean phytoplankton, the watershed protection functions of tropical forests, the pollution-cleaning and nutrient-trap functions of wetlands. For those people who believe that animals and plants have an intrinsic value, there can be no substitute.

Uncertainty

We cannot be certain whether or not we will be able to substitute for other environmental assets in the future and what the consequences of continually degrading nature will be. Scientists do not know enough about the functions of natural ecosystems and the possible consequences of depleting and degrading natural capital. And 'if we do not know an outcome it is hardly consistent with rational behaviour to act *as if* the outcome will be a good one'.

Irreversibility

The depletion of natural capital can lead to irreversible losses such as the loss of species and habitats, which once lost cannot be recreated through man-made capital. Other losses are not irreversible but repair may take centuries – for example, damage to the ozone layer and soil degradation.

Equity

There is an equity issue involved in replacing natural resources and environmental assets – that are currently freely available to everyone – with human-made resources that have to be bought and may only be accessible to some people in the future. Also, as we saw earlier in this chapter, poor people are more often affected by unhealthy environments than wealthier people. A substitution of wealth for natural resources does not mean that those who suffer are the same people as those who will benefit from the additional wealth.

Resilience

Human-made capital often lacks an important feature of natural capital – diversity. Diverse ecological systems are more resilient to shocks and stress. Biological diversity ensures that ecosystems are robust and more likely to survive disruption, disease and natural disasters. Even in economic systems, diversity helps to spread risks and maintain options.

Strong sustainability

Understandably, environmentalists generally reject the concept of weak sustainability even if it incorporates the idea of maintaining minimal environmental functions. They argue that the environment should not be degraded for future generations, even if the future generations are compensated with greater human-made capital. They claim that human welfare can only be maintained over generations if the environment is not degraded; in economists' terms, if natural capital is not declining. They point out that we do not know what the safe limits of environmental degradation are; if those as yet unknown safe limits are crossed, the options for future generations will be severely limited.

Secondly, many environmentalists do not agree that human and natural capital are interchangeable. They believe that a loss of environmental quality cannot be substituted with a gain in human or human-made capital without loss of welfare. Therefore, they argue, future generations should not inherit a degraded environment, no matter how many extra sources of wealth might be available to them. This is referred to as 'strong sustainability'.

The production and consumption values and absorption capacity provided by natural capital may be able to be replaced or extended, particularly through technological innovation. In this way it may make sense to speak of human capital compensating for natural capital. But this is not the case with other environmental values. To maintain recreational, spiritual and aesthetic values the environment must not be spoiled (Holland 1999: 56–9).

If an old growth forest is cut down, a commercial tree plantation may replace much of its economic value, but a plantation is unlikely to recreate the original ecosystem and support the biodiversity provided by the natural forest. Nor will it have the beauty or spiritual value of the original forest. The plantation will be an impoverished version of the original forest, with many of the values associated with forests gone (Humphreys 1999: 113).

Should we preserve these non-economic values of the environment for future generations? How can we know what sorts of environmental values future generations will appreciate? Visser 't Hooft (1999: 22) asks: 'If a majority is convinced that a worthwhile life depends on being able to walk in parks and forests, must it anticipate a possible fading out of that conviction in the minds of posterity?' Similarly, Bryan Norton (1999: 132) asks:

> … suppose that our generation converts all wilderness areas and natural communities into productive mines, farmland, production forests, or shopping centres, and suppose we do so efficiently, and that we are careful to save a portion of the profits, and invest them wisely leaving the future far more wealthy than we are. Does it not make sense to claim that, in doing so, we harmed future people, not economically, but in the sense that we seriously and irreversibly narrowed their range of choices and experiences? A whole range of human experience would have been obliterated …

Future people who have never experienced wilderness would not miss it and would make do with human-made landscapes. They would not know they were worse off. However, current generations would clearly have diminished the range of future choices and opportunities and impoverished future lives.

A professor of international and environmental law, Edith Brown Weiss (1990), argues that intergenerational equity consists of preserving options, environmental quality and access for future generations. Overdevelopment reduces options and reduces diversity. The principle of 'conservation of access' implies that current generations should ensure that future generations can also enjoy this access. Equity and fairness would seem to require that future generations not only be able to subsist but that they have the same level of opportunities to thrive and be happy as current generations.

Further Reading

Partridge, Ernest (2006) 'The Gadfly Papers', <http://gadfly.igc.org/papers/papers.htm>

Principles of environmental justice, Environmental Justice Net, October 1991, <http://www.ejnet.org/ej/principles.html>

Shrader-Frechette, Kristin (2002) *Environmental Justice: Creating Equality, Reclaiming Democracy*, Oxford University Press, Oxford.

Smith, Mark J (ed.) (1999) *Thinking Through the Environment*, The Open University, London & New York.

UNESCO Declaration on the Responsibilities of the Present Generations Towards Future Generations, 1997, <http://portal.unesco.org/en/ev.php-URL_ID=13178&URL_DO=DO_TOPIC&URL_SECTION=201.html>

Visser 't Hooft, Hendrik Ph (1999) *Justice to Future Generations and the Environment*, Kluwer Academic, Dordrecht.

Weiss, Edith Brown (1990) Intergenerational fairness and the rights of future generations, Foundation for the Rights of Future Generations, April, <http://www.srzg.de/ndeutsch/5publik/1gg/7jg2h3/weiss.html>

5

HUMAN RIGHTS PRINCIPLES

Human rights are entitlements based on morality, justice and fairness which, collectively, the nations of the world have agreed all people ought to have. They include the rights to life, liberty, health and wellbeing. Human rights apply to every human being throughout their life, no matter where they live or what their religion, occupation, race, colour, age or gender. (The gender bias found in some of the language used in the early human rights declarations and covenants should be seen only as an artefact of the times in which the rights were drafted.) Human rights are regarded as essential to human dignity and are inalienable, which means they cannot be taken away, sold, or given away.

Some rights are non-derogable, which means that they cannot be limited in any way, even in times of national emergency or war. Non-derogable rights include the right to life, the right to be free from slavery and the right to be free from torture. Other rights can only be limited or denied for reasons that have to do with the greater welfare of the community or the protection of others' human rights. Such limitations are detailed in human rights treaties, and no other limits are allowed. In other words, rights should always have priority over the preferences and desires of others, and governments have a duty to 'respect, protect and promote them' (Merrills 1996: 25–7; Rayner 2005a). Human rights are supposed to have absolute priority over any political lobbying or economic trade-off.

The Universal Declaration of Human Rights was adopted by the United Nations General Assembly in 1948, after World War II. Before the war it had been thought that rights were a matter for national governments to decide and implement, but the atrocities perpetrated by the Nazis during the war showed that this could leave millions of people without even the most fundamental rights. The United Nations was formed in 1945 in an effort to avoid future wars and to enable nations to sort out their differences in an international forum. The UN Charter affirmed 'faith in fundamental human rights, in the dignity and worth of the human person, in the equal rights of men and women and of nations large and small', and paved the way for the establishment of an international Commission on Human Rights (Bailey 2005).

The Universal Declaration (UDHR 1948) was compiled as a 'relatively short, inspirational and energising document' that could be easily understood by anyone. Being a declaration it was not binding on the countries which signed it, as a treaty would be, but nevertheless it was a significant statement of moral and political principles that has formed the basis of human rights treaties and national constitutions since. It has become part of international customary law. As customary law, all countries are bound by it, whether or not they have agreed to it (Bailey 2005).

The Universal Declaration was later reinforced by the International Covenant on Economic, Social and Cultural Rights and the International Covenant on Civil and Political Rights. These covenants, adopted by the UN in 1966, elaborate the rights in the Universal Declaration and are binding on the states that have signed them. Ratified or approved by over 130 nations, they came into force in 1976. The Universal Declaration was reaffirmed in 1993 by more than 150 nations at the World Conference on Human Rights in Vienna (Gleeson 2005). The Universal Declaration of Human Rights together with the two International Covenants make up the International Bill of Human Rights (see figure 5.1 below).

Figure 5.1 International Bill of Rights

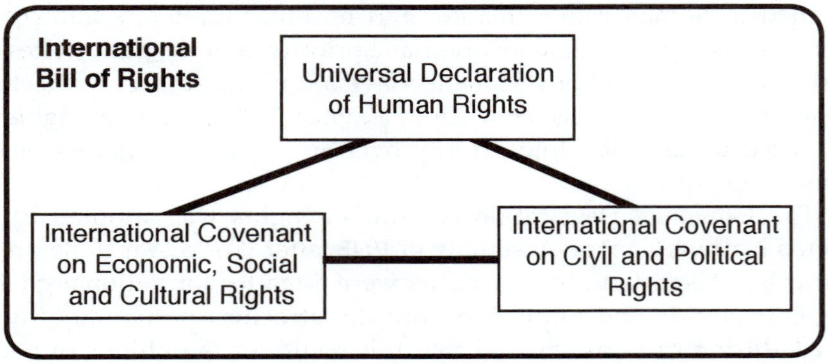

The International Covenant on Civil and Political Rights (CCPR 1966) includes the rights to freedom of thought, conscience and religion; freedom of association and peaceful assembly; the assumption of innocence until proven guilty at a fair trial; freedom from arbitrary arrest or detention; freedom from torture and cruel, inhuman and degrading treatment; freedom of movement to and from one's home nation; and freedom from slavery or forced labour. Countries which have signed up to it guarantee that every citizen will have these rights protected without discrimination and that anyone who feels that this is not the case is able to go to court to remedy the situation. Anyone who is unable to get redress for a breach of rights in their own country can complain to the UN's Human Rights Committee, which was established in 1977 to monitor whether governments are complying with their obligations under the Covenant (Rayner 2005b).

The International Covenant on Economic, Social and Cultural Rights (CESCR 1966) includes rights to an adequate standard of living, health, education, social security, work in proper working conditions for fair wages, participation in cultural life, and the benefits of social progress. These are rights that place an obligation on governments to adopt policies to ensure that individuals and groups are equally able to develop to their full potential. Because such policies cost money that a government may not have, the Covenant does not demand that these rights be guaranteed immediately but progressively, depending on the resources governments have available to achieve them. Nevertheless, governments are expected to spend money on ensuring the fulfilment of these obligations ahead of other non-rights-based objectives (Boyle 1996: 46). Governments have to report on their progress in this to the Committee on Economic, Social and Cultural rights but, unlike under the CCPR, 'there is no mechanism for individuals to make complaints about the breach of these rights' (Rayner 2005b).

The International Bill of Rights therefore 'defines in law the limits of authority that can be imposed on individuals, as well as the basic necessities required by them, so that all individual people, in every place, and at all times, can retain their human dignity' (Gosden 2000: 37; 2001). These rights 'protect the vulnerable and marginalized from being exploited or otherwise made to suffer under the self-interested politics of the powerful' (Hancock 2003: 2). The rights in the Bill of Rights were declared by the World Conference on Human Rights in 1968 to be *indivisible*, and by the UN General Assembly in 1984 and 1986 to be *interrelated*. This means the various rights are related to each other, complementary to each other and reinforce each other and cannot be separated off from each other (Trindade 1998: 120). The right to health is most obviously indivisible and interrelated to the right to life.

There are now many human rights conventions, treaties and instruments at global and regional levels. Other international human rights conventions include:

- Convention on the Prevention and Punishment of the Crime of Genocide (entry into force: 1951)
- Convention against Torture (entry into force: 1984)
- Convention on the Elimination of All Forms of Racial Discrimination (entry into force: 1969)
- Convention on the Elimination of All Forms of Discrimination Against Women (entry into force: 1981)
- Convention on the Rights of the Child (entry into force: 1989).

Various regions have also established human rights agreements, including:

- European Convention on Human Rights, 1950
- American Convention on Human Rights, 1969
- African Charter of Human and Peoples' Rights, 1981.

Many nations have also incorporated human rights into their constitutions. 'Respect for human rights is becoming a universal principle of good government' (Rayner 2005a).

ROLE OF ENVIRONMENTAL PROTECTION

The relationship between human rights and the environment was studied by the Special Rapporteur on Human Rights and the Environment for the UN Sub-Commission on Prevention of Discrimination and Protection of Minorities, Madame Zhohra Ksentini (1994), from 1991 to 1994. She reported on the human rights violations that result from environmental degradation, including climate change, deforestation, pollution and loss of biological diversity. Not only are human rights dependent on environmental protection but environmental degradation often entails the trampling of human rights. She noted that regional and international human rights bodies were increasingly allowing people to bring complaints of human rights violations based on environmental issues.

In 2002 a UN expert group (UNHCHR 2002) concluded:

> that respect for human rights is broadly accepted as a precondition for sustainable development, that environmental protection constitutes a precondition for the effective enjoyment of human rights pro-

> tection, and that human rights and the environment are interdependent and interrelated. These features are now broadly reflected in national and international practices and developments.

Similarly, Klaus Toepfer (quoted in CEDHA 2002b), Executive Director of the UN Environmental Programme, stated in 2001:

> Human rights cannot be secured in a degraded or polluted environment. The fundamental right to life is threatened by soil degradation and deforestation and by exposures to toxic chemicals, hazardous wastes and contaminated drinking water ... Environmental conditions clearly help to determine the extent to which people enjoy their basic rights to life, health, adequate food and housing, and traditional livelihood and culture. It is time to recognize that those who pollute or destroy the natural environment are not just committing a crime against nature, but are violating human rights as well.

A growing body of case law and more recent human rights agreements affirm that environmental protection is necessary for some of the most fundamental human rights, such as the rights to life, human health and wellbeing (UNHCHR 2002).

The rights to life, health and wellbeing

Life

The right to life is found in most human rights treaties. It can be argued that any environmental disaster or degradation that results in death breaches human rights. The UN Human Rights Commission recognises that environmental violations such as the transboundary movement of hazardous waste 'constitute a serious threat to the human rights to life, good health and a sound environment for everyone' (quoted in CEDHA 2002b).

The question is, does the right to life require governments to prevent people losing their lives from environmental causes, through ensuring clean air and water and reducing risks from other environmental contaminants? According to the Human Rights Committee, it does. Governments are expected to take positive measures to reduce infant mortality and increase life expectancy, and consequently are obliged to report on the public health and environmental measures they are undertaking to this end to the Committee (Churchill 1996: 90).

In 1980 the Port Hope Environmental Group complained to the Committee on behalf of present and future generations that the storage of radioactive waste near their homes in Ontario, Canada, posed a threat to their lives and those of future generations and therefore breached the

Covenant on Civil and Political Rights. While recognising that this was a legitimate complaint the Committee found that there were other avenues of appeal within the Canadian judicial system, including invoking the Canadian Charter of Human Rights and Freedoms, that the group could use to remedy the situation, and which they had not yet tried (Churchill 1996: 91; UNHRC 1982).

More recently the Federal High Court in Nigeria has ruled that gas-flaring by oil and gas companies violates constitutional rights to life and dignity. The gas-flaring by companies such as the Shell oil company, which continues in Nigeria despite an official ban, causes people to be exposed to toxic chemicals that pose serious health risks. The ruling has been contested by Shell (Hopkins 2005b).

Health and wellbeing

The Universal Declaration of Human Rights includes a person's 'right to a standard of living adequate for the health and well-being of himself and of his family' (Article 25). In addition, the International Covenant on Economic, Social and Cultural Rights includes the following provisions:

> The States Parties to the present Covenant recognize the right of everyone to an adequate standard of living for himself and his family, including adequate food, clothing and housing, and to the continuous improvement of living conditions. The States Parties will take appropriate steps to ensure the realization of this right, recognizing to this effect the essential importance of international co-operation based on free consent. (Article 11)

> The States Parties to the present Covenant recognize the right of everyone to the enjoyment of the highest attainable standard of physical and mental health.
> The steps to be taken by the States Parties to the present Covenant to achieve the full realization of this right shall include those necessary for ... the improvement of all aspects of environmental and industrial hygiene. (Article 12)

Although Article 11 is not specific about environmental protection, it is clear that an adequate standard of living will include a minimum environmental quality. What is more, the environment must be free of pollution and contaminants that might impinge on the right to the highest attainable standard of health in order to comply with Article 12, which does call for environmental improvement. The Commission on Human Rights resolved in 1991 'that all individuals are entitled to live in an environment adequate for their health and well-being' (quoted in Cameron & MacKenzie 1996: 130).

The Inter-American Commission has found that:

> [the] realization of the right to life, and to physical security and integrity is necessarily related to and in some ways dependent upon one's physical environment [and c]onditions of severe environmental pollution, which may cause serious physical illness, impairment and suffering on the part of the local populace, are inconsistent with the right to be respected as a human being (quoted in CEDHA 2002b).

Right to clean water

Interestingly, while the international covenants include a right to adequate food, they do not include a right to clean water. It may be that food was supposed to include water, or that in earlier times it was thought that water, like air, was so fundamental that it went without saying that it was implied in the rights to life, health and wellbeing (Gleick 1999). One might assume that other environmental benefits are likewise implied by other human rights.

The 1977 Mar del Plata Declaration states that 'all peoples, whatever their stage of development and their social and economic conditions, have the right to have access to drinking water in quantities and of a quality equal to their basic needs'. The UN Convention on the Law of the Non-Navigational Uses of International Watercourses (1997) also states that where there are conflicts over water use, priority should be given to 'the requirements of vital human needs', including drinking water and water to produce enough food to prevent starvation (quoted in Gleick 1999).

The right to clean water is explicitly included in the Convention on the Rights of the Child (UNICEF 1989), which recognises the extra vulnerability of children to environmental factors and, being of more recent origin, is more specific about what is required to achieve the right to health with respect to environmental protection:

> 1. States Parties recognize the right of the child to the enjoyment of the highest attainable standard of health and to facilities for the treatment of illness and rehabilitation of health …
>
> 2. States Parties shall pursue full implementation of this right and, in particular, shall take appropriate measures:
>
>   (a) To diminish infant and child mortality; …
>
>   (b) …
>
>   (c) To combat disease and malnutrition, including within the framework of primary health care, through, inter alia, the application of readily available technology and through the provision of adequate nutritious foods and clean drinking-water, taking into consideration the dangers and risks of environmental pollution …

Right to a healthy environment

The first regional charter to incorporate environmental requirements was the African Charter on Human and Peoples' Rights (ACHPR 1981), which states that 'All peoples shall have the right to a general satisfactory environment favorable to their development' (Article 24). An addition to the American Convention on Human Rights, the 1988 San Salvador Protocol (which came into force in 1999), similarly includes environmental requirements:

1. Everyone shall have the right to live in a healthy environment and to have access to basic public services.
2. The States Parties shall promote the protection, preservation and improvement of the environment.

Like the Covenant on Social Economic and Cultural Rights, this right to a healthy environment is limited by the resources available to a nation to achieve it. It is a progressive right rather than an immediate one. This means that for the poorer countries in South America, little will actually be done to advance this right (Churchill 1996: 99–100). However, the Awas Tingni people of Nicaragua have been able to use the San Salvador Protocol in a landmark case in the Inter-American Court to stop logging in their territories. The logging had been permitted by the government without consultation with the Awas Tingni, who argued that it violated their rights to cultural integrity, religion, equal protection and participation in government (CEDHA 2002; Taillant 2004: 28).

The rights to privacy, family life, and peaceful enjoyment of property

The European Convention on Human Rights (Council of Europe 1950) has been used as a basis of complaint by those living near airports. It states:

1. Everyone has the right to respect for his private and family life, his home and his correspondence.
2. There shall be no interference by a public authority with the exercise of this right except such as is in accordance with the law and is necessary in a democratic society in the interests of national security, public safety or the economic well-being of the country, for the prevention of disorder or crime, for the protection of health or morals, or for the protection of the rights and freedoms of others (Article 8).

Complainants have argued that the noise pollution from airports interferes with this right. Some such cases have been settled with compensation. However, in a case involving Heathrow Airport, the European

Commission found that the complainants' rights had been breached but that this was justified under clause 2 of the article above because the economic wellbeing of the nation depended on the airport and the complainants could move elsewhere (Churchill 1996: 91–3).

In a contrasting case in 1994, *Lopez-Ostra v. Spain*, the European Court of Human Rights found that the Spanish authorities had breached the human rights of a resident living near a tannery waste-treatment plant. The resident had suffered serious health problems as a result of the fumes from the plant and the Court ordered that she be compensated because the authorities had failed to find 'a fair balance between the interest of the town's economic well-being and the applicant's effective enjoyment of her right to respect for her home and private and family life' (Churchill 1996: 94).

This right to be free of interference with one's home and property is therefore limited, but the burdens on individuals must not be unreasonable. Similarly, environmental protection measures that interfere with a person's property can be justified in terms of protection of health or the economic wellbeing of the wider community (Churchill 1996: 94–5).

The right to self-determination

The international covenants have a common first article stating:

> 1. All peoples have the right of self-determination. By virtue of that right they freely determine their political status and freely pursue their economic, social and cultural development.
> 2. All peoples may, for their own ends, freely dispose of their natural wealth and resources without prejudice to any obligations arising out of international economic co-operation, based upon the principle of mutual benefit, and international law. In no case may a people be deprived of its own means of subsistence … (Article 1)

This article requires some protection of the environment to ensure it is able to support people – not only in terms of subsistence but also in terms of economic, social and cultural development – and that local people are able to choose how to deal with natural resources on their lands.

As the global environment is progressively degraded it is those peoples who subsist most closely to nature – the fishing communities, forest-dwelling peoples and subsistence hunters and farmers – who are most affected. The Inuit people of Alaska, northern Canada and the far east of the Russian Federation, for example, depend on their frozen environment for their sustenance and hunting culture. But global warming is causing the ice to thin out, which in turn is threatening the animals that live in these areas, including seals, walruses and polar bears. The Inuit can no longer predict the weather patterns and the conditions of their environment. The areas that were safe to cross in earlier times are becoming dangerous, killing some hunters who fall through the ice (Watt-Cloutier 2004: 10):

> Inuit believe there is sufficient evidence to demonstrate that the failure to take remedial action by those nations most responsible for the problem does constitute a violation of their human rights – specifically the rights to life, health, culture, means of subsistence, and property.

Because the survival, culture and self-determination of indigenous peoples is often so dependent on their local environment, their rights depend more closely on environmental protection than most other peoples. Many indigenous people have a special relationship to the natural environment which is central to their identity and culture.

The International Labour Organization's Indigenous and Tribal Peoples Convention (ILO 1991) accords indigenous peoples special collective rights that are distinct from those applying to minority groups and additional to the universal rights applying to all humans. This convention states:

> 1. Special measures shall be adopted as appropriate for safeguarding the persons, institutions, property, labour, cultures and environment of the peoples concerned.
> 2. Such special measures shall not be contrary to the freely-expressed wishes of the peoples concerned … (Article 4)

The right of indigenous peoples to self-determination in terms of social, cultural and political organisation and development, and control over their own land, reinforces the right of all people to self-determination as stated in the international covenants, while recognising their special relationship with and dependence on the land (MacKay 2002: 10–11).

Conflicting rights

Indigenous peoples' rights include the rights to hunt, fish and exploit their local resources, activities which may be at odds with environmental goals. In Africa, for example, over 100 000 of the pastoral Maasai people have been forced to leave their homes by governments establishing or extending national parks and conservation areas. The Maasai people have to subsist on ever-decreasing territories, with declining herds. Their land is particularly attractive for conservation because their practices have enabled wildlife to flourish. Generally they have had no say in government decisions about conservation and have received little or no compensation for their loss of land rights and livelihood (Veit & Benson 2004).

'Human rights activists see the challenge as protecting [the] environment *for* people and not protecting [the] environment *from* people'. Nevertheless, human rights and environmental protection can conflict. In the short term, the problem of human survival may conflict with 'long-term ecological security', in that the need for food and energy may cause people to disregard the health of the local environment (Dias 2000).

The right to 'continuous improvement of living conditions' could be interpreted as ever-increasing consumerism, which is of course detrimental to the environment. Similarly, the right to development (DRD 1986) can be seen as conflicting with environmental protection where development is interpreted narrowly as depending on environmentally damaging technologies and activities.

Some argue that environmental degradation is the necessary price paid to achieve economic development and increased prosperity, and that efforts to impose environmental obligations on developing nations are in essence a way of holding up their development. However, as Victor Ricco (2003: 2) of the Argentinian Centre for Human Rights and Environment argues:

> What good is economic development if we decrease our quality of life, if we cannot drink clean and safe drinking water, if we cannot breathe clean and safe air, if we do not have clean lands for our families and communities to grow and develop?

Potential conflict, however, is not a reason to neglect human rights that may give rise to that conflict. There have always been conflicts between different human rights and so rights have to be balanced against each other. It is for this reason that some individual human rights can be limited by the need for public order, morality and public health. One criterion which has been suggested by scholars for balancing rights is to prioritise basic needs and survival, which is another way of giving precedence to the right to life. This would place the value of increasing consumption below the value of a toxic-free environment, for example (Hancock 2003: 6–7, 16).

ENVIRONMENTAL HUMAN RIGHTS

As we have seen, the environment is protected to some extent by existing human rights, some of which explicitly refer to environmental protection while others imply environmental protection. Other human rights can be reinterpreted to give them an environmental dimension so that they include a concern for environmental protection. For example, the right to equality can be interpreted as a 'right to equal access to, and protection of, environmental resources' (Anderson 1996: 8).

Jan Hancock (2003: 1–3), in *Environmental Human Rights*, has argued that there need to be two new universal human rights: '(i) to an environment free from toxic pollution and (ii) to ownership rights of natural resources'. She argues that in capitalist societies, environmental protection is relegated to secondary considerations, subordinate to economic considerations, and that unless there are human rights to a healthy environment, this will continue, at the expense of the most vulnerable people in society.

New human rights have in fact been developed that explicitly recognise the importance of the environment to humans. The Stockholm Declaration (1972) created a right to the environment. Agreed to at a UN Conference on the Human Environment, it stated that:

> Both aspects of man's environment, the natural and the man-made, are essential to his well-being and to the enjoyment of basic human rights – even the right to life itself. (Preface)

> Man has the fundamental right to freedom, equality and adequate conditions of life, in an environment of a quality that permits a life of dignity and well-being, and he bears a solemn responsibility to protect and improve the environment for present and future generations. (Principle 1)

In 1984 the OECD agreed that the right to a 'decent' environment was a fundamental human right (Bosselmann 2005). A decade later the Special Rapporteur on Human Rights and the Environment, Madame Ksentini (quoted in Robinson 2002), claimed that the right to 'conservation' and 'prevention' of ecological harm was both an individual and a collective human right. Her final report (Ksentini 1994) included Draft Principles on Human Rights and the Environment (1994), put together by an expert group, which basically reinterpreted human rights in terms of environmental concerns. These Draft Principles have not yet been adopted.

National constitutions

The right to a healthy environment has nevertheless been incorporated into the constitutions of more than 90 nations since 1992, including nearly all constitutions enacted since that time (Robinson 2002). For example, the Argentinian Constitution gives all residents 'the right to a healthy, balanced environment' (article 31) and the Korean Constitution similarly gives citizens 'the right to a healthy and pleasant environment' (Chapter 11, article 35) (quoted in Dias 2000). The Brazilian Constitution (quoted in Bosselmann 2005) states:

> Everyone has a right to an ecologically balanced environment, an asset for common use by the people, and essential to the wholesome quality of life. This imposes upon Public Authorities and the community the obligation to defend and preserve it for present and future generations.

Other nations have interpreted the right to life, health and family life that is already in their constitutions as necessitating a healthy environment. This is particularly the case in South Asia and Latin America (Robinson 2002). In India, for example, the courts have found that the right to life includes the right to live in a clean, pollution-free, healthy environment (Dias 2000). One of the earliest cases where environmental human rights were tested was in Turkey, where the new constitution protects Turkish citizens' rights to a healthy environment. Farmers took the French-based mining company Eurogold to court for polluting their environment, and won (Sachs 1997).

Most recently France has adopted an environmental charter (Charte de l'environnement 2005) as part of its constitution. It was passed at a joint sitting of parliament in 2005 by a vote of 531 to 21. The charter guarantees every citizen the right to live in a balanced and healthy environment and embodies various environmental principles, including the polluter pays principle, the precautionary principle, the right to information, and an obligation to look after the needs of future generations (Case 2005).

Some argue that the right to a healthy environment cannot be enforced because of the difficulty of coming to an agreed definition of what comprises a 'healthy environment' or a 'satisfactory environment'. There will always be debate about what constitutes such terms. The 'threshold below which the level of environmental quality must fall before a breach of the individual human right will have occurred' is not defined, nor agreed upon at an international level (Korsah-Brown 2002: 81). However, the issue of whether a right is enforceable, or whether a breach of a right can be decided by the courts (its justiciability), should not determine whether a right exists and/or should be recognised (Trindade 1998: 135).

The rights of others

It has been argued that a human rights approach to environmental protection is particularly anthropocentric, that is human-centred. In other words, the environment is only protected to the extent that it serves human needs. Many environmentalists believe that other species should also have rights, particularly the rights to life, existence and wellbeing. They argue that the natural world has an intrinsic worth that does not depend on the value humans place on it. They point out that a purely human rights approach would still allow much environmental degradation to continue (Anderson 1996: 14; Bosselmann 2005).

However, whereas once it was thought that a pollution-free environment was all that was necessary for human wellbeing, modern thought is increasingly recognising that humans are a part of the natural world and that their welfare is dependent on the health of the ecosystems in which they live. For example, the Draft Principles on Human Rights and the Environment (1994) include the protection of flora and fauna: 'All persons have the right to protection and preservation of the air, soil, water, sea-ice, flora and fauna, and the essential processes and areas necessary to maintain biological diversity and ecosystems.'

The rights of future generations are also unclear in the arena of human rights. Such rights would have to be considered as collective rights, but who would be appropriate to 'claim and exercise' the rights of future generations (Merrills 1996: 32–3)? Thus we can see that human rights and even environmental human rights, while necessary, are not sufficient to protect the environment. Other principles, such as environmental sustainability and intergenerational equity, also have to be applied.

The Aarhus Convention (1998) 'is a new kind of environmental agreement' that 'links environmental rights to human rights'. Adopted in 1998 by the United Nations Economic Commission for Europe, the Convention covers access to information, public participation in decision making, and access to justice in environmental matters. It is covered in chapter 6 as part of the discussion on the participation principle, which includes both the right to information and the right to public participation.

Further Reading

Bosselmann, Klaus (2005) 'Human rights and the environment: redefining fundamental principles?' University of Melbourne, viewed 9 April, <http://www.arbld.unimelb.edu.au/envjust/papers/allpapers/bosselmann/home.htm>

Boyle, AE & MR Anderson (eds) (1996) *Human Rights Approaches to Environmental Protection*, Clarendon Press, Oxford.

Center for Human Rights and Environment (2006) Publications by CEDHA, <http://www.cedha.org.ar/en/documents/publications_by_cedha/>

Draft Principles on Human Rights and the Environment, E/CN.4/Sub.2/1994/9, Annex I (1994), University of Minnesota Human Rights Library, <http://www1.umn.edu/humanrts/instree/1994-dec.htm>

Ksentini, Fatma Zohra (1994) Final report – review of further developments in fields with which the sub-commission has been concerned: human rights and the environment, Commission on Human Rights, 6 July 1994, <http://www.unhchr.ch/Huridocda/Huridoca.nsf/0/eeab2b6937bccaa18025675c005779c3?Opendocument

Universal Declaration of Human Rights (1948) UN Office of the High Commissioner for Human Rights, <http://www.unhchr.ch/udhr/lang/eng.htm>

6

THE PARTICIPATION PRINCIPLE

Human rights include the right of individual citizens and groups to participate in shaping the decisions and policies that affect them. The International Covenant on Civil and Political Rights protects the right of citizens to participate in the governance of their nations. For example, article 25 guarantees the right to 'take part in the conduct of public affairs, directly or through freely chosen representatives'.

A number of declarations, treaties and conventions have reinforced and elaborated these rights. The importance and wisdom of providing the public with full information and encouraging public participation is recognised in the Rio Declaration of 1992:

> Environmental issues are best handled with participation of all concerned citizens, at the relevant level. At the national level, each individual shall have appropriate access to information concerning the environment that is held by public authorities, including information on hazardous materials and activities in their communities, and the opportunity to participate in decision-making processes. States shall facilitate and encourage public awareness and participation by making information widely available. Effective access to judicial and administrative proceedings, including redress and remedy, shall be provided. (Principle 10)

Similarly, Agenda 21, which was agreed to by over 100 nations at the Rio Conference in 1992, emphasises the need for public participation:

> One of the fundamental prerequisites for the achievement of sustainable development is broad participation in decision-making. Furthermore, in the more specific context of environment and

> development, the need for new forms of participation has emerged. This includes the need for individuals, groups and organisations to participate in environmental impact assessment procedures and to know about and participate in decisions, particularly those which potentially affect the communities in which they live and work. (Chapter 23.2)

Related human rights with respect to the environment include 'the right to receive prior notice of environmental risks' and the 'right to environmental impact assessments, the right to legal remedies including standing to initiate public interest litigation and the right to effective remedies where environmental damage is caused' (Dias 2000).

THE RIGHT TO KNOW

The right to information is recognised in most international human rights agreements. Shortly after the United Nations was formed, the General Assembly resolved: 'Freedom of Information is a fundamental human right and the touchstone for all freedoms to which the United Nations is consecrated' (quoted in CHRI 2005). Article 19 of the Universal Declaration of Human Rights states: 'Everyone has the right to freedom of opinion and expression; this right includes freedom to hold opinions without interference and to seek, receive and impart information and ideas through any media and regardless of frontiers.' This is reiterated in the International Covenant on Civil and Political Rights, Article 19.

What is more, other human rights cannot be realised without information. People need to have information to know when their rights are being threatened and by whom. The right to know is based not only on human rights but also in the requirement of open and transparent government for a well-functioning democracy: 'Right-to-know is grounded on the premise that a healthy democracy depends on a well-informed, active public that participates in important decisions affecting society' (Clean Water Fund et al. 2001).

The right to know is fundamental to ensuring that governments and the private sector are accountable. Accountability implies that an organisation's policies and actions are open to public scrutiny and regulatory investigation, and can therefore be compromised by secrecy. Accountability can be reinforced by regulatory agencies which are supposed to monitor the activities of the organisation, be it public or private, and to ensure that it abides by existing legislation and standards in its operations. However, the closeness of regulatory agencies to those they regulate, the interchange of personnel, and the power of the regulated to influence government, all suggest that full accountability cannot necessarily be guaranteed by regulatory agencies and that these agencies themselves need to be accountable. Public information is therefore vital to accountability.

Freedom of information

The Commonwealth Human Rights Initiative (CHRI 2005) has argued that because public officials create and collect information on behalf of the public, using taxpayer money, the public has a right to access that information, which essentially belongs to the public. The onus is then on the public authority to make a case for why any of their information is not available, rather than on the person requesting the information to make a case for why it should be available.

More than 40 countries have some form of freedom of information (FOI) laws. These generally apply only to information held by government departments and authorities, although they often include information about private companies held by these government bodies. FOI has various objectives:

> In the first place, it helps to make the government more accountable to the people being governed. Secondly, by facilitating the acquisition of knowledge, it encourages self-fulfilment. Thirdly, it acts as a weapon in the fight against corruption and abuse of power by state functionaries. Fourthly, it contributes to improving the quality of official decision-making. Fifthly, it enhances the participatory nature of democracy. Sixthly, it goes some way in redressing the inherent balance in power between the citizen and the state, and strengthens the hand of the individual in his dealings with government. (Iyer 2000)

The right to information is recognised by Commonwealth countries. In 2002, Commonwealth law ministers officially recognised that 'the right to access information was an important aspect of democratic accountability and promoted transparency and encouraged full participation of citizens in the democratic process' (quoted in CHRI 2005). In the USA, the 1966 FOI Act was amended in 1974 following the Watergate scandal:

> It allows ordinary citizens to hold the government accountable by requesting and scrutinizing public documents and records. Without it, journalists, newspapers, historians and watchdog groups would never be able to keep the government honest. (Rosen 2002)

The US FOIA applies to federal government agencies; each state has its own FOI legislation.

Principles

The US-based group OMB Watch (2001: 9) has formulated the key principles of a government information access programme. These include:

- In our democracy, all members of the public have an enforceable right to anonymous, timely, and unfiltered access to government information at low or no cost.
- Government has a duty to identify and collect data and information to protect and benefit the public, spur efficiency, ensure accountability, and strengthen democratic processes.
- Government has an affirmative responsibility to make information broadly available to the public in an equal and equitable manner and in formats that are timely, easily located, understandable, and useful. Those who seek to withhold information carry the burden of proof to justify their position.
- Government should strive to ensure that the information it releases is complete and accurate; however, questions about completeness or accuracy should not be permitted to restrict the free flow of information ...

How proactive should governments be?

Does the right to information mean that individuals have a right to get information if they seek it, or does it imply that governments should disseminate relevant information about proposed projects? Authoritative interpretations suggest that governments have an obligation to disseminate information and some agreements specify this.

In 1999 a group called Article 19 (after Article 19 in the Universal Declaration of Human Rights) put together *The Public's Right to Know: Principles on Freedom of Information Legislation*, which was subsequently formally endorsed by both the UN Special Rapporteur on Freedom of Opinion and Expression and the Organization of American States Special Rapporteur on Freedom of Expression. The principles were:

1. Maximum disclosure – a presumption that all information should be subject to disclosure with minimal exceptions or limitations.
2. Obligation to publish – information that is of public interest should not only be accessible but published and disseminated by government authorities where feasible.
3. Promotion of open government – encouraging a culture of open government and informing citizens of their rights to information.
4. Limited scope of exceptions.

5. Processes to facilitate access.
6. Costs – individuals should not be deterred from making information requests by excessive costs.
7. Open meetings – meetings of government departments, public authorities and agencies should be open to the public.
8. Disclosure takes precedence over other laws.
9. Protection for whistleblowers.

Environmental right to know

With respect to the environment, the right to know would include 'the right to be informed about the environmental compatibility of products, manufacturing processes, industrial installations and their effect on the environment' (Douglas-Scott 1996: 115). The preparation and publication of environmental impact assessments and statements would also be included.

The right to know can apply to consumers, workers and the community. With regard to chemicals, for example, consumers have a right to know about the hazards associated with consumer products and the safe handling of those products. Workers have a right to know about the chemical hazards in their workplace and the safety procedures associated with them. And the community has a right to know about chemicals that might threaten their health and safety or the environment (PIAC 1994: 3). The right to know with respect to chemicals might include:

- Information about chemicals
  - Quantities and properties of chemicals at a particular site
  - Chemical inputs and outputs at a chemical plant
  - Chemical components of products
  - Chemicals to be used, manufactured, mixed, packaged, disposed etc.
- Information about processes involving chemicals
  - Are they to be sprayed, heated, pressured etc?
- Information about the management of chemicals
  - How chemicals are to be disposed of, including accidental releases
  - Data on accidents and incidents
  - Information on injuries that might arise from an accident
  - Data that is collected and provided to government
  - Details of enforcement activities carried out by government
  - Licences, approvals, hazard and risk assessments (PIAC 1994: 12–3).

Armed with this sort of information people can make informed decisions, take action to protect themselves, and monitor industrial activity and government measures, so that private companies and governments are more accountable.

Methods of providing this sort of information include national registers and inventories, state of the environment reports, local community monitoring panels, and labels.

The right to know is a well-established principle in the USA and Europe. It is recognised that such a right needs to be legislated and cannot be voluntary, as many governments and private companies are reluctant to divulge this sort of information if they have a choice. 'Only mandatory obligations to prepare annual emissions and chemical use reports would ensure uniform disclosure, bring into existence information which most companies would not prepare otherwise, and provide national and regional perspectives' (Gunningham & Cornwall 1994: 1–5).

According to Agenda 21: 'The broadest possible awareness of chemical risks is a prerequisite for achieving chemical safety. The principle of the right of the community and of workers to know those risks should be recognized' (Chapter 19.8). Various international treaties also require nations to provide environmental information, including: the UN Framework Convention on Climate Change, the Convention on the Prevention of Marine Pollution by Dumping of Wastes and Other Matter, and the Montreal Protocol on Substances that Deplete the Ozone Layer.

European Union

In 2003 the European Commission (EC 2003b) passed a directive on public access to environmental information which replaced an earlier (1990) directive on the same topic. It aimed 'to guarantee the right of access to environmental information held by or for public authorities' to anyone without their having to demonstrate or state their interest and 'to ensure that, as a matter of course, environmental information is progressively made available and disseminated to the public in order to achieve the widest possible systematic availability and dissemination to the public of environmental information'.

The Directive defines environmental information in broad terms including the state of the environment; the state of human health and safety; administrative measures including policies, plans and programmes; economic analyses and assumptions; and reports on implementation of environmental measures.

The Directive applies to public authorities, including non-government organisations (NGOs) undertaking public administrative functions, having public responsibilities or providing public services relating to the environment. This is important, because otherwise the privatisation of public services would result in the removal of public information from the public domain. Whether public services are provided by private or public bodies, those bodies need to be accountable and open to public scrutiny.

In compliance with the EU Directive, the United Kingdom introduced Environmental Information Regulations (EIR) in 2005 that replaced earlier regulations. As does the EU Directive, the UK EIR applies not only to public authorities and advisory groups but also to private companies carrying out public services impacting on the environment such as energy, water, waste and transport (Information Commissioner 2005).

Limitations

FOI laws are not really adequate to fulfil environmental right to know requirements, because the environmental information collected by agencies is restricted to what is reported to government as part of administrative and regulatory responsibilities, and can be both fragmentary and spread around different government departments or authorities. The type of information available through FOI is limited. For example, information on emissions may be limited to the information that companies have to provide as part of their licence conditions yet not include total emissions for the year. Information about private firms sometimes requires permission from those firms for it to be released (CEPA 1994: 3; Gunningham & Cornwall 1994: 4). What is more, people can only make one-off requests for particular existing information rather than gaining access to databases of integrated information. FOI requests can also be expensive.

Even the EC Directive (2003) includes a number of exceptions. It does not cover internal communications (although it may if public interest can be shown). Nor does it include information bearing on international relations, public security, national defence, intellectual property rights, personal privacy, confidential proceedings where confidentiality is provided for by law, and confidential commercial or industrial information where confidentiality is provided for by law. Information may also be withheld to protect the interests of those who supply information voluntarily.

The UK EIR includes the same exceptions. The exceptions are, however, subject to a public interest test whereby disclosure is to be allowed if it is in the public interest. Moreover, commercial confidentiality cannot be given in the United Kingdom as a reason for not disclosing emissions data (Information Commissioner 2005).

Pollution inventories

The right to know includes 'routine, systematic, mandatory, public reporting of toxic chemicals or other environmental health hazards' (Orum & Heminway 2005: 2). Pollution inventories or registries are one way of contributing to such reporting through disseminating information on the pollution emitted by private companies and thus bypassing the need for individuals to request it. Agenda 21 states that governments should:

- Direct information campaigns such as programmes providing information about chemical stockpiles, environmentally safer alternatives and emission inventories that could also be a tool for risk reduction to the general public to increase the awareness of problems of chemical safety;
- Establish ... national registers and databases, including safety information, for chemicals; (19.60)
- Consider adoption of community right-to-know or other public information-dissemination programmes, when appropriate, as possible risk reduction tools. (19.61)

Inventories of pollutants have been established in a number of countries, including the USA, Canada, the United Kingdom, the Netherlands, Norway and Australia, as a contribution to fulfilling the public's right to know. Collectively these inventories are referred to as Pollutant Release and Transfer Registers (PRTRs). The design of PRTRs varies from country to country, particularly with respect to which chemicals have to be reported.

Such inventories or registers generally provide information about the emission of a number of specified chemicals and by identifying trends and hot spots provide a useful database for government environmental regulation. That the extent of their pollution is made public can encourage individual companies to voluntarily reduce their chemical waste discharges. Emission levels are not necessarily directly measured; often they are estimated. The ensuing inventories do not measure the total load of pollutants in the environment but are meant to provide some indication of load (CEPA 1994: 1).

USA

The earliest right to know legislation was introduced in the USA in the Emergency Planning and Community Right-to-Know Act 1986 (EPCRA). It was the result of public pressure following a disaster in Bhopal, India, where thousands of people were killed by the release of methyl isocyanate from a Union Carbide factory. Americans began demanding the right to know what was being released, or might accidentally be released, by factories near them (USEPA 2004).

The law requires facilities in particular industries – including manufacturing, metal and coal mining, electric utilities, and commercial hazardous-waste treatment plants – and federal facilities (not state government facilities) to submit to the relevant authorities emergency planning information; an inventory of hazardous chemicals kept on their premises and their location; and annual estimates of the amounts of particular chemicals (from a list of 650 out of potentially thousands) they discharge to the environment (USEPA 2004). As part of their emergency planning information, companies have to report 'worst case scenarios for the release of regulated substances and risk management plans to prevent or deal with them' (Douglas-Scott 1996: 118).

The information about chemical discharges is compiled annually as the Toxic Release Inventory (TRI), which is kept electronically as a geographically-based information system (GIS). The public is able to access data for individual firms as well as for particular regions, industries, chemicals or environmental media – air, water, land. In 1990 this database was expanded by the Pollution Prevention Act to include information on waste disposal and source reduction activities being conducted by each company:

> Armed with TRI data, communities have more power to hold companies accountable and make informed decisions about how toxic chemicals are to be managed. The data often spurs companies to focus on their chemical management practices since they are being measured and made public. In addition, the data serves as a rough indicator of environmental progress over time. (USEPA 2004)

In the first few years of its operation the TRI highlighted the vast amount of chemicals being discharged into the environment, much of it unregulated, and brought action by government and industry to reduce it. 'From 1988 to 2000, for example, releases of chemicals subject to TRI reporting dropped by a remarkable 48 per cent' (CPR 2005c). NGOs produced 'league tables' of polluters, which shamed some companies into going beyond their legal obligations to reduce emissions. Other companies which hadn't previously estimated their total annual discharges realised they were losing money by allowing so many chemicals to go down the drain, so to speak (Gunningham & Cornwall 1994: 8–9).

The TRI is limited by the number of chemicals it covers, which are but a small subset of the total chemicals produced, used and emitted; by the fact that small firms and some non-manufacturing sources of pollution – including oil wells, medical waste incinerators and agricultural producers – are not included; and the fact that the information provided is not linked to specific products (Orum & Heminway 2005: 3).

Australia

In Australia, the National Pollutant Inventory (NPI) includes only 90 chemicals, compared with a list of 1000 possibilities (CEPA 1994: 20), and compared with 150 considered in determining acceptable water quality under Australian Water Quality Guidelines for Fresh and Marine Waters. The NPI does not include data on hazardous chemical storage, use or disposal – only emissions. These emissions are estimated by the polluters themselves on the basis of their own self-monitoring with occasional random assessments of reported data by regulating authorities.

The NPI, like the US TRI, focuses on manufacturing. Again, the agricultural industry, which uses a great deal of chemicals, is not included (CEPA 1994: 6; Gunningham & Cornwall 1994: 17). Companies in the sectors covered can gain a reporting exemption on the basis of national security or commercial sensitivity but they have to prove that such issues are at stake; in the case of commercial confidentiality, the public interest must be taken into account in deciding whether to grant an exemption.

OECD and Europe

In 1996 the OECD, referring to Agenda 21 requirements with respect to public information and participation, passed a recommendation on implementing pollutant release and transfer registers, which stated:

> That Member countries take steps to establish, as appropriate, implement and make publicly available a pollutant release and transfer register (PRTR) system … PRTR systems should provide data to support the identification and assessment of possible risks to humans and the environment by identifying sources and amounts of potentially harmful releases and transfers to all environmental media. (OECD 1996)

A PRTR, as defined in the OECD Guidance Manual for Governments (OECD 2000), 'is an inventory of pollutants released to air, water and soil, and waste transferred off-site for treatment and/or disposal'.

The EU's 1998 Integrated Pollution Prevention and Control (IPPC) directive requires member nations to report the emissions of 50 substances to air or water to the European Pollutant Emission Register (EPER). The EPER (2005) first published a set of pollutant details from across Europe for 2004. The thresholds for reporting these 50 substances have been set so as to capture 90 per cent of emissions from industrial plants. It currently covers around 10 000 plants in 15 EU countries plus Norway and Hungary (EA 2005a).

The UK Environment Agency (EA 2005b) is responsible for the national Pollution Inventory, which 'collects information on releases and transfers of waste off-site' from the businesses it regulates in England and Wales. The information from this inventory feeds into the EPER and a National Atmospheric Emissions Inventory (NAEI). The NAEI (2005) collects information from several government departments and 'compiles estimates of emissions to the atmosphere from UK sources such as cars, trucks, power stations and industrial plant'.

In 2003 the Protocol on Pollutant Release and Transfer Registers was attached to the Aarhus Convention (Aarhus Convention 1998; see page 119) and signed by 36 European states and the European Community. It requires nations to establish a PRTR which is free, online, user-friendly;

covers at least 86 of the pollutants listed in the Protocol; covers releases from specific types of facilities – 'e.g. thermal power stations, mining and metallurgical industries, chemical plants, waste and waste-water treatment plants, paper and timber industries' – as well as some spread-out non-point sources; and releases to air, land and water. PRTRs have to be designed with public participation and are mandatory for the industries covered. People should be able to look up specific firms, locations, mediums and pollutants.

Gaps

Ironically, communities in many developing countries like India, site of the Bhopal disaster that prompted the right to know legislation in the USA, still do not have the right to know about risks and emissions from US-owned and other foreign companies operating in their neighbourhoods (IRTK 2003). There is now an International Right to Know campaign supported by Amnesty International and various environmental, labour and development groups, which aims to redress this inequity.

Inventories provide some key information but there is much environmental information that is still not readily available to the public in most countries, including:

- **Untested ingredients** in specific pesticides and other products (labeling), and the flow of chemicals into the environment through product streams from industrial facilities (chemical use data, also known as 'materials accounting');
- **Compliance records** of producers and emitters of pollution; also, information on enforcement actions against violators, and the filing and status of citizen suits;
- **Facility ownership**, such as the identity of parent companies;
- **Geographic and climatic information** related to pollution outfalls and point sources (e.g., the height of smokestacks, the direction of prevailing winds, groundwater plume modeling);
- **Total volume flows, release durations, and the size of peak releases** of toxic emi-ssions; and the total environmental loading of pollutants within geographic areas;
- **Health of ecosystems**;
- **Workplace illness and injury records**; and
- **National environmental trends,** such as landuse trends, drinking water safety, and human health indicators (e.g., asthma, birth defects and chronic diseases). (OMB Watch 2001: 25)

State of the environment reporting addresses the last of these points and, to some extent the health of ecosystems, but most are not covered by either inventories, right to know or FOI legislation.

PUBLIC PARTICIPATION

The right to public participation goes beyond the right to information. The importance of public participation in environmental decisions is internationally recognised (Saladin & Dyke 1998: 1). According to the UN's Special Rapporteur on Human Rights and the Environment: 'Failure to take part in decision-making, whether internationally or nationally, has been and still is at the origin of development choices or the imposition of development strategies which have had serious adverse effects on the environment' (Ksentini 1994).

Lack of public participation in decision making has resulted in development strategies oriented to economic growth and financial considerations. The Global Consultation on the Right to Development as a Human Right (quoted in Ksentini 1994) concluded that these economic strategies 'failed to a large extent to achieve social justice, human rights have been infringed, directly and through the depersonalisation of social relations, the breakdown of families or communities, and of social and economic life' (para 153).

The Louisville Charter for Safer Chemicals (Orum & Heminway 2005: 5) defines participation this way:

> Participation includes traditional and innovative means of engaging communities and workers in decisions about environmental health hazards and solutions. At the broadest level, these means include voting, freedom of speech and assembly, literacy, and the right to petition for a redress of grievances. They include service on local boards and commissions, citizen lobbying, notice and comment on government regulations, and the use of initiatives and referendums. In the workplace, participation includes training on health hazards and safer alternatives, labor-management committees, rights to organize, whistleblower protection, access to technical expertise, and opportunities to seek and accompany both occupational and environmental health inspections.

International agreements

Many international agreements emphasise the right of citizens to participate. One of the earliest was the 1982 World Charter for Nature (UN 1982) which states:

> All persons, in accordance with their national legislation, shall have the opportunity to participate, individually or with others, in the formulation of decisions of direct concern to their environment, and shall have access to means of redress when their environment has suffered damage or degradation. (Principle 23)

In 1991 Commonwealth countries agreed to the Harare Declaration (quoted in CHRI 2005), which recognises 'the individual's inalienable right to participate by means of free and democratic political processes in framing the society in which he or she lives'.

Other international agreements emphasise the desirability of public participation, such as the Protocol on Water and Health (UN/ECE 1999), which states:

> Access to information and public participation in decision-making concerning water and health are needed, inter alia, in order to enhance the quality and the implementation of the decisions, to build public awareness of issues, to give the public the opportunity to express its concerns and to enable public authorities to take due account of such concerns. Such access and participation should be supplemented by appropriate access to judicial and administrative review of relevant decisions. (Article 5)

Agreements that promote participation include:

- ECE Convention on Environmental Impact Assessment, 1991
- Biological Diversity Convention, 1992
- Council of Europe Convention on Damage resulting from Activities Dangerous to the Environment, 1993
- UN Framework Convention on Climate Change and its Kyoto Protocol, 1997.

Professor Dinah Shelton (1999: 226), of Notre Dame University, notes that:

> In sum, the right to participation is so widely expressed that almost no international environmental treaty omits it from its operative provisions. In human rights law, it is one of the fundamental rights guaranteed by all human rights instruments, being inherent in the rule of law and democratic governance. As such, the right to participation may be considered to form part of the corpus of general international law.

Electoral representation

Participation of the governed gives governments and their policies legitimacy. Representation, whereby citizens are able to elect representatives to make decisions on their behalf, is a very weak form of participation. Citizens can influence decisions in that representatives can be voted out periodically if they do not perform well, but that influence is very indirect.

Representative democracy, on its own, has not been effective in allowing citizens' views to directly influence technological and development decisions. When decisions are made by elected governments without direct public participation:

- the opinions of minorities can be ignored;
- politicians are most concerned about the period up to the next election – at most 4 or 5 years;
- politicians rely on advice from experts who may have different priorities and values from the majority of people (NENT 1997: 11).

For these reasons citizens have increasingly demanded more direct participation in such decisions, including environmental decisions. Mechanisms such as consultation on environmental impact statements, public enquiries and the membership of community spokespersons on committees have all been used to meet the public demand for greater participation.

What is genuine participation?

True public participation, also known as citizen participation, requires 'the genuine involvement of all social actors in social and political decision-making processes that potentially affect the communities in which they live and work'. Used effectively, public participation can help in establishing priorities, finding solutions and coming to decisions. 'The community is hence transformed into a promoter of ideas and an active actor in the public realm', while the government is merely 'advisor and technical implementer of publicly agreed upon works' (Picolotti 1999: 3–4).

The collection and provision of information, including that covered by freedom of information and right to know legislation, does not in itself constitute public participation, although it is clearly necessary to enable public participation to be effective and genuine. For participation to be effective the community must be fully informed and have access to information.

Much environmental decision making involves public consultation. This might include surveys of citizen views, public hearings, and calls for public comments on proposed developments. However, the party doing the consulting is not legally obliged to act in accord with its findings. Consultation allows citizens to express their views, but there is no guarantee that those views will be considered or taken into account. Appointing members of the public or community representatives to advisory boards and committees is also a form of consultation that falls short of real participation.

Genuine participation requires that the public has a real chance to determine the outcome. Those conducting the participation exercise must be committed to listening to and heeding community opinion and all those with a stake in the outcome need to be identified and given an opportunity to take part. But more than this, participation requires a redistribution of power so that those taking part have a say in any decisions: 'Participation in decision-making implies commitment and exercise of power in the decision-making process' (Picolotti 1999: 4–5).

Aarhus Convention

The statements of principle included in international agreements do not go into detail about how public participation should be implemented, nor of what it consists, and so in 1995 the environmental ministers of the UN Economic Commission for Europe (UNECE), which includes European and North American nations, agreed to some guidelines on public participation (Saladin & Dyke 1998: 1). The Aarhus Convention on Access to Information, Public Participation and Access to Justice in Environmental Matters was subsequently adopted in 1998 and came into force in 2001. Although it applies to national decision making, the Convention also requires parties to it to promote the principles of public participation in international decision making.

The Aarhus Convention recognises:

> that every person has the right to live in an environment adequate to his or her health and well-being, and the duty, both individually and in association with others, to protect and improve the environment for the benefit of present and future generations [and that] to be able to assert this right and observe this duty, citizens must have access to information, be entitled to participate in decision-making and have access to justice in environmental matters. (Aarhus Convention 1998)

It also recognises that to achieve these rights 'citizens may need assistance in order to exercise their rights'.

The Convention requires that information on the state of the environment be collected regularly and systematically by the relevant authorities and that the public be informed of upcoming decisions and their ability to participate in them. Such decisions can range from policies, programmes and plans at the highest level, to regulations, specific permits and approvals at the local level.

The Convention recognises that people will only be interested in participating if they can feel confident that their views will be seriously considered and taken into account in the decision, and thus details some minimum requirements for a public participation process. These include the need for people to be given effective notice of the decision in time to be able to prepare their input; that they be told how they may participate; and that they have good opportunity to submit comments, information and analyses. When the decision is made it should take account of the public input and the public should be informed of the decision in writing with the reasons for it.

Finally, the Convention requires a mechanism for people to seek remedies if they are not informed and given the opportunity to participate fully, or 'to challenge the substance of a decision' by appealing to an independent and impartial review body whose decisions are binding on public authorities. Such appeals should not be too time consuming or expensive and appropriate remedies should be available (Saladin & Dyke 1998: 10).

Benefits of public consultation

Participation can be time consuming and expensive and lead to or highlight conflicts, and also means that governments are not able to control the final outcome. However, the benefits are many. Ann Richardson (1983: 52–61), in her book *Participation*, gives three main arguments for advocating genuine participation in government decision making. Firstly, it is the fairest system of government. This rests on the idea that those who will be affected by decisions should have a right to influence those decisions. She points out that it can also be argued that those who bear the costs of these decisions should have the sole right to determine them.

Secondly, participation is important to the wellbeing of participants. It gives dignity to those involved and affected. It helps in the development of individual capability and awareness and helps to create a well-informed, responsive, involved citizenry, which is necessary for a vibrant democracy.

Thirdly, public participation usually leads to better decisions. In this way increased participation is an aid to policy makers, for because of it they have more information about what services are required, the limits of public tolerance, the problems, concerns and issues involved, and are aware of various other forms of feedback. Members of the public who are immediately affected by a development often devote much time and energy necessary to researching the problem and can become experts in their own right. Their expertise may be more focused on the immediate problem at hand. For example, they may become, over time, expert in emissions from municipal incinerators of the type that is planned for their neighbourhood from having read everything they can find on this topic.

Additionally, local people often have knowledge and experience of their local environment, and contextual or relevant knowledge in an area which technical experts involved in a project don't have, such as familiarity with local weather patterns, sea conditions, and flora and fauna in the area. It could also be argued on moral and ethical grounds that local people have special knowledge about their own situation and how a development in their neighbourhood will affect them.

Further Reading

Aarhus Convention (1998) Convention on Access to Information, Public Participation in Decision-Making and Access to Justice in Environmental Matters, United Nations Economic Commission for Europe, <http://www.unece.org/env/pp/>

Boyle, AE & MR Anderson (eds) (1996) *Human Rights Approaches to Environmental Protection*, Clarendon Press, Oxford.

Picolotti, Romina (1999) Agenda 21 and human rights: the right to participate, Center for Human Rights and Environment (CEDHA), <http://www.cedha.org.ar/docs/doc21-eng.doc>

Saladin, Claudia & Brennan Van Dyke (1998) *Implementing the Principles of the Public Participation Convention in International Organizations*, Center for International Environmental Law, Washington DC, June.

Shelton, Dinah (1999) A rights-based approach to public participation and local management of natural resources, Paper presented at the 3rd IGES International Workshop on Forest Conservation Strategies for the Asia and Pacific Region, 7–9 September, Tokyo, <http://www.iges.or.jp/en/fc/phase1/3ws-26-dinah.pdf>

What is the right to information?, Commonwealth Human Rights Initiative (CHRI), viewed 27 May 2005, <http://www.humanrightsinitiative.org/programs/ai/rti/rti/what.htm>

PART III

ECONOMIC METHODS OF ENVIRONMENTAL VALUATION

7

MEASURING ENVIRONMENTAL VALUE

A central theme of sustainable development is the integration of economic, social and environmental concerns. This principle is at the heart of the Bruntland Commission report, the Earth Summit agreements and various national policies and strategies. Chapter 8 of Agenda 21 (UN 1992), agreed to at the Earth Summit on Integrating Environment and Development in Decisionmaking, states:

> A first step towards the integration of sustainability into economic management is the establishment of better measurement of the crucial role of the environment as a source of natural capital and as a sink for by-products generated during the production of man-made capital and other human activities.

In this view, integrating environment and economy means appreciating the role of the environment as a component of the economic system that provides raw materials for production and as a receptacle for wastes from production. David Pearce and his colleagues (1989: 5), in their report on sustainable development, interpreted the principles of sustainable development as recognising that 'resources and environments serve economic functions and have positive economic value'. Similarly, DJ Thampapillai (1991: 5) states in his text on *Environmental Economics*:

> Clearly, the natural environment is an important component of the economic system, and without the natural environment the economic system would not be able to function. Hence, we need to treat the natural environment in the same way as we treat labour and capital; that is, as an asset and a resource.

The economists' view

Economists claim that environmental degradation has resulted from the failure of the market system to put any value on the environment, even though the environment serves economic functions and provides economic and other benefits. They argue that environmental assets, because they are free or underpriced, tend to be overused or abused, thereby resulting in damage. Because they are not owned, and do not have price tags, there is no incentive to protect them.

The word 'value' is derived from the Latin *valere*, meaning 'to be strong or worthy', and has a moral dimension for most people: values are what they teach their children. However, economists use value to mean 'that amount of some commodity, medium of exchange, etc., which is considered to be an equivalent for something else; a fair or adequate equivalent or return' (*Oxford English Dictionary* quoted in Waring 1988: 17). So when economists talk about environmental values they are speaking of something quite different from the environmental values that environmentalists speak of.

Economists argue that unless the environment is valued in monetary terms – that is, given a price – it will be undervalued. They claim that most people are used to dealing with monetary values and can more easily relate to them. Also, because other things are valued in monetary terms, if environmental benefits are converted into monetary terms they can be compared with the benefits of other ways of spending money. For example, the benefits from preserving a wetland can be compared with the benefits of filling it in and building a housing estate.

Some environmental resources – such as timber, fish and minerals – are bought and sold in the market. But their price often does not reflect the true cost of obtaining them, 'because their valuation has invariably been based on the resource as an entity by itself and not as the component of a resource system' (Thampapillai 1991: 15). Thus the price of a resource may include the partial but obvious cost of obtaining it, but not the cost of the environmental damage caused in the process.

Other environmental goods, such as clean air, the ozone layer and aesthetic landscapes, are not bought and sold, and so are said to have a zero price in the market place. They are referred to as public goods.

The treatment of public goods

The market does not deal very well with resources that are not individually owned – such as the atmosphere, waterways and some areas of land – referred to as public (or social) goods by economists. Public goods all have the following characteristics to some degree, which are what prevents them from being priced by the market:

1. 'Consumption by one person does not reduce the quantity available to others.' For example, when a bushwalker goes to a scenic lookout her action does not reduce the amount of view available for others to see.
2. Benefits automatically accrue to everyone – 'enjoyment cannot be made conditional upon the payment of a price or upon ownership'. For example, if the ozone layer is not depleted, everyone benefits. Conversely, no one can be prevented from benefiting, even if they do not pay to prevent its depletion.
3. 'Individuals cannot avoid using the good.' For example, the air is something that no one can avoid breathing (HRSCEC 1987: 11).

Public goods include some types of information, most scientific knowledge, lighthouses and national defence, as well as environmental benefits. In reality, there is a continuum from 'pure' public goods to private goods, with many goods and services having some but not all the characteristics of a pure public good. For example, a water supply can be charged for, and is sometimes privately controlled and sold. The world's supply of fertile soil, forests and even beaches can be seen as a common heritage, but parts can be owned by individuals.

One of the reasons that public goods are not usually bought and sold is that it is difficult to exclude non-payers from using or taking advantage of them. This means it is hard to make a profit from providing them, and there is little incentive for private firms to supply or maintain them. However, public goods often cost money to supply or maintain, and their provision and protection has traditionally been a government responsibility.

There is some debate about how well governments fulfil this responsibility. Economists agree that the environment could be more effectively protected if people and firms were charged real prices for using it. This would ensure that environmental considerations were incorporated into market decisions and the environment was properly priced to reflect the relative scarcity of natural resources and assets.

NATIONAL ACCOUNTS

Chapter 8 of Agenda 21 recommends that one means to integrate environment and development into decision making is for nations to establish 'systems for integrated environmental and economic accounting'. The best known aspect of national accounting is the gross national product (GNP), a measure of all the goods and services bought and sold in and by a nation, and commonly accepted as a measure of a nation's standard of living. If the GNP rises it is assumed that everyone is better off. If the GNP goes down, even over a short period of time, economists say there is a recession and critics say the government is not managing the economy properly. The GNP of a country divided by the number of people in the country gives an average figure for the standard of living of the population as a whole.

Problems with GNP as a measure of welfare

However, GNP does not give any indication of the state of a nation's environment and does not take into account environmental depletion that may result from rising GNP. The ways in which GNP neglects the environment are:

GNP only measures market transactions

GNP only includes services that are legally bought and sold. It does not include components of the environment such as wilderness areas or native birds that are not bought and sold. Keeping trees in a forest is not counted in GNP, and is not counted as contributing anything towards a nation's wellbeing; but when a tree is cut down and sold as timber it adds to GNP and therefore to economic growth. Marilyn Waring (1988: 1) discovered, as a politician in New Zealand, that in the system of national accounts:

> the things I valued about life in my country – its pollution-free environment; its mountain streams with safe drinking water; the accessibility of national parks, walkways, beaches, lakes, kauri and beech forests; the absence of nuclear power and nuclear energy – all counted for nothing.

Similarly, Robert Repetto (1989), Director of the Economic Research Program of the World Resources Institute, points out that a nation 'could exhaust its mineral reserves, cut down its forests, erode its soils, pollute its aquifers, and hunt its wildlife to extinction' without affecting its measured income. Repetto argues that GNP as a measure confuses the using up of valuable assets with the earning of income, and that this is a particular problem for countries dependent on natural resources for employment and revenues, because they are using a system of accounting that ignores their principal assets.

GNP does not discriminate between costs and benefits

Hospital bills, car repairs and insurance costs add to economic growth because they are services that are provided and paid for. If there is a toxic spill which damages water supplies, GNP does not decline; in fact, it goes up if people spend money getting medical treatment for health problems or injuries caused by the spill. If the government spends millions of dollars cleaning up the damage, GNP goes up because the money spent is considered to be a purchase of goods and services. In fact, in the year that the ship *Exxon Valdez* spilt its cargo of oil in Alaska, that state's GNP rose dramatically because of all the money spent trying to clean up the spill.

The destruction of environmental resources and the costs of cleaning up after the destruction are labelled 'growth' and 'production' in GNP measurements.

Depreciation of the environment is not counted

Natural resources which have been used up or degraded – such as open space, wildlife, scenic landscapes, and the quality of air and water – are not counted in the national accounts, even though it is obvious that these things contribute to a nation's social wellbeing. Repetto (1989) gives the example of a farmer who cuts down some timber and sells it to pay for a barn. In the farmer's accounts, she or he has lost the timber but gained the barn. In the national accounts, income and investment would rise when the farmer sold the timber *and* when the farmer built the barn. No losses would be recorded.

In the past, economists have not thought of the environment as being used up or worn out in the same way as are buildings and equipment. This is because they assumed that natural resources – the resources obtained from the environment – were so abundant that a small loss would not be noticed. Also, they have assumed that natural resources were 'free gifts of nature' because they required no investment to obtain them. However, as economists usually value things according to what price they can be sold for, rather than how much it has cost to produce them, this stance is inconsistent. Repetto (1989: 40) argues that the true measure of depreciation 'is the amount that future income will decline as an asset decays or becomes obsolete'. Soils depreciate as they are degraded, and become less fertile, in just the same way that machines depreciate as they get older.

Modifying GNP

In recent years, the problems associated with national accounting and GNP have been widely recognised. Many people have called for national accounts to be adjusted to take account of environmental resources lost in the process of generating wealth so that they will provide a better indication of the true wealth of a nation.

Various modifications to GNP have been proposed over the years as a way of incorporating social and environmental factors. As early as 1972, economists William Nordhaus and James Tobin (1972) recommended modifying GNP by subtracting the cost of pollution and other 'negative' goods from the final figure, and adding services which do not get paid for, such as housework. They called their new indicator 'net economic welfare' (NEW).

Alternative indicators have been resisted by governments because they are seen as too difficult to measure. Additionally, politicians prefer to use indices that emphasise and even exaggerate progress. However, in 1985 the OECD made a commitment to develop 'more accurate resource accounts', and in 1987 the Brundtland Commission recognised the need to take full account of the improvement or deterioration in the stock of natural resources in measuring a nation's economic growth (Repetto 1989: 42).

In order for the environment to be integrated into national accounts, however, it has to be valued in monetary terms – and this creates problems. It is relatively simple to assign a value to minerals and resources that have a market value, but not so easy to put a value to non-commercial wild species, for example, or ecosystems.

The people who put together the United Nations' system of national accounts, based on GNP, have decided that there should not be any major changes to them. Rather, they suggest that a separate system of satellite accounts should be worked out that would give measures of natural resources; and that, at some time in the distant future, these might be incorporated into the main GNP figures. Norway, Canada and France have instituted extensive systems of resource accounts which are separate but supplementary to their national economic accounts. These are physical measures of the country's natural resources such as forests, fish and minerals.

COST–BENEFIT ANALYSIS

Cost–benefit analysis (CBA) is another way of integrating environmental and economic goals in policies and activities. CBA is a tool which decision makers use to choose between alternative courses of action. It has experienced a resurgence in use worldwide in association with environmental policy making. It can be used in a variety of circumstances.

Uses of CBA

Assessing government projects

CBA has traditionally been used to weigh the benefits that would arise from a government project against the costs associated with it. A private firm that is producing goods or services for a market will make an investment decision on the basis of whether it thinks it can make a reasonable profit from the investment. However, governments tend to provide services for which there are no buyers, or services for which there is a market but no profit objective. The provision of urban infrastructure – such as roads, water and sewerage – cannot be adequately evaluated on the basis of financial return on investment. CBA therefore provides a means of evaluating such projects and comparing them to assess priorities so that public money is spent wisely and efficiently. It is also used by international banks and aid agencies to evaluate projects.

Integrating environmental considerations

It has been argued that CBA should be applied to all private as well as public projects as a way of ensuring that environmental and social costs and benefits, as well as profit potential, are included in all project decisions. Indeed, undertaking a CBA is now a formal requirement for many large-scale projects undertaken by private enterprise, such as those in the mining sector and the building industry.

Assessing natural resource use and environmental projects

CBA can be applied to other matters requiring decisions, such as the rate of exploitation of scarce natural resources and the management of wilderness areas. Economists and business people are now arguing that it should be used more often as a way of deciding which way to proceed towards sustainable development. 'In Britain, the growth of an audit culture has led to growing demands for monetary expressions of the benefits of environmental projects' (O'Neill 1996: 98). It is also being used to evaluate greenhouse gas reduction strategies.

Assessing the merit of government regulations and policies

CBA is commonly used in the USA 'to weigh the various interests at stake' in a decision by government to introduce a regulation (de Sadeleer 2002: 199). Similar assessments are also made in Australia for environmental measures. In the USA, government agencies must undertake a full risk assessment and CBA before any major regulation can be introduced. The rationale embodied in the legislation is to 'provide more cost-effective and cost-reasonable protection to human health and the environment' by using 'scientifically objective and unbiased' consideration of risks, cost and benefits as a basis for decision making. Opponents of legislation argue that CBA is being used as a way of delaying and obstructing environmental regulation (see chapter 8).

The rationale behind CBA

In order to weigh costs against benefits, CBA usually attempts to put a monetary value on both so that they are expressed in the same units. The costs of a road project would include the cost of labour and materials used in construction, as well as other costs such as the loss of parkland and homes to make way for the road, and the resulting pollution, disruption to neighbourhoods, and loss of peace and quiet. The benefits of such a project might include time saved to motorists, increased predictability of journey times, and increased accessibility of a particular location.

When the US EPA decided to phase all the lead out of petrol in the 1980s, it justified this decision on the basis of CBA, which calculated medical costs from lead poisoning as well as 'the costs of remedial education for children whose cognitive development had been impaired by lead, and the children's expected loss of future income due to their lowered IQs'. It valued the loss of each IQ point to children exposed to lead at $8346 (Ackerman & Heinzerling 2004: 4).

Obviously, some costs and benefits are very difficult to put into monetary terms. But proponents of CBA see it as helping to make the decision-making process more objective and rational. They argue that it is rational to choose a course of action in which the gains outweigh the losses and that, by putting the gains and losses in numeric terms, it is easier to be objective, consistent and rational in the assessment:

> The use of money as a measure of these costs and benefits should not be controversial since it is simply a practical device which enables us to compare them. The issues of real importance in the evaluation are the amounts of money to be associated with each cost and benefit and the aggregation of these amounts so that the decision-maker can determine the most beneficial course for society. (Abelson 1979: 197–8)

Economists argue that whenever people make a decision, they weigh the pros and cons of that decision, but often do so unconsciously or intuitively. By undertaking a formal CBA, the values they are attaching to the costs and benefits are made explicit and are recorded for everyone to see rather than remaining inside someone's head. This means that people have to think about those values in a more systematic and reasoned way.

Discounting under CBA

Normally, future costs and benefits are discounted (reduced) because it is assumed that they are not worth as much to people as present costs and benefits. The reasoning behind discounting is as follows: if a person has the choice of receiving a sum of money now or waiting to get it later, most economists assume that, even if he or she ignores inflation, the person would prefer to get the money now. He or she will only be interested in getting it later if the sum has become larger by then.

For the economist, $1 this year is worth $1 + r (the discount rate) next year. Therefore, $1 next year is worth less than $1 this year; it has to be discounted (reduced) if we are to consider it in today's values.

Whether a project goes ahead or not will often depend on what discount rate is used. Small differences in discount rates can make big differences in the final ratio of benefits to costs if long-term costs or benefits are being considered. For example, the net present value of an income or cost of $200 million in 50 years' time would be:

- \$1.7 million if the discount rate is 10 per cent
- \$ 17 million if the discount rate is 5 per cent
- \$ 74 million if the discount rate is 2 per cent.

Objectivity of CBA

Proponents of CBA argue that, by placing explicit numbers on proposed actions, the process is more open to scrutiny by others. However, what tends to happen is that the analysis is highly technical, and neither available nor accessible to the public. The inevitable value judgments involved in attaching a price to environmental and social benefits are hidden beneath a mass of figures that give the impression that the analysis is rational, neutral and objective. Public debate over the options is therefore inhibited.

Even in the case of a willingness to pay (contingent valuation; see page 135) survey, which is supposed to objectively reflect values of the population, economists exercise value judgments about which answers are to be included in the analysis. In the case of the North Carolina study of the value of chronic bronchitis described later in this chapter, the answers of only two-thirds of those interviewed were included. Some answers were excluded because the economists judged the interviewees to be inconsistent. Other answers were excluded because they were thought by the economists to be far too high or too low (Ackerman & Heinzerling 2004: 96).

In reality, environmental value is highly subjective:

> The same patch of trees can be valued by international conservationists and scientists as an embodiment of the world's precious biological diversity, mapped by an Indonesian commercial timber concession as merely another block containing so many cubic feet of exportable tropical hardwood, or seen and claimed by a local Dyak community as the site of a cultivated forest garden, inhabited by orchards of fragrant Durian trees and memories of family members gathering honey. (Zerner 2000: 6)

Averaging such values does not give an objective outcome. Nor does converting them into some sort of universal measure.

Justifying projects

CBA, far from being an objective source of information, is often used to justify projects. Ian Barbour (1980: 170), a professor emeritus of Science, Technology and Society, argues that the 'formulation of problems and the preselection of alternatives, which are frequently the most important decisions, occur before the analysis is made. In the analysis itself, an agency typically overstates benefits and understates costs'. He claims that environmental effects and other indirect costs tend to be neglected, while indirect benefits are searched for: 'While the assignment of monetary values appears to be a technical question, it often reflects the biases of analysts or their judgments of what the public wants'.

Barbour's claims have been borne out by various studies and reports. In 2000, for example, an internal Pentagon investigation found that the US Army Corps of Engineers had been manipulating CBA's to justify civil works projects that the Corps wanted to undertake (Ruch 2000). Similarly, the numbers of people who will be displaced by dam projects around the world are often grossly underestimated to ensure that CBAs support the projects (Corner House 1999).

The same bias can be found in estimates of national assets. During the Clinton presidency the US Forest Service estimated that by 2000, recreation in the nation's forests would contribute $111 billion to its GDP. In contrast, the Forest Service under the George W Bush presidency estimated that it was worth only $11 billion in 2002. The new figure provides much more justification for logging and mining in national forests (Eilperin 2005).

Undermining environmental regulations

CBA is also used to attack environmental regulations. When new environmental regulations are being proposed, the industries affected tend to exaggerate their compliance costs, which influences government estimates of the cost of regulation. A 1997 study by the Economic Policy Institute in the USA of 'all emission reduction regulations for which successive cost estimates' were available, found that in 11 out of 12 cases the initial pollution-control cost estimates were double, and often much more than double, the actual costs (Hodges 1997).

A recent study by the Center for Progressive Reform in the USA found that the Office of Management and Budget (OMB) had consistently used CBA to argue for less and weaker regulation (Driesen 2005). Ackerman and Heinzerling (2004: 9, 213) argue that CBA is in fact used to promote deregulation under the cover of scientific objectivity. They claim opponents attack environmental regulations as being uneconomic, and use complicated and contrived economic analyses to discredit legislation, rather than publicly debating its merits.

What is rational?

Economists argue that weighing costs against benefits is the only rational way to make a decision. They argue that trade-offs are necessary and can only be made rationally if measurement is involved. However, even if one agrees that trade-offs are necessary, this bureaucratic method of deciding trade-offs by measuring costs and benefits is not necessarily the most rational way of making a decision. People make decisions all the time that do not involve converting everything to a single measure for simple comparison.

> Good judgement is founded on the existence of capacities of perception and of knowledge based in education and experience. Indeed, it is attempts by economists to force the measuring rod of money or any other unit onto rational deliberations which lead to arbitrariness, contrivance and obstruction of the process of reasoned debate. (O'Neill 1996: 98)

In fact, some would argue that the attempt to find a common measure for ranking 'all objects and states of affairs' is actually *ir*rational or, at the very least, limiting (O'Neill 1996: 98). Values cannot be reduced to one overarching measure. Larry Lohmann (1997) points out:

> Looking to criteria such as weight and monetary value to define rational choice is insufficient in contexts in which people need to reason not just about means but also about clusters of interlocked, mutually irreducible ends and how to develop them in light of those means.

Similarly, John O'Neill (1996: 98) comments that the 'fact that I prefer A to B with good reason is not evidence that A possesses more of some overarching super-value that is present in all my other potential choices as well'. A person may make one choice on the basis of cost and another on the basis of friendship. There is no single measure (money or utility etc.) that can encompass both decisions. Nor is the balancing of costs and benefits appropriate to both decisions.

ENVIRONMENTAL VALUATION IN PRACTICE

The integration of environmental gains and losses into either national accounts or CBA requires that they be converted into money terms, although it is recognised that these gains and losses would not in reality be bought and sold on the market.

Direct costs and benefits are the easiest to estimate. These might include estimating the value of production forgone because of environmental damage or the value of earnings lost through health problems associated with air and water pollution. However, direct monetary costs tend to underestimate the real costs and benefits provided by the environment. Improved health resulting from a cleaner and safer environment is worth more than just the medical bills saved, for example. A clean beach is worth more than just the value of having healthier beachgoers.

Measuring the values that people place on the environment is very difficult – some say impossible. For example, the reasons for preventing losses of species, and maintaining ecosystems and biodiversity, are many and wide-ranging; the social, ethical, aesthetic and cultural values of plants and animals have been recognised in religion, art and literature throughout history.

For most economists, however, the environment can be priced because all these values can be translated into the preferences of individuals. This is usually done in one of the three ways described below:

Willingness to pay (contingent valuation)

Market prices for environmental benefits are often derived from surveys. These surveys may ask people how much they are willing to pay to preserve or improve the environment (willingness to pay), or how much monetary compensation a person is willing to accept for loss of environmental amenity (willingness to sell). Values for 'willingness to pay' and 'willingness to sell' are based on surveys that are likely to be inaccurate, because people may inflate or deflate the amounts they are willing to pay or accept.

With willingness to pay (also known as 'contingent valuation'), it is thought that people will understate the amount they would pay if they think there is a chance they might actually have to pay that amount. This is because people know that if others pay and they do not they will get the benefit anyway – they can become 'free riders'. On the other hand, if people believe they will never be asked to pay up, they may exaggerate the amount they are willing to pay.

Surveys based on willingness to sell tend to obtain a much higher figure for what the environmental quality is worth (assuming people want a maximum price for something that they are selling). Willingness to sell surveys, therefore, tend to generate values that economists believe are too high. For example, surveys found that US households were willing to spend $100 each to prevent another disaster like the *Exxon Valdez* oil spill, but when they were asked how much money they would want before they would allow another spill to happen, not only were the sums much higher but many people said they would not allow it to happen no matter how much they were paid (Ackerman & Heinzerling 2004: 156).

Opportunity costs

Opportunity costs can be used to put a value on an area of the environment which is to be preserved from development. To work out the opportunity cost for such an area, economists list all the possible alternative activities that could take place in that area. For example, the value of preserving a wetland may be estimated by working out what the land would be worth if it were used for agriculture or housing. For each alternative activity, the economist works out what benefits would have been gained that could not be gained in any other way and then subtracts the costs that would be involved in getting these benefits. So, for the housing alternative, the cost of building the houses and providing services for them would be subtracted from the value of the houses. And if those same houses could just as easily be built somewhere else, the opportunity cost would only consider the additional benefits from building them in the area being assessed.

The highest amount of net benefits (after subtracting costs) that one can get from any alternative course of action that has been forgone is the opportunity cost of preserving that area. This indicates the minimum value placed on the area, since the decision to preserve it has meant that those making the decision were willing to forgo at least those benefits, and maybe more.

This method can be used before a decision is made, so that decision makers or the public can decide whether they believe the area is indeed worth what has been worked out as the opportunity cost. If they decide not to preserve the area, environmental losses can be worked out in terms of the amount it would take to restore the environment to its original state after development has occurred – for example, after mining or logging. Environmentalists do not believe that all areas can be restored in this way, and thus reject this approach for not reflecting the full measure of environmental loss.

Opportunity cost can only be a partial measure of environmental value. The value of the area for housing may have no relationship whatsoever to the ecological or aesthetic or spiritual value of the area it will be destroying. A wetland, for example, might be providing a breeding ground for fish and other aquatic organisms as well as performing a cleansing function, filtering out pollutants that flow through the area.

Using proxies (hedonic pricing)

This method assumes that the value of environmental assets can be found by considering the prices of the closest market substitutes. For example, a lake that is used for fishing, boating and swimming might be valued by calculating what people spend on private fishing, boating and swimming facilities. Another market substitute commonly used is property values. The idea is that houses in a polluted area will be worth less than houses in a non-polluted area, and part of the difference in house prices will reflect the value the market puts on clean air or on the cost of pollution. Differences in property values will arise for other reasons as well, such as the quality of accommodation and accessibility to the central business district or public transport routes. The analyst must be able to work out what part of the difference is due to the environmental factors, and must be able to infer from that how much people are willing to pay for improved environmental quality.

Proxies are also used in the willingness to pay method to avoid asking people directly how much the environment or their health is worth. For example, a contingent valuation study was undertaken in North Carolina in the late 1990s to work out the value of a chronic case of bronchitis. The surveyors thought that if they asked people directly what they would pay to avoid getting chronic bronchitis they would get unrealistically high amounts because people would not actually have to pay the amount they stated. Instead, they asked shoppers in a shopping mall if they would prefer to live in a more expensive area, where the risk of getting bronchitis was lower, or stay living where they were, given a particular bronchitis risk. The interviewees were told what the effects of bronchitis were. The surveyors altered the cost of living and the risk of bronchitis until the shopper being questioned would be equally happy living where they were or moving to the new location with the lower risk of bronchitis. From this survey they calculated that a case of chronic bronchitis was worth $883 000 to these shoppers. The results of that same survey were later used, with figures adjusted for inflation, to put a value on bladder cancer (Ackerman & Heinzerling 2004: 95–7).

The next chapter, chapter 8, evaluates the concept and practice of converting environmental value to a monetary value, be it through CBA or in order to integrate environmental assets into national accounts. Each of the principles outlined earlier in the book, apart from the polluter pays principle, will be applied to these methods.

Further Reading

Abelson, Peter (1979) *Cost Benefit Analysis and Environmental Problems*, Saxon House, London.

Ackerman, Frank & Lisa Heinzerling (2004) *Priceless: On Knowing the Price of Everything and the Value of Nothing*, The New Press, New York.

O'Neill, John (1996) Cost–benefit analysis, rationality and the plurality of values, *The Ecologist* 26 (3), May/June, pp. 98–103.

Pearce, David, Anil Markandya & Edward B Barbier (1989) *Blueprint for a Green Economy*, Earthscan, London.

Repetto, Robert (1989) Wasting assets: the need for national resource accounting, *Technology Review*, January, pp. 39–44.

Waring, Marilyn (1988) *Counting for Nothing: What Men Value and What Women are Worth*, Allen & Unwin, Wellington.

8

IS MONETARY VALUATION PRINCIPLED?

THE PARTICIPATION PRINCIPLE

Bypassing public debate

Conflict often arises over resource use and development projects because every individual accords different values to the environmental benefits of clean air and water, unspoilt wilderness areas, ecological balance and biological diversity. Differing values are also placed on social benefits such as community feeling and a sense of security. Each person's valuations will include economic, ecological, aesthetic and ethical components. It is because people put different values on the environment that conflict arises in the first place. Such conflict is normally resolved politically.

Depoliticising environmental issues

One of the attractions of cost–benefit analysis (CBA) is that it turns a highly charged political decision into one that appears to be technical and impersonal, one that can be dealt with by the appropriate professional experts – economists – in a calm and rational manner free from emotion and bias.

> Value conflicts that should be resolved politically are concluded in what look like rational, neutral, objective calculations. This may appeal to administrators, but it hinders public debate of the policy issues and lessens the accountability of bureaucratic officials. Numbers carry an unwarranted authority when used to legitimate decisions that are basically political in character. (Barbour 1980: 170)

Public debate over the options – a 'reasoned discussion of choices' – is therefore inhibited, and public participation is replaced by a technocratic process (O'Neill 1996: 100).

Frank Ackerman and Lisa Heinzerling (2004: 9, 213) argue in their book *Priceless* that using CBA as a governmental decision-making tool allows a 'small sample of nameless individuals who answer a survey' to dictate public policy, rather than politicians showing leadership and basing policy on rights and principles that they are willing to defend in public debate. They point out:

> By proceeding as if its assumptions are scientific and by speaking a language all of its own, economic analysis too easily conceals the basic human questions that lie at its heart and excludes the voices of people untrained in the field. Again and again, economic theory gives us opaque and technical reasons to do the obviously wrong thing.

The benefits of public debate

Public debate and discussion is not only an essential part of public participation but it can also enable people to learn about an issue, reason together, change their positions, modify their demands, negotiate with each other and understand each other's positions. All this is curtailed when debate and discussion are replaced by surveys of individual uninformed preferences or economic calculations.

Instead of people being able to form their values in a way that allows for give and take, for learning over time, and being able to express their values themselves – whether in a comprehensive, hesitant, impassioned or nuanced way – an anonymous surveyor demands that they convert their values into prices on the spot, often before they have had a chance to even think about an issue or find out more about it. The prices obtained from individuals are then translated by economic experts into a set of numbers that are aggregated with others. Members of the public have no chance to persuade others or be persuaded. They have no opportunity to explore compromises or alternatives that might suit several parties.

The outcomes of using methods such as willingness to pay are not influenced by reasons for people's choices or preferences. Whether their reasons are based on falsehoods, ignorance or prejudice, or are well founded, immoral, irrational or sensible, is not considered relevant. All that matters are the preferences themselves. Public debate, on the other hand, can uncover falsehoods and prejudice, enlighten ignorance and tease out moral and ethical issues. It ensures that people's views are more likely to be well informed and sensible.

Resource economists have found a certain reluctance by the public to co-operate with contingent valuation surveys. This is because

> respondents believe that environmental policy – for example, the degree of pollution permitted in national parks – involves ethical, cultural, and aesthetic questions over which society must deliberate on the merits, and that this has nothing to do with pricing the satisfaction of preferences … (Daly and Cobb 1989: 91)

Individual preferences vs social good

Environmental questions have traditionally been determined by a political process that enables community influence through voting, campaigning and protesting. Yet some economists and market enthusiasts argue that the market is more democratic than the political process because individual consumers can express their preferences by choosing how they spend their money. They argue that it is only when a person puts a money value on environmental quality that economists can get a true measure of the strength of feeling and the degree of concern individuals have for an environmental asset.

However the market allocation of natural resources is not democratic because not everyone has an equal vote. The power of the consumer is not evenly distributed (the wealthy, businesses and bureaucracies have far greater consumer clout), and consumers do not get to choose from a full range of alternatives.

Economist Peter Self (1990: 9) claims the idea that markets rather than governments are more efficient at giving people what they want is based on the fallacious assumption that there is no such thing as the common good outside of individual wants and preferences. He disagrees with this proposition, claiming that when people vote they often consider wider interests than their own self-interest. They see themselves as part of a group – be it an occupational group, an ethnic group, a class, a nation or whatever. Politically, people are not only concerned about their self-interest, they also consider the 'good of society'.

This is why people support ideas such as public education when they do not have children, and environmental protection beyond their own lifetimes. 'As consumers they seek to maximise their own materialistic wants, whilst as citizens they are concerned with what constitutes a "good" society' (Cooper & Hart 1992: 22). Clearly, asking people to treat the environment as if they are consumers of the environment does not clarify their views about whether it should be preserved (Corner House 1999).

Moreover, by reducing environmental debates to calculations of aggregate preferences, discussion of wider social goals is avoided. CBA 'completely obscures the underlying dispute about the nature of 'development' and 'environment' (Corner House 1999). By confining decisions to a comparison of costs and benefits, not only are broader policy and political issues ignored, but there is an underlying assumption 'that efficiency in allocation is the criterion that society deems paramount when making a decision'. However 'other criteria such as equity and political acceptability may be of greater concern to environmental policymakers' and to the community (Cooper & Hart 1992: 26).

Beyond price

Oscar Wilde described a cynic as 'one who knows the price of everything and the value of nothing'. EF Schumacher (quoted in Pearce 1983: 1–2), who wrote the well-known book *Small is Beautiful*, said of CBA:

> To press non-economic values into the framework of the economic calculus, economists use the method of cost/benefit analysis ... In fact, however, it is a procedure by which the higher is reduced to the level of the lower and the priceless is given a price. It can therefore never serve to clarify the situation and lead to an enlightened decision. All it can do is lead to self-deception or the deception of others; ... the pretence that everything has a price or, in other words, that money is the highest of all values.

CBA, and the integration of environmental values into national accounts, assume that environmental 'goods' and human-made goods are interchangeable and that what matters is the aggregate value of both types of goods. If the aggregate is what matters, then environmental goods can be traded off for human-made goods and this is, after all, the underlying principle of CBA. But are some values beyond trade-offs?

Many argue that attaching a price to something devalues and cheapens it. This is certainly the case for praise, friendship and even sex. For many people, putting a price on nature is as abhorrent as putting a price on family, justice or freedom. It represents the further creep of the market and economics into areas of life that have traditionally been considered above material concerns. Like the packaging and marketing of religion, sex and body organs, it is somehow unsavoury and definitely unwelcome.

The idea that some things are beyond price is a way of saying that they have special value beyond their value as tradeable commodities. If a thing can be priced in the same way as a sack of potatoes, then that special quality is lost (Kelman 1994: 144–5). O'Neill (1996: 99) argues that asking people what they 'would be willing to pay to forego a good to which they are committed' is in fact an 'attempt to corrupt the relationships constitutive of a culture. Only someone corrupted by a lifetime in markets' would be able to give a realistic price.

Many environmentalists believe that other living creatures have a value independent of any monetary value that individual humans can accord to them. Contingent valuation and other methods of finding a price for parts of the environment are completely anthropocentric (human-centred) and take no account of the preferences of other living creatures. This, economists believe, is as it should be. For them value is defined in terms of exchange between humans. For many environmentalists, however, especially deep ecologists, this is unacceptable and arrogant. It denies other living things any intrinsic value, that is, any value apart from their value to humans.

Morality

Just because the benefits of an action outweigh the costs, it does not mean that the action would necessarily be considered moral by the community. An individual may not gain personally from giving money to charity but may believe it is the right thing to do. Conversely, a US jury was disgusted, as most people would be, with the decision of the Ford Motor Company not to fix the hazardous placement of the petrol tank on its Ford Pinto because it estimated the costs of doing so outweighed the benefits in terms of the economic value of lives saved (Corner House 1999).

Child labour or slavery would be considered immoral even if the economic advantages to the whole society outweighed the costs to some individuals. In fact in most circumstances the fact that someone benefits from wrong compounds the crime rather than justifies it. Killing someone for money is, in the eyes of the community, thought to be worse than killing someone in a fit of passion. Yet CBA reverses this logic. Pollution and its consequences are okay as long as there is much money to be made from it (Corner House 1999).

CBA tends to be used to avoid considering the moral dimensions of a decision. New Zealand politician Marilyn Waring (1988: 20) says that the moral value of averting injury, saving life and ensuring healthy working conditions are ignored in a CBA: 'The value of safety is its costs and benefits relative to lost or gained production, possible legal suits, different groups of workers, and the allocation of scarce resources'.

Most people consider species preservation to be an ethical question, but efforts to price environmental benefits miss that dimension altogether. For example, surveys have found that US householders are collectively willing to pay $18 billion to protect humpback whales. Yet they would be outraged if someone offering a larger amount, say $30 billion, were allowed to kill all the remaining humpback whales (Ackerman & Heinzerling 2004: 162). The public participation curtailed by CBA would enable ethical and other non-economic values to be considered.

THE EQUITY PRINCIPLE

Distribution of costs and benefits

CBA is about total costs and benefits, and does not deal with who gets the benefits and who suffers the costs. As long as the sum of the benefits outweighs the sum of the costs, even if a small group of people get the benefits and a whole community suffers the costs, the society as a whole is assumed to be better off: 'we are not only comparing apples and oranges, as is often the case in CBAs, but also dealing with situations where "apples" are taken away from one group of people to provide "oranges" to another group' (W Fisher quoted in Corner House 1999). For example, where people are displaced by the building of a dam, their land (and often livelihood and culture) is taken away to provide others with electricity.

The theory behind CBA says that a change is an improvement if the winners *can* fully compensate the losers and still be better off themselves. In reality, the winners seldom compensate the losers. It is sometimes argued that although the distribution of benefits and costs may be unfair in particular instances, it will all balance out in the end. But the tendency in our society is for winners to frequently win and for losers to usually lose – so that poor people are the ones who tend to suffer the costs of hazardous, dirty or unwelcome developments (see chapter 4). CBA hides these distributional consequences and appears neutral when in fact a certain section of the community is benefiting while other sections are losing.

Although CBA is based on a principle of compensation, economists generally don't ask people how much they would require as compensation for environmental losses because there is no limit to how much they might require. Rather, they ask how much people are willing to pay to avoid these losses, a different question altogether which elicits a different answer, governed by how much that person can afford. The first question is more relevant to the theory behind CBA, the second is more about affordability.

Reinforcing existing inequities

CBA and national accounting do not discriminate between needs and wants, between luxury items and necessities. All are converted to numbers and treated the same. In fact, luxury items are accorded higher values than necessities because wealthy people are willing to pay more for them. Naturally, a person's willingness to pay will be limited by their income, assets and ability to borrow. It will also be shaped by his or her perceptions of monetary value; for example, $1000 is a huge amount to someone living on $3 a day in a poor country. Within any community, people's willingness to pay will be dependent on their incomes.

Because a person's willingness to pay depends on their financial security and income level, any survey of willingness to pay is likely to be distorted, giving greater weight to the values of those with the highest incomes who are able to pay much more for what they value. In this way the time saved by a wealthy executive when an airport is sited close to the city is valued highly but the cost of the added noise generated by the airport in a depressed neighbourhood with low property values may be worth little.

CBAs reflect and reinforce existing inequities within society. For example, siting a dirty industry in an already dirty area will be less costly than siting it in a low-pollution area – because the costs of pollution, if measured in terms of decline in property values, will be lower. Similarly, siting the polluting industry in an area that has depressed property values for other reasons – but is nevertheless unpolluted – will also be less costly, according to willingness to pay surveys or hedonic pricing, than siting it in an affluent area; again, the poor are disadvantaged.

In 1992, *New Scientist* reported on a leaked World Bank memo which argued that it was better policy to pollute areas where poor people lived. In this memo, the bank's chief economist, Lawrence Summers, suggested the bank should be encouraging dirty industries to move to less developed countries because wages were lower and therefore the costs arising out of death and illness (usually measured as wages forgone) would be lower. He was quoted as saying, 'I think the economic logic behind dumping a load of toxic waste in the lowest wage country is impeccable and we should face up to that' (Pearce 1992).

Although Summers later claimed that his memo was a joke, it is unlikely his fellow economists at the World Bank would have appreciated his black humour. The reality is that cost benefit analysis and environmental pricing do reinforce the tendency for environmental burdens to be imposed on those who are poor and who already live in degraded neighbourhoods (see chapter 4).

A few years later a group of economists led by British economist and CBA expert David Pearce calculated the costs of global warming. Using willingness to pay, they found that the value of lives in poor countries was $100 000 and the value of lives in wealthy countries was $1.5 million. Naturally, many people were outraged at this discrepancy, which highlighted the inequities involved in willingness to pay methods (cited in Raghavan 1995).

Another equity issue in terms of willingness-to-pay surveys is the question of which populations are surveyed. It will make a difference to the outcome if the survey is limited to local populations or includes broader populations who know less and care less about the environment in question. But is it fair that people living outside an area should determine the environmental quality within it? Alternatively, should local people be able to decide to destroy a unique feature of their environment, something that is part of the greater human heritage, without input from others?

The uses of proxies are similarly iniquitous. For example, the use of wage premiums paid to those who work in hazardous environments as a proxy for what that risk to health is worth assumes that everyone has the same preferences as the workers, 'who do not have many choices or who are exceptional risk-seekers' (Kelman 1994: 142). The value of the time environmentalists spend fighting to protect an area can also be used as a proxy for what they think it is worth. But this can be problematic; if one environmentalist earns more money in his or her day job than a fellow environmentalist, does that mean one person's spare time is worth more than another's?

Discounting future generations

In terms of environmental costs, the higher the discount rate that is used, the greater is the bias towards the present and against the future. The further the costs extend into the future, the less they will be worth in today's values – but future generations will still have to put up with them. An extreme example is the storage of radioactive waste, which can be radioactive for hundreds of thousands of years into the future. Environmental and health problems arising from this radioactive waste hundreds of years hence would be worth almost nothing in today's values.

Because costs that are more than 30 years away become almost valueless using discounting at normal rates, long-term environmental costs such as resource depletion may be effectively ignored: 'Except at very low discount rates, a tree that takes 40 years to grow would have a very low value today to show against its costs' (ESD Working Group Chairs 1992: 14). Discounting therefore discriminates against future generations.

Economist David Pearce and his colleagues (1989) put forward the following reasons for discounting:

- Money obtained now can be invested and earn interest.
- People tend to be impatient.
- The person might die before he or she gets the money.
- One cannot be sure of getting the money in the future.
- People in the future will probably be better off so money will not be worth as much then.

While discounting money may make sense, discounting environmental values seems to be an example of what economists Herman Daly and

John Cobb (1989: ch 7) call 'misplaced concreteness': in other words, getting mixed up between the measure (in this case, money) and the real world (the environment), and assuming that the real world behaves as the measure does. Just because people would rather have money now than later, so they can invest it or be sure of having it, does not mean that they will value the maintenance of an area of environmental significance less each year into the future.

In reality, an area of environmental significance is likely to increase in value as areas like it become scarce and our knowledge about ecosystems increases. Such areas are also likely to become more valuable as populations increase, and especially if leisure time increases. Discount rates based on individual private preferences are inappropriate for societal decisions regarding environmental protection because, as we saw earlier, people treat private consumption decisions differently from political decisions about what is good for society.

The idea that someone would like to consume now rather than in the future is also not applicable to public goods, which can be enjoyed now *and* in the future; only consumption that uses up the environment, such as logging or pollution, fits the discounting model. Society gets the benefits of environmental preservation, and therefore the risk of one person dying before he or she gets the benefits is meaningless.

Discounting is also applied to human health impacts in a similarly inappropriate way. Future cancer cases are discounted so that 100 cancer cases in 20 years are equivalent to 26 cancers today (using a 7 per cent discount rate) (Ackerman & Heinzerling 2004: 196–7). 'At a discount rate of 5 per cent, one death next year counts for more than a billion deaths in five hundred years' (Shrader-Frechette 2002: 168). This clearly favours benefits today very heavily against future deaths, which become in the calculation almost worthless. Daly and Cobb (1989: 153–4) declare:

> The prize for nonsensical discounting must go to those who discount future fatalities to their 'equivalent' present value ... one is left with the suspicion that the motivation underlying the whole ludicrous calculation is simply to convert a 'very large number' into a very small number under the cover of numerological darkness.

Not only are future lives discounted, but some CBAs also discount future years of an individual life. In the USA economists use life years rather than lives as a measure of benefit or cost. In this measure a 65-year-old is worth less than a 20-year-old because they have less life years left, unless that 20-year-old already has a life-shortening disease. On top of this, the Office of Management and Budget (OMB) discounts future life years so that the 75th year of a child living now would be worth only a few days when discounted to present value, and a child who is killed at the age of a five loses only 14 present-value years of life. In this way the OMB calculated that the benefits of a regulation for child restraints that would have saved 36–50 children aged three years old amounted to 'a present value of only 25 to 35 children, each with a present value life expectancy of only about fourteen years' (Ackerman & Heinzerling 2004: 196–7).

HUMAN RIGHTS PRINCIPLES

Economic valuation and cost–benefit analysis would seem to allow any treatment of the environment or individual human beings so long as the aggregate benefits outweigh the estimated costs incurred; that is 'any cost is allowable, provided the benefits are greater'. This can be challenged, however, 'by arguing that some costs are preventable evils that ought never to be allowed, even for countervailing benefits' and that 'some unfair distributions of risk or costs are so unacceptable that no benefits could counterbalance them' (Shrader-Frechette 2002: 168).

Human rights conventions are the ultimate arbiters of what are unacceptable burdens and of how people should be treated. Avoidable activities that result in human deaths or degrade the environment to the extent that people in a neighbourhood cannot enjoy an adequate standard of health and wellbeing infringe human rights and cannot be justified, no matter what the benefits. Thus CBA is an inappropriate decision-making tool whenever such consequences are likely to result. Human rights must take precedence over the satisfaction of individual preferences and tastes as measured by willingness-to-pay surveys and market values. 'The market cannot tell us the worth of, or the rights of, other people' (Ackerman & Heinzerling 2004: 229).

Human rights are inalienable, which means they cannot be taken away, sold, or given away. Yet that is just what a CBA does – it trades away people's rights in return for benefits that may even go to others. Similarly, individuals have the right 'not be sacrificed on the altar of somewhat higher living standards for the rest of us' (Kelman 1994: 141).

If clean air and water and a healthy environment are human rights there is no point trying to put a price on them with a view to trading them off for other benefits. In this respect, some environmental benefits are priceless: 'Wherever economists encounter losses that are inconsolable by money – serious injury and death are common examples – their methods cannot work' (Adams 1996: 3). Yet, as we saw in the previous chapter, economists are ready to put a monetary value on serious diseases such as chronic bronchitis and bladder cancer, and then trade them off for the benefits others get from imposing these diseases.

Economists may argue that such losses can be accorded infinite value in a CBA, but this is effectively the same as putting a veto on the cost–benefit calculation, for infinite value trumps all else. This is why, in practice, economists put a finite value on human life. One US study in the early 1990s found that the value of human life varied from $70 000 to $132 million per person (Lohmann 1997). In 2000 the US EPA valued American lives at $6.1 million each for a CBA aimed at justifying the removal of arsenic from drinking water (Ackerman & Heinzerling 2004: 61). Such exercises, even though they are sometimes used to justify environmental measures, are contrary to human rights principles because they imply that lives can be sacrificed so long as the economic gains are high enough.

THE SUSTAINABILITY PRINCIPLE

Pricing environmental goods

The market value accorded to parts of the environment clearly depends on who is doing the valuing and how it is done. CBA 'privileges some forms of expertise at the expense of others'. The economists who carry out the willingness-to-pay surveys become the central experts, while those who have knowledge of local environments and how they might be threatened are sidelined and may not even have a chance to inform the wider public of these threats because of the way in which public debate and discussion is curtailed (Corner House 1999).

But how can economists, or the laypeople they survey, know how to accurately value an ecosystem when they don't even know all the functions it performs? Consider the functions that a simple tree performs (see table 8.1) and how much more difficult it is to know the functions of a complex ecosystem. Willingness-to-pay surveys take account of the functions of parts of an ecosystem only to the extent that the people surveyed are knowledgeable about them and are influenced by this knowledge in their responses.

Individual preferences are shaped to a large extent by the information available to people about the consequences of their choices – and that information is usually partial, often distorted and mostly shaped by the media. Those surveyed may think a wetland area is unattractive and not worth anything, and thus be unwilling to pay to protect it, even though the wetland has important ecological values – which they are unaware of.

Table 8.1 Some of the tasks performed by trees

stabilising the soil	recycling nutrients
cooling the air	modifying wind turbulence
intercepting the rain	absorbing toxic substances
reducing fuel costs	neutralising sewage
increasing property values	enhancing social awareness
providing beauty	cutting noise
giving privacy	promoting tourism
encouraging recreation	reducing stress
improving personal health	providing fruit for humans
providing habitat for birds	regulating the water table
preventing salination	providing shelter

Source: (Beckham 1991: 16)

What is more, many people, when asked about what they are willing to pay to protect the environment, give an amount that they would make as a donation to a good cause rather than the amount they actually think that part of the environment is worth. This is probably why surveyors 'found that people were willing to pay the same amount for saving 2000 birds, as for 20,000, or 200,000' (Ackerman & Heinzerling 2004: 163).

Each of the methods of valuation used by economists provides only a partial measure of environmental value. The use of proxies such as travel costs, for example, assumes that people only travel to an area if the cost of getting there is less than the benefits they get from being there. It also assumes that use of the area for recreation constitutes its sole value, and that the cost of travel reflects how much people are prepared to pay for its preservation. However, an area may be valuable for other reasons; and people may be restrained from going there more frequently, not because of the cost of travel, but because of other commitments. For all these reasons, the true value of the area to the community and to the health of local ecosystems is undervalued by such methods.

Will market pricing save the environment?

Those in favour of valuation admit the difficulty of getting an accurate dollar value, but answer that 'even a partial valuation in monetary terms of the benefits of conserving biological resources can provide at least a lower limit to the full range of benefits'. They are therefore 'important in crystallizing those issues involving implicit value judgements that may otherwise be ignored' (McNeely et al. 1990: 26–7).

David Ehrenfeld (1988: 213), a US professor of biology, points out that attaching a dollar value to a species still does not guarantee its survival. He points to a study done by a mathematician in 1973 which showed that:

> it was economically preferable to kill every blue whale left in the oceans as fast as possible and reinvest the profits in growth industries rather than to wait for the species to recover to the point where it could sustain an annual catch.

Some environmentalists favour the idea of pricing the environment, believing that decision makers will not protect it unless they can see how much it is worth. They hope that by incorporating environmental costs into national accounts figures and CBAs, more notice will be taken of the environment. British environmentalist Jonathon Porritt (quoted in Lohmann 1991: 194) argues that 'when you are talking to the people who are really in the business of destroying the environment, you have to use concepts that will allow them to begin to understand what we're saying'.

Larry Lohmann (1991: 194) responds to Porritt by pointing out that more environmental battles are won by local people chanting and demonstrating in their own language, and forcing leaders to listen to them, than by people 'who allow their views to be phrased in consultants' cost–benefit terms'.

Other environmentalists argue that adapting CBA and national accounts to include environmental values will not change the power structure, and that it will not be environmentalists who put monetary values on the environment but economists employed by industry and government. Also, while CBA may save individual areas of the environment that are threatened by less profitable developments, they are only saved until a more profitable development comes along. In the meantime, other parts of the environment are progressively traded off for economic benefits.

Substitutability

Whereas profits can be made from a variety of activities, the loss of environmental quality cannot be so easily replaced. CBA, by converting environmental values into monetary terms, assumes that all 'goods' are interchangeable and replaceable without overall loss of welfare. It assumes that a community can continue to use up its natural resources and degrade its natural environment just as long as it is increasing its wealth and infrastructure by an equivalent economic value. The fact that a region is becoming a more sterile, artificial and dangerous place in which to live is supposedly compensated for by the comforts and entertainments residents are able to buy.

Similarly, an adjusted GNP figure is merely a way of measuring weak sustainability. It assumes that as long as total capital, human plus natural, is increasing then welfare is increasing. But this allows for the gradual deterioration of the environment as long as the total capital stocks are increasing. As was seen in chapter 4, however, there are several reasons for maintaining a certain level of 'natural capital', including the irreversibility of much environmental depletion; the fact that such substitution reduces the resilience of natural systems; our inability to know which parts of the environment can be replaced, and the long-term consequences of continual degradation.

The strong sustainability position, which is the precautionary position, is that some environmental values are not replaceable and their loss should not be weighed against economic benefits. This is incorporated into the US Endangered Species Act, which accords endangered species an 'incalculable value' (de Sadeleer 2002: 171).

THE PRECAUTIONARY PRINCIPLE

Cost–benefit analysis is in many ways contradictory to the precautionary principle. It is a quantitative measure aimed at replacing the deliberation, reasoning and wisdom that is central to the precautionary principle. Ackerman and Heinzerling (2004: 171) note the impact of CBA on environmental decision making: 'The EPA's role under the Clean Water Act has been converted from identifying the best ways to avoid environmental harm to embarking on a lengthy and obscure inquiry into the monetary value of not killing fish'.

The idea of modifying a project to prevent adverse consequences is not encouraged by CBA because CBA is, for reasons of practicality, applied to total projects rather than to the design process. If the benefits of the total project outweigh the costs, there is little reason to search for ways to reduce the environmental costs. The idea promoted is that the consequences of the project are an inevitable part of the project – and we either accept them with the project or reject the project. This is not in keeping with the precautionary principle, which would seek to minimise the project's impacts even if the benefits outweigh the costs.

A major problem with valuing the environment according to individual preferences is that a value that reflects current willingness to pay might not be consistent with long-term welfare or survival. Individuals might, for example, prefer to continue adding to greenhouse gas emissions rather than cut back on energy use because they don't know of or believe in the consequences; but in the long run such behaviour threatens lives and is not precautionary.

Reversibility

The assignment of monetary values to the environment relegates issues such as irreversibility and irreplaceability to the background, whereas they are central to the precautionary principle. For example, CBA ignores the fact that the decision to preserve an area is reversible, whereas the decision to develop an area may be irreversible. No provision is made in standard CBA for the importance of keeping options open for the future.

Similarly, CBA does not allow a full consideration of the consequences of wrong assumptions and predictions. Wrong thinking could go either way, of course. If a new chemical turns out to be less hazardous than was assumed, the consequence might be unnecessary regulation and over-investment in health and environmental protection, which could lead to extra expense to industry for emission controls and technologies. But the overall social consequence of this extra spending might actually turn out to be good for the economy in terms of job creation and new industries (Ackerman & Heinzerling 2004: 227–8).

However, if the chemical turns out to be more hazardous than was assumed, the cost may be many deaths or irreversible ecosystem damage. In assigning costs and benefits to the regulation of the chemical, these asymmetrical consequences of being wrong in different ways are not accounted for. A precautionary approach would prefer to risk extra investment in environmental and health protection rather than extra deaths and destruction, yet few CBAs take account of such preferences.

CBA takes no account of the relative risk aversion that people may feel for different outcomes. It assumes risk neutrality. Pearce (1994: 133) suggests that CBA could be modified so that some losses were more heavily weighted than gains to take account of people's risk preferences. The problem then becomes working out what weightings are appropriate. Others argue, however, that some risks are never acceptable and should be prevented, rather than being calculated and compared with the benefits of taking those risks, as occurs with a CBA. This is in keeping with the precautionary principle.

Uncertainty

Identifying all the consequences of a particular project or policy option is difficult because it involves predicting the future and dealing with the uncertain interactions between human activities and the ecosystems in which they take place. Moreover, there will be unintended and unexpected indirect effects arising from any large project. While this is a problem whether one is doing a CBA or not, it can be crucial for the outcome of a CBA, and could make the difference between a project being considered justifiable or not.

> The problem of valuing environmental resources does not lie primarily in the lack of markets but in the difficulties of determining the value of any particular species or example of habitat type to the system as a whole. Decisions rarely involve stark choices between survival and extinction for particular species or eco-systems. Rather

> they involve questions of more, or less. Opting for less increases the risk of extinction, but by how much? And if extinction does follow how does one value this? The world's stock of genetic material is depleted, but what is the probability that a particular species or ecosystem will contain the key to future survival or welfare? And if we knew that how should we appraise it? How risk averse should we be? The scientific community has no answers to these questions; what can one hope to obtain by asking the public? What one gets from the contingent valuation is a willingness to pay, but is that the relevant measure in a context of extreme uncertainty about the significance of the decision? (Bowers 1990: 17)

In situations where the consequences of an action are uncertain, economic values cannot be attached to them and CBA becomes rather meaningless. Yet uncertainty is often ignored in order to be able to carry out a CBA:

> There is enormous pressure, in effect, to ignore all uncertainty and develop a single best estimate based on what is known today. If researchers offer high and low estimates to reflect the uncertainty, there is a strong tendency to use the average and ignore the extremes. (Ackerman & Heinzerling 2004: 224)

Alternatively, where there is disagreement about a potential cost, it is likely to be ignored altogether.

Biologist David Ehrenfeld (1988: 215) points out that our society is ignorant of most species that exist, the role they play in their ecosystems, how they interact, and the use or value they might be to humans now and in the future. He asks: 'How do we deal with values of organisms whose very existence escapes our notice?' and 'What sort of value do we assign to the loss to the community when a whole generation of its children can never experience the streams in their environment as amenities?'

Bryan Norton (1988: 204) uses the argument that biodiversity is necessary for survival to argue against the placing of dollar values on species so that they might be weighed against such things as 'the value of real estate around reservoirs and kilowatt-hours of hydroelectric power'. He compares such reasoning to hospital administrators trying to work out which parts of a life-support system can be disconnected and sold to raise money for the hospital.

Cumulative impacts

Individual CBAs are unable to take into account the cumulative loss of many small decisions in many communities. Over time these could in fact destroy ecosystems, cause extinctions of species and threaten human survival. Ecological systems are not like economic systems where you can plot trends in smooth continuous lines. Rather, such systems may be able to withstand many small assaults and then collapse suddenly once a threshold is crossed: 'If we think we are in the region of a threshold, valuation could be irrelevant'. But scientists are often unable to identify such thresholds and so the precautionary principle suggests that when a threshold may be close, we should act to avoid crossing it by preventing activities that may do so (Pearce 1994: 148–9).

PART IV

ECONOMIC INSTRUMENTS FOR POLLUTION CONTROL

9

PRICES AND POLLUTION RIGHTS

When individuals or firms make decisions about production, consumption and investment, they generally consider only their own costs and benefits, not the environmental or social consequences (externalities). Consideration of the pollution they create does not enter into their decisions. It is laws which force the polluter to take notice of these external costs by prescribing limits to what can be discharged or emitted. Economic instruments are intended to make these external costs part of the polluter's decision by adding a charge or in some way providing a monetary incentive for considering the environmental and social costs.

While legislation is aimed at directly changing the behaviour of polluters by outlawing or limiting certain practices, economic instruments, in theory, aim either to make environmentally damaging behaviour cost more or to make environmentally sound behaviour more profitable. Economic instruments do not tell polluters what to do; rather, polluters find it expensive to continue in their old ways. Individuals or firms can then use their superior knowledge of their own activities to choose the best way of meeting environmental standards.

Not all pricing and taxation measures employed by a government are aimed at environmental protection. They may be used to promote other goals and may in fact have adverse impacts on the environment. Economic instruments differ in that they are intended to:

- provide a financial stimulus to change
- encourage voluntary action
- involve government authorities
- maintain or improve environmental qualities.

Economic instruments are supposed to be more economically efficient than legislative measures in that pollution reductions can be made for less cost. Regulations are said to be inefficient because they require polluting discharges from all firms to meet uniform standards regardless of the firm's ability to meet them. Alternatively, they require all firms to install particular pollution control technologies regardless of a firm's ability to pay for them. While this will improve environmental quality it is said to be at a high cost. Economic instruments, on the other hand, are said to permit 'the burden of pollution control to be shared more efficiently among businesses' (Stavins & Whitehead 1992: 9).

There are two main types of economic instruments:

- *Price-based measures*, which use fees, charges and taxes to internalise environmental costs and benefits.
- *Rights-based measures*, which 'create rights to use environmental resources, or to pollute the environment, up to a pre-determined limit, and allow these rights to be traded' (Commonwealth 1990).

Advocates of price-based measures argue that better use should be made of pricing and taxation arrangements to achieve a more efficient allocation of natural resources. For example, with an effluent charge, each firm would pay a set rate for each unit of pollution and those firms which find it cheaper to reduce their pollution than to pay the charge can do so. Those for which it would cost more than the charge to reduce their pollution can choose to pay the charge instead. In this way, pollution is reduced most by those who can do it cheaply, and is therefore a more cost-efficient way of achieving a limited amount of pollution reduction.

With rights-based measures, rights – for example, to discharge a certain amount of pollution – are assigned by government, and markets are set up to allow those rights to be bought and sold. Firms which can reduce their pollution more cheaply than others can sell their excess rights to firms for which it would be expensive to reduce their pollution. In this way, economists argue, a given level of air or water quality could be achieved more efficiently with a lower aggregate cost to the firms involved.

Both price-based and rights-based measures are based on market principles. In the case of price-based measures, an economist would say that a price is set and demand determines the quantity of pollution that is discharged. In the case of rights-based measures, the quantity of pollution is set and demand determines the price to be paid to discharge it.

PRICE-BASED MEASURES

Fees, charges and taxes

The most common form of price-based measure is a charge, fee or tax. Charges 'make attractive tools for managing the environment because they attach an explicit cost to polluting activities and because sources can easily quantify their savings if they reduce the amount of pollution they emit' (NCEE 2004: 3). Charges, fees and taxes are supposed to provide an incentive to change behaviour but their effectiveness will depend on how high they are. Governments can use the money raised in this way for environmental protection, such as collective waste treatment and research into pollution-control technologies, although often they do not.

Effluent charges or fees

A charge or fee can be considered as a 'price' that is paid for polluting the environment. Effluent fees have been used mainly in the area of water-pollution control and are based on the quantity, and sometimes content, of a firm's discharges to waterways or sewers. A few countries also charge air emission fees.

Effluent fees are often charged for the purposes of raising revenue and to cover the administrative costs of the relevant regulatory agency and thus in most cases are too low to provide any sort of incentive for environmental protection. In some countries, such as Germany and the Netherlands, the fees are higher and supposed to cover the cost of treatment, but not to act as a disincentive to discharge. In some countries effluent charges are based on easy-to-measure parameters such as volume and weight of suspended matter or organic matter and in others, such as France, are based on parameters such as salinity, toxicity, nutrients, halogenated hydrocarbons and heavy metals (NCEE 2004: 9–10).

User charges

User charges are fees imposed for using a resource or for being provided with a service. They are commonly used for the collection and treatment of municipal solid waste. Householders normally pay a flat rate for waste disposal while the rate for industrial users depends on volume. The aim of such charges is to cover the cost of the disposal service. In Denmark, where rates are very high, the quantity of waste going to disposal facilities has been reduced and reuse of building waste has increased. Both Denmark and the Netherlands use higher fees for landfill disposal to encourage companies to favour incineration of waste. Several European countries and Australia impose separate charges for hazardous waste disposal (NCEE 2004: 18–9).

Water-use charges are increasingly being introduced as well. Royalties on resource use – such as timber, minerals and oil – are another form of user charge. Royalties increase the price of resources and can encourage people to be more efficient in using them, because the less they use the less they will have to pay.

Product charges

These are charges added to the price of products. They are generally used to discourage disposal or encourage recycling. For example, a charge could be made according to how much packaging a product uses. Product disposal charges are also sometimes placed on items such as paper to encourage waste-paper recycling.

> Levied in numerous industrialized countries, product charges are imposed either on a product or some characteristic of that product. Although some of these charges may discourage consumption, many of them are advance disposal fees intended to finance the proper disposal of the products after their use. (NCEE 2004: 20)

In Germany, charges are imposed on lubricating and other mineral oils to cover the costs of their collection and disposal. Other products that attract product charges in Europe and Canada include car air-conditioners, batteries, building materials, dry cleaning solvents, fertilisers and pesticides, lubricating oil, packaging and tyres. Energy taxes are also a type of product charge, and many countries, including Australia and the United Kingdom, have used a differential tax to encourage drivers to buy unleaded petrol (NCEE 2004: 20–1).

Sales and excise taxes

Environmental taxes are commonly used in Europe to discourage environmentally harmful activities or products (Robinson & Ryan 2002: 14). A sales tax is a percentage of the price of a purchase which is paid to the government. An excise tax is a fixed amount of money per product sold which does not depend on the price for which the product is sold. Both types of tax are often paid by consumers and can be used to provide incentives for consumers to buy environmentally friendly products. For example, some governments encourage people to buy solar water heaters by exempting them from sales tax.

The imposition of different amounts of sales tax on competing goods or services can ensure that environmentally friendly products have a price advantage over polluting products. For example, some governments exempt refillable bottles from sales tax, thereby giving them an advantage over non-refillable bottles which add to the litter problem (Robinson & Ryan 2002: 14).

Subsidies

Subsidies are payments from governments to producers which effectively reduce the price of their goods or services, and therefore encourage their sale. Subsidies include payments to firms that reduce their pollution, and tax concessions and rebates for environmentally friendly products and technologies. Some environmentally beneficial activities – like investment in recycling schemes and donations to environmental groups – are tax deductible in a few countries.

Subsidies are also used to encourage resource conservation, particularly in the area of energy use. In Australia solar water heaters are subsidised. In Denmark there are grants for renewable energy generation and energy-saving measures. In Switzerland investment in energy savings can be a tax deduction. Reforestation is also subsidised in many countries. In several Asian nations taxes, tariffs or import duties are reduced for pollution control and wastewater treatment equipment (NCEE 2004: 34–5).

Many countries provide subsidies or income tax concessions for agricultural practices that are less harmful to the environment than others. Canada has a Land Management Assistance programme. In Germany, Finland, Norway and Sweden, grants are available to farmers who convert to organic farming. In the United Kingdom, farmers are rewarded for not spraying near the perimeters of their crops, for maintaining hedges and woodlands, and for limiting the use of nitrogen-containing fertilisers and animal manure in nitrate-sensitive areas (NCEE 2004: 33).

Australia has a National Landcare Programme, and various states offer financial incentives to farmers for protecting areas of wildlife habitat on their properties. Farmers can also claim tax rebates and deductions for money spent on preventing land degradation, eradicating pests, reducing problems such as salinity and placing a conservation covenant on their land (ATO 1999; National Heritage Trust 2004: 6; Robinson & Ryan 2002: 22).

Deposit-refund systems

A potentially polluting product may be given a price that includes an amount which is refundable if it is returned. The aim is to discourage improper disposal. Deposit-refund systems combine product charges (the deposit) with recycling subsidies (the refund). Although these systems can be quite effective they can also be expensive to administer. For this reason '[d]eposit-refund systems appear best suited for products with high value, or whose disposal is difficult to monitor and potentially harmful to the environment' (NCEE 2004: 23).

The best-known deposit-refund system is that for soft-drink bottles, which often end up as unsightly litter. This traditional mechanism for encouraging people to return bottles for recycling is very common around the world. A German scheme, introduced in 2003, has resulted in a reduction in the use of non-refillable cans and bottles of 60 per cent (NCEE 2004: 25).

In South Korea, the producer or importer, rather than the consumer, pays a deposit on various types of food and drink packaging, detergents, batteries, tyres, household appliances and other items. Money is refunded in accordance with the amount of packaging the companies are able to collect and treat (Lease 2002).

Scandinavian countries have mandatory deposit-refund systems for motor vehicles. A deposit is paid on purchase that is refunded when the vehicle is returned to an authorised scrap dealer (NCEE 2004: 25).

Financial enforcement incentives

Financial enforcement incentives include non-compliance fees for those who do not comply with regulations. In theory, the fee should be more than the profit made by not complying.

Performance bonds are enforcement incentives that seek to avoid the court costs usually associated with fines. Payments made by companies – often mining, timber, oil and gas companies – to the authorities are refunded if compliance is achieved. In this way they are like a deposit-refund system. If compliance is not achieved, the bond is forfeited and it is the company that has to go to court if it disputes the decision. Performance bonds aim to shift the burden of risk from the community and the government to the developer or business carrying out an activity that may harm the environment.

Performance bonds have been used in Australia, China, Indonesia and the Philippines. The Philippines has a Forest Guarantee Bond, for example, while mining companies in Indonesia have to post a reclamation guarantee to cover the environmental damage they might cause (NCEE 2004: 25–6).

Liability insurance schemes are also sometimes used to cover compensation for possible environmental damage. In this case the insurance is supposed to cover full rehabilitation costs. The incentive for potential polluters to clean up their production processes is that lower premiums will be charged if there is only a low probability of those processes causing damage.

TRADEABLE POLLUTION RIGHTS

Tradeable pollution rights are a rights-based alternative to pollution charges. They allow firms to trade the right to emit specified amounts of particular pollutants. Such rights are increasingly being used as 'a major policy tool in both domestic and international strategies' to deal with pollution (Drury et al. 1999: 239). Emissions trading is used in Chile, Canada, Australia, Europe and the USA (Robinson & Ryan 2002: 26).

Tradeable pollution rights first emerged in the USA in the 1970s when it was felt that economic growth would be constrained by air quality laws enacted as part of the Clean Air Act. Under these laws, maximum allowable concentrations for specific pollutants were set for each region. The problem for regions which were already over the maximum allowable concentrations (non-attainment areas) was how to achieve economic growth when industrial growth was likely to add to the air pollution load and therefore would be illegal.

Offsets

US regulators adopted an 'offset policy' in 1976. Initially, offsets occurred within companies. Firms that wanted to expand had to reduce the emissions from existing facilities so that the total amount of pollution emitted after they began operating any new plant was no more than they had previously been discharging.

This practice spread to external offsets. In Oklahoma City, for example, oil companies were persuaded by the local chamber of commerce to reduce their hydrocarbon emissions enough to allow a new General Motors car manufacturing plant to be established in the area. In other cases, government facilities reduced their emissions to offset the effect of new private industries moving into their areas.

Companies wanting to establish in a non-attainment area could make way for their own pollution by paying to reduce the pollution of others. For example, an oil company planning to build a petroleum processing plant that would discharge sulphur dioxide and hydrocarbons arranged to pay for the pollution-control equipment for a dry-cleaning business, to buy and close down a chemical factory, and to buy low-sulphur fuel for some ships in San Francisco Bay (Seneca & Taussig 1984: 233).

Such arrangements have now been formalised into a market for offsets – in fact, offsets are mandatory for major new sources of pollution in non-attainment areas. Trade in pollution rights allows firms sited in an over-polluted area to voluntarily reduce their emissions and get 'emission reduction credits' which in turn can be sold to firms wanting to move into the area. Offsets created by the closure of a pollution source may be owned by the local government. New firms have to buy or be allocated 1.2 emission reduction credits for each unit of emission that will come from their plants.

Germany has an offset programme for new companies wanting to establish in polluted areas (NCEE 2004: 27). Few other countries apart from the USA use offsets in this way, although offsets are an integral part of the Kyoto greenhouse protocol (see page 168).

Bubbles and banking

It was soon realised by US authorities that offset policies were not enough to reduce pollution to acceptable standards. Additional 'bubble policies' were introduced in 1979 to deal with established industries, policies which also started off being applied to individual companies. An imaginary bubble with a single opening is placed over an industrial complex which actually has more than one point of discharge. This means that discharges are not regulated individually, but standards are set for the total emissions from the complex.

In this way, the company can meet the standards by reducing the emissions from those of its operations where it can be done cheaply while leaving other operations with above-standard emissions. The concentrations and volumes of emissions from the various operations are averaged, and it is this average that must meet the standard. The regulator does not have to negotiate what pollution-control equipment should be installed at each outlet point. This is left up to the company to decide.

The bubble concept has since been extended from individual companies to cover several industrial facilities owned by different companies. A 'virtual bubble' is placed over a whole region and standards are set for average concentrations and/or volumes of emissions from facilities in that region. Firms that reduce their pollution below the required standard get emission reduction credits which can be 'stored' (in an emissions bank) for later use when the firm wants to expand, or sold to another company in the region that cannot afford to meet the standard.

The chemical company DuPont has estimated that its 52 plants achieved cost savings in the early 1980s of over 86 per cent from the use of regional bubbles (Seneca & Taussig 1984: 232).

Cap and trade emissions trading

Cap and trade emissions trading was first introduced in the USA after the Clean Air Act was amended in 1990 to include a national emissions trading programme for acid rain and to authorise states to set up their own emissions trading programmes to reduce smog in cities (Drury et al. 1999: 241).

Under cap and trade programmes, a limit is set for the total emissions of a specific pollutant, or set of pollutants, that may be emitted over a particular period – usually a year – by specific industries in a particular region. A limit or cap is chosen that is intended to protect the environment. This cap is then divided into allowances that are allocated to specific firms, generally the larger firms in a particular industry sector with significant emissions, for example electricity-generating plants. A firm can sell any allowances surplus to its requirements to another firm that needs extra allowances, or save them for the future when they might be needed. In other words, the allowances become tradeable pollution rights (USEPA 2004a: 1).

Allocation

The two main ways of initially allocating allowances are usually referred to as 'grandfathering' and 'auctioning'. Grandfathering involves allocating allowances to firms on the basis of their past emissions. Firms that polluted more in the past are thus allocated a larger share of allowances. Alternatively, a pre-specified number of allowances can be auctioned off to polluters. In either case the total allocation – the cap – is supposed to be within the estimated capacity of the environment to assimilate the specified type of pollution, or at least a step towards achieving that goal.

Acid rain

The first cap and trade emissions trading programme was established in March 1993 when the US EPA auctioned off rights to emit sulphur dioxide (SO_2), which is a primary cause of acid rain. The programme set a cap that required the total amount of SO_2 discharged by power stations to be reduced by 2010 to half the levels discharged in 1980. Each allowance gives the owner the right to emit one ton of SO_2. In addition, regulations limiting the SO_2 discharged in particular areas were maintained as a safety net to ensure that air quality standards would still be met in each region, despite trading (USEPA 2002a: 6).

SO_2 allowances are now auctioned every year by the Chicago Board of Trade. Before 2005 they cost around \$150–\$200/ton, much cheaper than paying for flue-gas scrubbers to remove SO_2 from plant emissions. It is claimed that this programme saves industry hundreds of millions of dollars each year compared with complying with legislation aimed at cleaning up SO_2 to the same level. Limited reductions in SO_2 emissions have been made with cheaper methods such as using low-sulphur coal (Kinsman 2002: 26; USEPA 2004a: 1).

Smog trading

The first smog trading scheme in the world was the Los Angeles Regional Clean Air Incentives Market, RECLAIM, introduced in 1994. This is a cap and trade programme in which 431 large firms were allocated tradeable allowances of smog-causing nitrogen oxides (NO_x) and sulphur oxides (SO_x) based on their past emissions. The cap has decreased over time (Drury et al. 1999: 247–8). Trading programmes of this kind have since proliferated around the USA for NO_x and other air pollutants.

The Clean Air Interstate Rule (CAIR), introduced by the EPA in 2005, allows states to require power stations to comply with either the EPA's interstate NO_x cap and trade programme or state-based NO_x legislation of whatever type the state chooses (USEPA 2002a; 2005: 1).

Europe

Emissions trading has been used far less in Europe, particularly with respect to NO_x. A UK scheme in the early 1990s for SO_2 failed to generate much trade. The Slovak Republic has a trading scheme for SO_2 from large industrial sources, including power plants. A trading scheme for NO_x began in 2005 in the Netherlands. Elsewhere these gases are covered by standards and regulations. The United Kingdom is considering a cap and trade scheme to control SO_2 and NO_x from large industrial sources such as iron and steel works and oil refineries. The power industry, however, seems uninterested in such a scheme because local opposition would prevent its buying up emissions allowances (Keats 2005: 20–1).

Open market emissions trading

Open market emissions trading began in the early 1990s in various states in the USA. It allows companies to earn emission reduction credits (or discrete emission reductions) for voluntary reductions in a particular time period of specified air pollutants discharged from their plants – usually nitrous oxides and volatile organic compounds that contribute to smog. These can be either reductions from the usual emission rates for a particular facility, or reductions below the regulated standards which the facility is required to meet, whichever is the lesser. Reductions are often expressed in terms of concentrations of pollutants or rates of discharge per hour rather than total quantities of emissions discharged over a year. These programmes may also be referred to as 'rate-based trading' (USEPA 2002b: 2). Table 9.1 shows how emission reduction credits differ from emission allowances.

Table 9.1 Allowances vs credits

Emission reduction credit	Emission allowance
Scheme: 'Open market emissions trading'	Scheme: 'Cap and trade'
Only emission reductions can be traded	All emissions can be traded
Credits are generated when a source reduces its emissions below an agreed baseline	Allowances are allocated by the regulatory authority
Participation in the credit market is voluntary – sources can just meet existing standards	Participation in the program is mandatory – the overall emission cap still applies even if sources do not trade
Applies to emission reductions below defined baseline	Applies to all emissions

Source (Sorrell and Skea 1999: 11)

Firms that reduce the rate of emissions from a particular facility can sell the credits they earn to other firms which are not otherwise able to comply with emission regulations, or for whom buying credits is cheaper than reducing emissions to comply with the regulations. Trading is usually open to all firms. The money that can be earned from selling credits is supposed to provide an incentive for firms to come up with innovative ways to reduce their emissions rates.

Some open market emission trading schemes allow firms to gain credits from reducing pollution from a variety of small mobile sources such as old cars, leaf-blowers and lawnmowers. Credits can be exchanged between different types of sources and industries, and in some cases different types of pollutants are covered under the one scheme so that reductions in emissions of one chemical can be used as credits for increased emissions of another.

The trade is done through an Emission Trading Registry, which acts like a clearing house. These registries do not usually check whether the emission reduction credit is valid or legitimate, however – it is up to the buyer to do that (Leonardo Academy 2005).

> The 'creator' or 'generator' demonstrates that they have exceeded their regulatory requirements and that the reductions are 'surplus'. They describe the steps they have taken or technology they have installed to reduce their emissions to show they are 'real' and the result of an emission reduction activity. They document their emissions before installing the technology, document their emissions after the technology is installed, and, using accepted engineering practices, 'quantify' the emissions in a workable and replicable manner. They must also show the reductions are 'permanent' for the life of the emission reduction program. (Clean Air Action Corporation 2002: 13)

The US EPA developed a model for this type of trading, the Open Trading Market Rule, which was adopted in 2001 when it was incorporated into the EPA's Economic Incentive Program (Clean Air Action Corporation 2002: 24).

Tradeable water pollution rights

Tradeable pollution rights can also be applied to water. This is mainly done in the USA and Australia, and often applied only to nutrient loads (nitrogen and phosphorus) in discharges to water. Nutrient trading is being considered for the Danube Basin in preparation for an increase in industrial activity in the countries of Eastern Europe as their economies grow (Hawn 2005b). The OECD (cited in Robinson & Ryan 2002: 24) has suggested that water trading markets are necessarily limited because of:

- transaction costs (that is, costs of administering a tradeable rights system)
- being limited to one catchment or river system
- being limited to trades with users downstream
- the importance of time and place of allocations or discharges.

In the USA, where some 40 per cent of waterways are in poor condition (Faeth 2000: 1), a national Water Quality Trading Policy was introduced in 2003. The US EPA encourages water trading to achieve reductions in nutrients and sediment (USEPA 2004b). Nutrients can create dead zones in waterways where algal blooms block the light, oxygen is used up, and fish and other aquatic or marine life cannot survive. The trading of nutrient credits generally involves factories or industries, with large individual dischargers paying for nutrient reduction credits from several smaller sources, usually farmers in the same watershed. Farmers can reduce the nutrient run-off from their land relatively cheaply by changing their tilling, planting or fertilising methods, while factories can find it quite expensive (Hawn 2005b; Sokulsky 2005).

Such schemes have already been introduced into a number of states with the aim of meeting water quality standards for least overall cost. Many states have a limit or total maximum daily load (TMDL) for industrial point sources discharging into waterways. Trades can be facilitated by a central body that acts as a pollutant exchange or broker, and sometimes buyers and sellers do deals with each other directly, with the approval of the regulatory authority. Normally trade is confined to a particular waterway or watershed and each trade includes a bit extra for the environment.

The EPA is open to the idea of trading to reduce some pollutants such as selenium, which comes from agriculture, but is opposed to trading in 'persistent bioaccumulative toxic pollutants' (USEPA 2004b).

Water pollution bubbles

The US EPA (1996) has also been supportive of water pollution bubbles or 'intra-plant' trading, where a company has a total discharge limit for all its outfalls but is able to decide how much each individual outfall discharges. This concept has also been adopted by the NSW EPA in Australia. For example, the South Creek Bubble Licence sets a maximum aggregate load for nutrients from several of Sydney Water Corporation's treatment plants discharging into South Creek, which flows into the Hawkesbury-Nepean river system – a system significantly stressed by nutrient loads. Sydney Water can decide how much of that aggregate load will come from each plant (James 1997).

GLOBAL WARMING MEASURES

The Kyoto Protocol came into force in February 2005, although neither the USA nor Australia has ratified it. The agreed targets (see table 9.2) are meagre compared with the 60–70 per cent reduction in greenhouse gases that the UN Intergovernmental Panel on Climate Change (IPCC) estimates is necessary by 2050 to prevent serious and irreversible climate change.

Table 9.2 Kyoto Protocol targets for greenhouse gas reductions by 2012

Australia	+8%	Lithuania	–8%
Bulgaria	–8%	Monaco	–8%
Canada	–6%	New Zealand	0%
Croatia	–5%	Norway	+1%
Czech Rep.	–8%	Poland	–6%
Estonia	–8%	Romania	–8%
EU	–8%	Russia	0%
Hungary	–6%	Slovakia	–8%
Iceland	+10%	Slovenia	–8%
Japan	–6%	Switzerland	–8%
Latvia	–8%	Ukraine	0%
Liechtenstein	–8%	United States	–7%

The signatory nations have agreed to allow nations to pay to exceed their targets using a range of mechanisms. These are:

- Emissions trading, which allows countries to buy the rights to discharge emissions above their agreed target from countries that reduce emissions below their agreed targets.
- Joint implementation (JI), which allows countries to offset their excess emissions by paying for emissions reductions or carbon sinks in other countries which have agreed to the Protocol.
- Clean development mechanism (CDM), which allows countries to offset their excess emissions by paying for emissions reductions or carbon sinks in countries which are not signatories to the Protocol; that is, developing nations.

Carbon sinks are to be created by projects such as tree planting that absorb carbon dioxide. CDM allows for afforestation, reforestation and avoided deforestation to offset greenhouse gas emissions. Offsets could also be generated by providing renewable energy generation projects and energy-efficient technologies to developing countries or by the closing down of old, dirty plants in Eastern Europe. In the case of both JI and CDM, the emissions reductions in other countries are supposed to be additional to what would otherwise have occurred – thus if a polluting facility goes out of business because of financial difficulties, the resulting emissions reductions cannot be claimed as additional because they would have happened anyway.

Each nation, in deciding how to meet its targets, may allocate greenhouse gas allowances to companies and allow them to use the same mechanisms of trading and offsets to meet them. In this way, individual corporations can also invest in projects in other countries to offset their emissions. The need to invest in JI or CDM schemes to offset emissions is supposed to provide an incentive for greenhouse gas generators to lower their own emissions, and income for developing countries to invest in environmentally-friendly technologies.

There is some disagreement between nations about the extent to which they should be allowed to meet their targets using emissions trading and other flexibility mechanisms; but many large corporations are pushing for there to be no limits in this regard, and nations such as Japan, Canada and Norway have acceded to this stance (Bachram et al. 2003: 1; CEO 2000: 9).

Emissions trading

The emissions trading system under the Kyoto Protocol is a cap and trade system that will begin in 2008 and cover the 38 nations which are signatories to the Protocol. The cap for each nation is the emissions target it agreed to (shown in table 9.2). If nations are unable to meet their cap by the end of 2012 they will be penalised by having the excess plus a 30 per cent penalty included in their cap for the next 5-year compliance period (Bachram et al. 2003: 18). More effective penalties and fines for non-compliance have been opposed by the same nations that have been pushing for maximum use of market measures such as emissions trading (CEO 2000: 9).

In most countries, corresponding emission allowances will be distributed for free to large polluting companies on the basis of their past emissions (grandfathering). Corporations did not wait for an official international emissions trading scheme to be set up, and by 1999 were already trading $50 billion worth of emissions (CEO 2000: 13). The London International Petroleum Exchange deals in greenhouse gas emission credits and the Sydney Futures Exchange deals in credits from forestry projects (Rising Tide 2005b). Various states in the USA have introduced emissions trading schemes for greenhouse gases from power plants, including Massachusetts, New Hampshire and Oregon (Sonneborne 2002: 2).

There are now several active emissions trading markets:

- The UK system was the first to be established, in 2002. It is an emission reduction scheme rather than a cap and trade scheme. Reduction credits are earned by reducing emissions below a baseline based on past emissions. Companies which agreed to participate received an 80 per cent discount on the Climate Change Levy – a carbon tax on industrial and commercial energy use (IETA 2005: 34; Royal Society 2002: 37).
- The NSW Greenhouse Gas (GHG) Abatement Scheme began in 2003. All electricity retailers have to take part and are required to reach set reduction targets or buy credits to cover any excess (IETA 2005: 35).
- The Chicago Climate Exchange (CCX 2005) was set up in 2003. It claims to be the world's first 'voluntary, legally-binding rules-based greenhouse gas emissions allowance trading system'. Its purpose is to demonstrate how an emissions trading system could work. There is also a Chicago Climate Futures Exchange where investors can gamble on what the price of allowances will be in the future. The CCX deals in all six greenhouse gases and includes carbon offsets projects.
- The EU emissions trading system began in 2005 and covers some 13 000 companies including electricity and heat generators, and producers of cement, ceramics, ferrous metal, glass and paper (Chatterjee 2005).
- Individual European countries have also set up trading programmes. Denmark, for example, has set up a cap and trade programme to cover its electricity sector. The Netherlands has also set up a domestic greenhouse gas emissions trading system (Rising Tide 2005a; Bachram 2004: 5).

Carbon offsets

Both joint implementation and the clean development mechanism include a wide variety of projects providing carbon offsets. For example, the World Bank's Prototype Carbon Fund (PCF) 'counts energy efficiency in the Czech Republic, waste management in Latvia, afforestation in Romania, waste incineration in Mauritius, landfill gas extraction in South Africa and soil conservation in Moldou as eligible for carbon offset credits' (Bachram et al. 2003: 26).

One of the earliest carbon offset projects was created in 1988 when a proposal to build a coal-fired power plant in Virginia, USA, was justified by a $2 million project to pay farmers in Guatemala to plant pine and eucalypt trees and manage them to offset the power plant's CO_2 emissions. Similarly, in 1998 American Electric Power, which uses coal to generate electricity, pledged it would preserve 2.7 million acres of a tropical rainforest in Bolivia in the hope that this would exempt it from having to reduce its greenhouse gas emissions, which would be far more expensive. By that time there were around 100 such projects worldwide, including projects in Costa Rica, Uganda, Mexico and Australia (Lohmann 1999; Lynch 1998).

Australia

In New South Wales a *Carbon Rights Legislation Amendment Act*, passed in 1998, 'enabled State Forests to acquire and trade in such rights as well as to procure land and manage it for investors of such rights'. Under this legislation Tokyo Electric Power Company (TEPCO) paid NSW State Forests to plant 40 000 hectares of trees. In return TEPCO will get both the revenue from the timber when it is logged and from the carbon offsets from the growing trees. Queensland has similarly amended its legislation to separate 'ownership of timber harvesting rights and carbon rights in a stand of trees from ownership of land' (Robinson & Ryan 2002: 27). A National Carbon Accounting Standard has also been developed to enable other organisations and individual landholders to get credit for their carbon sequestration activities (Salvin 2000).

Australia is one of the first countries to introduce legislation that enables carbon rights to be separated from land and resource ownership and to be owned and traded separately. This has enabled the Australian Sustainable Investments Fund to be established as a carbon fund which buys the carbon rights to Australian forests and plantations (Dickie 2005).

Global market in carbon offsets

The global market in carbon credits is expected by 2010 to be worth some $27.5 billion, according to the International Energy Agency (IEA) (cited in Marriott 2005). In 2004, some 107 million metric tonnes of greenhouse emission reductions, generated mainly by JI and CDM projects, were being traded. This was an increase of 38 per cent on 2003. Sixty per cent of these were bought by European buyers and just over 20 per cent by Japanese buyers. Almost 70 per cent were bought by private buyers as opposed to governments. They sell for between $3 and $7 per tonne of CO_2 equivalent, much less than the price in emissions trading systems. The emissions reductions were mainly generated in India, Brazil and Chile (IETA 2005: 3–4, 21). Most emission reductions are earned by reducing greenhouse gases other than CO_2 (see figure 9.1).

Figure 9.1 Source of emission reduction credits, 2004–5

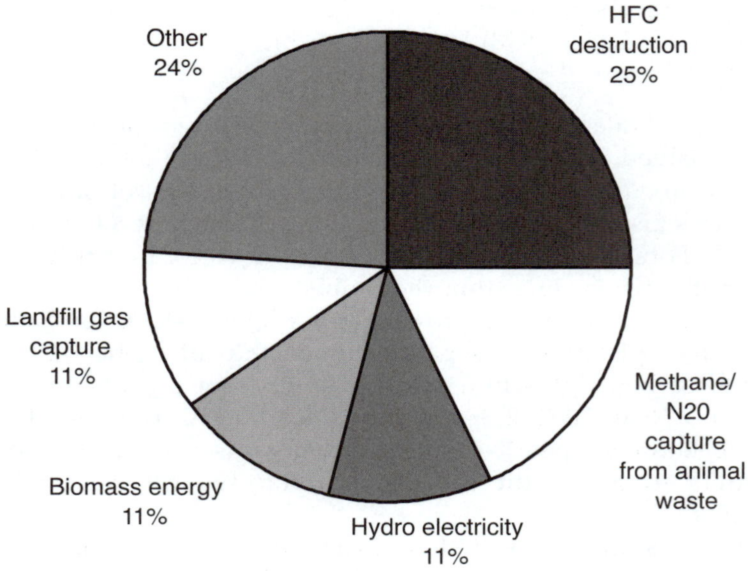

Note: HFC is a refrigerant and a greenhouse gas
Source: (IETA 2005: 3)

Carbon neutral

A number of companies, such as the Carbon Neutral Company and Carbonfund.org, now sell the opportunity to be carbon neutral to people taking aeroplane trips, driving cars and engaging in other greenhouse gas generating activities. The 2005 G8 meeting was advertised as carbon neutral. Various bands, like the Rolling Stones, and celebrities have also made international tours that are supposed to be carbon neutral (McCallin 2005). Organisers of the 2006 Commonwealth Games in Melbourne proposed to make it carbon neutral through the mass planting of trees. The UK-based Carbon Neutral Company (previously Future Forests) had a turnover of £1.4 million in 2004 and expects that to increase to £2.5 million in 2005 (Hopkins 2005c).

Carbon taxes

A carbon tax is a tax on the carbon content of fossil fuels such as coal, natural gas and oil. The tax is imposed in order to raise revenue and to encourage people to use less of these fuels, which contribute to greenhouse gases in the atmosphere. Because so much carbon is used in affluent countries, even a fairly small tax could raise large amounts of money.

Carbon taxes are most prevalent in Europe, being levied in Belgium, Denmark, Finland, France, Italy, Luxembourg, the Netherlands, Norway and Sweden (NCEE 2004: 21). However, they 'are not applied to all fossil fuels or based on the quantity of CO_2 emitted'. For example, the UK's Climate Change Levy is a tax on energy rather than a carbon tax, and excludes household energy use. Only in New Zealand was a genuine carbon tax proposed, but it was subsequently abandoned because of concerns that its cost (estimated at NZ$4 per week per household) would not be justified by sufficient reduction in emissions (New Zealand Scraps Kyoto Carbon-Tax Plan 2005).

Are economic instruments, whether based on prices or property rights, appropriate policies for environmental protection? Chapter 10 considers whether the economic instruments used for pollution control comply with the sustainability principle. Chapter 11 considers whether they comply with the polluter pays principle and the precautionary principle, and chapter 12 evaluates these economic instruments in terms of human rights principles, the equity principle and the participation principle.

Further Reading

Clean Air Markets (2006) US EPA, <http://www.epa.gov/airmarkets/>

International experiences with economic incentives for protecting the environment (2004) National Center for Environmental Economics, US EPA, Washington DC, November, <http://yosemite.epa.gov/ee/epa/eermfile.nsf/vwAN/EE-0487-01.pdf/$File/EE-0487-01.pdf>

OECD (2003) OECD/EEA launch new database on economic instruments used in environmental policy, 2003, <http://www.oecd.org/document/15/0,2340,en_2649_34487_2505231_1_1_1_1,00.html>

Robinson, Jackie & Sean Ryan (2002) A review of economic instruments for environmental management in Queensland, CRC for Coastal Zone, Estuary and Waterway Management, <http://www.coastal.crc.org.au/pdf/economic_instruments.pdf>

Water Quality Trading (2006) US EPA, <http://www.epa.gov/owow/watershed/trading.htm>

10

THE SUSTAINABILITY PRINCIPLE AND ECONOMIC INSTRUMENTS

In most cases economic instruments aim to maximise economic efficiency rather than environmental protection. That is, they aim to achieve a given level of environmental protection at least cost to industry, and to enable continued economic growth despite restrictions on pollution. An OECD report (1989: 118) states:

> More consensus seems to exist regarding advantages of emissions trading in terms of economic efficiency than with respect to its environmental effectiveness. Substantial cost savings are reported by many authors on this subject. An important advantage of emissions trading over direct regulations is that it has facilitated continuous economic growth in dirty areas.

Open market emission trading does *not* ensure that the growth of total emissions in the environment is controlled. Unlike cap and trade emissions trading, there is no limit on the total amount of a pollutant allowed into the air in a region. When emission reduction credits are sold, the quantity of emissions they represent is usually reduced by 10 per cent, which is supposed to ensure that the environment benefits from the transaction – however, if more facilities are established in a region aggregate emissions can still rise.

The use of price-based instruments such as tax incentives and grants has not been particularly successful at promoting environmental protection either, because often they are not worth enough to motivate companies to earn them. An Asia-Pacific study found that 'tax incentives and grant schemes appear to be an area where numerous initiatives have been established through APEC, but with very little effect or benefit'. It found that measures such as technology transfer which inform and teach companies about what they might do, and the removal of 'perverse incentives' such as fossil fuel subsidies, were more effective at achieving environmentally beneficial changes (Gunningham & Sinclair 2002: 29–30).

Limited vs substantial reductions

Economic instruments 'encourage change by those who can achieve the change most cheaply' (National Heritage Trust 2004: 3), which is fine if only limited pollution reductions are required – that is, if reductions can be limited to what can be done cheaply. However, they tend not to work if substantial reductions are required.

The US EPA (2004b) notes that water pollution trading works best when 'the necessary levels of pollutant reduction are not so large that all sources in the watershed must reduce as much as possible to achieve the total reduction needed – in this case there may not be enough surplus reductions to sell or purchase'. The same is true of air pollution trading.

If substantial pollution reductions are necessary, more expensive reductions have to be made, and there is little point in setting up markets that enable some firms to avoid making those expensive reductions to minimise aggregate costs to the industry. This became evident in Germany when the government was considering implementing an acid rain emissions trading programme, the aim of which was to be a 90 per cent reduction in SO_2 between 1983 and 1998. By comparison, the US emissions trading programme aimed at only a 50 per cent reduction by 2010. This meant that in the USA there was much greater scope for power stations to find cheaper ways to reduce their emissions than in Germany, where every power station would have little choice but to retrofit their plants with flue-gas desulphurisation and selective catalytic reduction for nitrogen oxides – which meant that there was no scope for trading (Schärer 1999: 144–5). The Germans therefore decided against an emissions trading programme and achieved their goal using legislation.

In other words, the more rigorous the emission reduction required the more likely it is to require state-of-the-art technology to be achieved and the less scope there is to find cheap solutions and sell excess allowances or reduction credits.

The US acid rain cap and trade scheme is consistently cited as a success because it has achieved some reductions at minimal cost – but how do those reductions compare with what can be achieved with traditional regulation? 'US sulphur emissions now exceed those from the EU Member States by 150%' (EA 2003: 8). Despite overall national reductions, levels of SO_2 increased in 16 states, and 252 out of 600 power stations increased their emissions (Moore 2004a: 11). Even according to its champion, the US EPA:

> The Acid Rain Program has enjoyed an unusually high level of emission reductions and near-perfect compliance. However, it is becoming increasingly clear that the program's emission targets may not be sufficient to achieve its environmental goal of ecosystem recovery. For example, some Adirondack and other sensitive ecosystems remain acidic, and visibility in the East, including the Great Smokies [Smoky Mountains], remains impaired. Scientists believe that emissions from electric generating facilities that cause acid rain must be reduced by two-thirds or more beyond current requirements to allow ecosystems to recover. (USEPA 2002a: 9)

The EPA intends to continue the cap and trade programme to achieve these reductions.

SETTING THE BASELINE OR CAP

Efficiency vs environment

Even proponents of trading admit that there will inevitably be a conflict and an implicit trade-off between the goals of reducing costs and improving environmental quality (Atkinson & Tietenberg 1991: 20–6; Hahn & Hester 1989: 147). This conflict can be seen in the setting of baseline standards or caps for tradeable emissions programmes. The various possible reasons for choosing a particular cap or baseline emission standard include:

- environmental and health protection
- technical feasibility – available technology
- economics – balancing costs
- politics – influence of vested interests and political acceptability.

In practice, baselines and caps tend to be based on economics and politics rather than on what is technically feasible to protect the environment and human health. Emissions trading in greenhouse gases, for example, aims to reduce the emissions from industrialised nations by an average of 5 per cent rather than the 50–70 per cent that is thought to be necessary to prevent global warming (Bachram 2004: 2–3; Moore 2004a: 2–3).

What is good for the environment is not necessarily good for encouraging trade in a market. If the cap is too low and too few allowances are issued, or the baseline standard is too low, there will be few allowances or reduction credits for sale – because few firms will be able to reduce their pollution levels below the allowances they are allocated or the emissions standards set. Yet a low cap may be essential to protecting the environment.

Political factors are also influential, as they are with legislation. Nutrient trading hasn't really taken off in the USA, partly because caps on nutrient levels are not strict enough to force point sources to buy allowances from farmers. But stricter caps have not been imposed because they would be politically unpopular with the industrial polluters that would be the buyers (Hawn 2005b).

Baseline air emission levels are usually set in the USA by making them the same as existing licence limits. Opponents of emissions trading point out that these established licence limits have not enabled states to meet air quality goals so that, logically, while further reductions in emissions are needed, surplus rights should not be traded.

Several US states have allocated allowances on the basis of what a firm has been discharging in the past – that is, grandfathering. But if a firm's actual emissions are overestimated, so that allowable emission rates are set higher than actual emission rates to start with (which, it has been argued, happens in many states), a firm may get more allowances than it needs or credit for reductions it has not actually made. This is one reason why offsets have often not resulted in any noticeable improvement in air quality (Hahn & Hester 1989: 122).

Los Angeles Regional Clean Air Incentives Market

The Los Angeles Regional Clean Air Incentives Market (RECLAIM) programme was designed to reduce emissions of sulphur dioxide and nitrous oxides by 13 000 tons in ten years. It began operation in 1994, but by 1997 no significant reductions had occurred, according to an internal audit by the South Coast Air Quality Management District. Air pollution allowances had been issued on the basis of each company's worst emissions in the previous five years – which meant that companies were able to inflate the baseline of allowable emissions by some 40 000 tons overall above the level they were emitting in 1994 (Belliveau 1998; Drury et al. 1999: 264–5).

As a result, allowances were very cheap for a few years, many being given away for nothing because few companies needed them. There was therefore no pressure to install pollution controls. Whereas nitrous oxide (NO_x) emissions from industrial facilities had been reduced by around 37 per cent between 1989 and 1993 under the previous regulations, in the new trading regime they were reduced by less than 3 per cent between 1994 and 1996, as opposed to a forecast 30 per cent (Drury et al. 1999: 265–75).

By 2001 it was clear that the 30 per cent goal was not going to be met. What is more, the rate of emissions reductions had slowed to a crawl, and concentrations of NO_x in the air were actually increasing. By this time, however, NO_x allowances were in short supply because of economic growth. Speculation caused their price to rise to $45 000 per ton in a very short time, causing panic among companies now needing to buy allowances. As a consequence of power industry pressure, the government was forced to withdraw power plants from the RECLAIM programme. They are now required to meet traditional pollution control regulations (CPR 2005; Moore 2004a, 2004b).

EU emissions trading

When the EU emissions trading system was introduced in 2005, analysts believed that many governments had been too generous in allocating allowances to local firms because they feared these industries would be at a competitive disadvantage if they had to buy extra allowances. A study by Ilex Energy Consulting (2005) for WWF examining six EU countries found that none of them had set caps that went beyond business as usual and none of the six would meet their agreed Kyoto obligations. Because allowances were not in great demand, the market opened at €8 per tonne and settled around €23 a few months later, far less than would be necessary to provide an incentive to reduce emissions (Pearce 2005a).

In the United Kingdom, 'with the exception of power generators, the UK government has ended up giving rights to most industrial sectors to emit yearly at least as much carbon dioxide as they annually emitted *de facto* between 1998 and 2003' (Lohmann 2004: 12). *New Scientist* reported:

> The UK, despite publicly banging the drum for action on climate change, has ended up being one of the worst offenders. When environment secretary Margaret Beckett published her draft allocations for British industry in May 2004, they added up to a total of 736 million tonnes of CO_2 over the next three years. This, according to calculations by the Department for Environment, Food and Rural Affairs, would require a reduction of less than 1 per cent compared with business-as-usual emissions. Even so, intense lobbying by industry followed … in October 2004, the expected business-as-usual emissions were substantially raised, and the permitted emissions raised to 756 million tonnes. (Pearce 2005a)

PHONEY REDUCTIONS

The evidence of how well tradeable pollution rights have worked in practice is mixed. While proponents claim that a given environmental standard can be met for much less cost than by using legislation, opponents argue that the environment benefits little from such schemes. This is because the emissions reductions that are bought and sold are often phoney.

LA Rule 1610

Rule 1610 was introduced in Los Angeles in 1993. It enabled companies to offset their emissions by reducing emissions from mobile sources. This could be done by:

- reducing emissions from vehicles through repairs or retrofitting
- purchasing low-emission vehicles
- scrapping old, high-emission vehicles
- purchasing low-emission lawn and garden equipment (Drury et al. 1999: 249).

Some 20 000 cars were scrapped under this scheme in the first five years. It was assumed that these cars would otherwise have continued to be driven for three more years, for 4000–5000 miles per year. Companies wanting to increase their allowable emissions paid around $600 for each car scrapped. In fact, many cars that were at the end of their lives and would not or could not have been driven any longer were included in the scheme, although no environmental benefit was gained from their inclusion. Between 100 000 and 200 000 old vehicles were scrapped or abandoned each year anyway, and it was by no means clear that the cars scrapped under Rule 1610 weren't part of this group:

> … market forces encourage people who were planning to scrap an old car for its $50 value as scrap metal to obtain $600 for it through the Rule 1610 program instead. This practice is encouraged in Los Angeles because many licensed scrappers are operated jointly with junkyards, where people bring their old cars to be destroyed. While this is rational economic behavior for the car owner, it creates false emission credits. (Drury et al. 1999: 261–2)

Auditors also found that the engines of cars that were supposed to have been scrapped to earn emissions credits were in fact being sold for reuse. Only the car bodies were crushed. This, of course, defeated the purpose of the exercise.

Greenhouse gas emissions trading

The introduction of emissions trading as a mechanism for greenhouse gas reductions has the potential to enable similar phoney reductions. The most obvious is the trading of emissions credits with Russia and other Eastern European countries in economic decline. This has meant that some countries in Eastern Europe, already emitting 30–45 per cent less carbon dioxide than in 1990 because of lowered production, can sell rights to emissions they were not going to make to the USA or Japan in return for hard currency, with no net benefit to the planet (CEO 2000: 13; Pearce 1997). In other words, the reductions that would have occurred *without* emissions trading are now available to affluent countries to avoid making their own emissions reductions. These are referred to as 'hot air' or 'phantom' emissions reductions.

Companies were given millions of dollars in incentives to take part in the UK's voluntary emission trading scheme. An independent non-government group, Environmental Data Services (ENDS), found that three chemical companies, including DuPont, claimed credit for reductions that they had been required to make previously under EU laws. In addition to the millions they got in taxpayer incentives, they made millions from selling the credits they did not deserve. It has been alleged that other companies have also claimed phoney reductions (resulting from plant closures), thus 'securing a baseline against a "false" projection of economic activity which exaggerates output and hence emissions' (Bachram 2004: 5).

In New South Wales, Australia, the Greenhouse Abatement Scheme issues certificates to those who reduce greenhouse gas emissions which can then be sold to electricity retailers who have to meet mandatory emissions reductions. However, a study by researchers at the University of NSW has found that 95 per cent of the certificates issued in the 18 months leading up to June 2004 were for projects established before the introduction of the scheme, and that more than 70 per cent were awarded for emissions reductions that would have occurred anyway. A government spokesman defended the scheme, which is predicted to cost taxpayers some $2 billion over nine years, saying: 'It is not possible to distinguish between production or investment decisions made as a result of the scheme and those that would have been made anyway' (Frew 2005).

Carbon offsets

Those claiming credits for carbon offsets under the joint implementation (JI) and clean development mechanism (CDM) schemes must supply a 'brief explanation' of how emissions of greenhouse gases caused by human activity 'are to be reduced by the proposed CDM project activity, including why the emission reductions would not occur in the absence of the proposed project activity' (Pearson & Loong 2003).

The company getting the credits is therefore able to 'conjure up huge estimates of the emissions that would be supposedly produced without the company's CDM or JI project'. The company investing in a gas-fired power plant, for example, can argue that the alternative would have been a coal-fired power plant – and there is no onus on the company to prove that the coal-fired plant would have been built, nor that the gas-fired plant would not have been built without the CDM credits. Nor does it matter that a wind farm would have reduced CO_2 emissions far more. Using the credits gained with 'imagined' reductions, a company or country can increase their emissions from existing plant in countries that have signed the Kyoto protocol. The benefit to the environment is doubtful, however, since a gas-fired power plant may have been built anyway (Bachram 2004: 4; Lohmann 2004: 29; Pearson & Loong 2003).

In some cases projects that are already underway belatedly claim CDM credits, even though it is obvious they would have gone ahead anyway. An example is the Esti Dam in Panama, which was more than half complete when the Dutch government applied for 3.5 million tonnes of CDM credits for it. Thus CDM credits are being claimed without any genuine emission reductions being made. This non-reduction then allows more emissions in signatory countries than would otherwise have been permitted, in fact diverting funds from genuine reductions to subsidise business as usual (Pearson & Loong 2003).

The Climate Justice Network (Rising Tide 2005b) points out that transnational companies with operations in developing countries can earn credits from taking measures to reduce emissions that they should have taken anyway: 'An example of a horribly easy emission reduction would be Shell stopping gas flares on the oil fields which have already been poisoning people in the Niger Delta for decades – and actually getting paid for it with emission credits!'

The CDM mechanism also provides a disincentive for governments in poor countries to introduce 'programmes supporting renewables or other climate-friendly projects', as this might disqualify them from receiving CDM funding – since the projects might no longer be seen as additional to what would normally happen without CDM funding: 'There is evidence, for example, that Mexico City has held back several "climate-friendly policies" in order not to jeopardise CDM investment'. This means that government policies that would have reduced global greenhouse gas emissions are substituted for by project financing that avoids corresponding emission reductions in affluent nations, so there is no global benefit (Lohmann 2004: 29).

The CDM also provides an incentive for industrial facilities to be designed without pollution controls so that they present an attractive emission-reduction opportunity. It is conceivable, for example, that future landfill dumps could be designed without methane capture in the hope that foreign investors looking for credits would be attracted to pay for the methane capture. On top of this, there is an incentive for governments to not enforce the environmental regulations they do have in order to justify CDM projects: 'some proposed CDM projects are claiming carbon credits simply for obeying the environmental laws of the host country on the grounds that, without the projects, it can be predicted that the law would be violated' (Lohmann 2004: 29).

MONITORING AND ENFORCEMENT

It is often argued by economists that markets are more efficient than centralised government decision making because they automatically gather information and ensure that supply and demand are balanced and resources allocated efficiently. This line of argument cannot be applied to artificial markets such as those created for pollution rights, since the need for monitoring and enforcement remains and is, in fact, arguably greater.

For charges and fees to work properly, the regulator still needs to know what volumes and concentrations of wastes are being discharged, and also needs to ensure that the firm is paying the correct amount for the quantities discharged. For emissions trading to work properly, the regulator needs to know whether a firm deserves emission reduction credits and whether it is keeping within its allowance. 'Any system of environmental control needs inspectors to check whether claimed emissions, discharges or resource extractions are correct: they are not less "bureaucratic" because they are tax inspectors rather than regulatory ones' (Jacobs 1993: 7). Too often inspection and verification does not happen.

Incentive to cheat

Under a technology-based system, as the Clean Air Act used to be in the USA, monitoring and enforcement was fairly straightforward. It was a matter of monitoring emissions and ensuring that the appropriate pollution control equipment was installed (Moore 2004a: 6). A major problem with schemes that rely on some degree of self-assessment to measure emission reductions is that they are notoriously difficult for government authorities to monitor and verify. Emissions trading increases the incentive to cheat because claimed reductions are worth money (Drury et al. 1999: 259).

Environmental groups sued a number of companies in the RECLAIM programme, including United Airlines and the Southern California Gas Company, for failing to purchase sufficient credits to cover their pollution. The companies settled the case by agreeing to either reduce their emissions or buy more credits. The problem was that the regulator simply verified transactions after they had been made, often being able to do little more than check the paperwork because of a lack of personnel and resources to physically measure each claimed reduction (Drury et al. 1999: 282; Moore 2004b).

Under emissions trading schemes, companies often do not report actual measured emissions but estimated emissions, based on models that are frequently far from accurate. Drury and his colleagues (1999: 260–1) report that although such models underestimated oil company emissions by factors of between 10 and 1000, these estimates were accepted by the regulatory authorities. In the case of Rule 1610, auditors found that companies were under-reporting their emissions so they didn't have to buy so many allowances (CPR 2005).

Monitoring difficulties

Some pollutants are particularly problematic:

> Emissions of VOCs [volatile organic compounds] are difficult to monitor accurately because millions of sources release VOCs from everyday activities, and VOCs evaporate into the air instead of being emitted from a stack. VOC trading was dropped from the original RECLAIM proposal because the monitoring and enforcement challenges were so severe ... For example, most VOC emissions are from leaks from thousands of pieces of equipment (so-called fugitive emissions) or evaporation from direct use of thousands of VOC-containing products (e.g. spray paints). (Drury et al. 1999: 181)

Monitoring numerous small and medium-sized firms is also difficult in an emissions trading scheme, which is why many such schemes, such as the US acid rain programme, only include large companies. Open market emissions trading, however, covers not only small and medium enterprises but also many different sources and multiple pollutants. This makes monitoring even more difficult, and is usually beyond the ability of state or federal agencies to enforce with their existing resources.

In 2002 the New Jersey Environmental Protection Commissioner claimed that the state's Open Market Emissions Trading programme had not only failed to clean up the environment but had endangered gains that had previously been made with respect to reducing air pollution (Twyman 2002). Environmentalists had earlier pointed out that there was no mechanism for verifying reported reductions in traded emissions, which included nitrous oxides and volatile organic compounds. Not only that, but companies were able to gain credits for emissions reductions they had made some years earlier (Biello 2002; Fichthorn & Wood 2002: 28). The programme was officially repealed in 2004.

Global warming measures

The difficulties of monitoring and enforcing statewide emissions trading programmes is multiplied many times when it comes to monitoring emissions and claimed reductions worldwide, as well as the 'countless transactions around the globe that are brokered by far removed "middle men"' (Belliveau 1998). This is particularly the case in developing countries, where the regulatory infrastructure and skilled personnel required to measure and monitor emissions reductions may not be well developed (Richman 2003: 166). It is also a problem in affluent countries, where monitoring is often neglected:

> At the same time as hundreds of millions of dollars are invested in setting up trading schemes all over the world, virtually no financial support is channelled into vital regulatory infrastructure. The UK alone has spent UK £215 million on their trial trading scheme. As brokers, consultants, accountants, speculators, energy corporations and politicians all scramble for a piece of the emissions trading pie, no equivalent level of activity is seen from credible verifiers or monitors. This imbalance can only lead to an emissions market dangerously reliant upon the integrity of corporations to file accurate reports of emissions levels as well as emissions reductions from projects. (Bachram et al. 2003: 37)

Where emissions reductions are verified, it is often done by transnational corporations which at the same time are acting as consultants and accountants to the very companies whose emissions they are auditing. 'This can only lead to a severe conflict of interests, resulting in fraud and ultimately little guarantee of actual emissions reductions' (Bachram et al. 2003: 37).

There is even more scope for cooking the books when it comes to carbon sinks, such as tree plantations, because of the lack of accepted methods for calculating how much carbon is temporarily taken up by growing trees. The trees might release their carbon early as a result of fires, disease or illegal logging. Thus, while plantations need to be monitored long term, throughout their life-cycles, to ensure the carbon credits earned by planting them are deserved, governments are only concerned with meeting targets within a comparatively short compliance period (Kill 2001: 10).

Water pollution trading

Nutrient trading is difficult to monitor because of the inclusion of non-point sources, such as farms which have dispersed run-off, because 'non-point discharges are episodic and cannot be directly measured, only estimated' (Faeth 2000: 3). Nutrient loads are also influenced by extraneous factors such as weather changes and soil characteristics, so it is difficult to measure reductions from many small farms. The National Wildlife Federation (NWF) in the USA has pointed out that water pollution trading therefore involves 'trading federally-enforceable point source discharge limits for unenforceable nonpoint controls ... without enforceability there would be no assurance that polluted runoff controls would actually reduce pollution' (NWF 1997).

Additionally, the 'EPA has little regulatory authority over politically powerful farmers and ranchers' (Sokulsky 2005). The conflict between environmental and economic goals becomes evident when a ratio between non-point and point trades is established. A higher ratio (for example, 5 kilograms from a non-point source is equivalent to 2 kilograms from a point source) is required to make up for the difficulties in monitoring, but a lower ratio ensures that allowances or credits will more readily be traded (Hawn 2005b).

In a water-pollution trading system, monitoring for pollution from point sources is normally done by the factories themselves. This involves taking a sample each week to ensure that a monthly average is met. But a single sample is not necessarily typical of the outflow throughout the week, and although regulations require sampling to be 'representative', it is too easy for the discharge to be sampled at times when pollutants are low (Caton 2002). Self-monitoring is often required under non-market regulations as well, but when a commercial value is added to discharges the temptation to cheat is increased.

Price mechanisms

There is also scope and incentive for fraud and illegal activity with charges and fees. A system of charges will only work if there is strong policing and enforcement – and there is no reason to suppose that where traditional legislation failed for want of that enforcement, charges will succeed. For example, when South Korea introduced a system of fees for authorised garbage bags for the collection of household waste in 1995, the amount of waste going to landfills went down by some 40 per cent in the first six months. 'Unfortunately, a large quantity of the decrease was attributable not to waste reduction or recycling, but rather to uncontrolled incineration or private disposal.' This illegal activity occurred even though the bag fees were not high enough to cover disposal costs (NCEE 2004: 19).

In the United Kingdom a landfill tax was introduced in 1996 to make it expensive to dump contaminated waste. However, instead of avoiding the creation of waste, or treating the waste themselves to save money on the landfill tax, some of the companies responsible for the waste began dumping it in illegal places, like golf courses. While the Department of Environment claimed a 10 million tonne reduction in waste at landfills because of the tax, the *Guardian* reported that the excess waste:

> [was being] disposed of as land-raising material at golf courses, retail development parks, sports facilities and even private residential developments ... Often the first indication of something going wrong is when a resident rings up to say a cricket pitch has risen 10 feet overnight... Altogether 30 golf courses are under investigation for illegal dumping. (Hencke 2000c)

Fraud

The introduction of markets into environmental protection brings profit-making opportunities and with it the opportunity for fraud. In California, one of the designers of the RECLAIM programme set up an auction house for the trading of emissions reduction credits, but was later found guilty of fraud in her work as credit broker. She apparently traded in bogus credits and made 'fishy transactions' that included selling the same credits to two different companies. Environmentalists claimed that programmes that turn pollution control into a profit-making opportunity invite such fraud (Bustillo & Rosenzweig 2004).

In the UK landfill tax scheme describe above, the waste firms were able to avoid 20 per cent of their due landfill tax by donating the money to an independent environmental trust. The idea was that money raised from the polluter – hundreds of millions of pounds – would be used for conservation purposes. Although the waste firms were not allowed to profit from such donations they were able to set up environmental trusts, with their own people as directors, trusts which received millions of pounds from the scheme. In some cases the trust directors themselves received unauthorised fees of over £100 000 (Hencke 2000a, 2000b).

Several of these trusts were charged with fraud. Five had their registration revoked within the first three years of the scheme being set up. Two others were under investigation in 2000 for fraud amounting to £5 million. A parliamentary inquiry found in 2001 that the scheme, worth some £340 million, had benefited the waste companies and that the private regulator of the scheme, Entrust, was unfit to supervise it (Hencke 2000a, 2001).

PERPETUATING BAD PRACTICES

Avoiding change

Emissions trading tends to protect very polluting or dirty industries by allowing them to buy emission rights rather than meet environmental standards. In this way, trading can reduce the pressure on polluting companies to change production processes and introduce other measures to reduce their emissions. Some environmentalists argue that it is preferable in the long run for firms that cannot make the environmental grade to go out of business and make way for other firms which can produce substitute products in a cleaner way.

The fossil fuel-dependent companies which want to continue expanding their businesses are the very ones that are promoting emissions trading in the knowledge that it will enable them to continue to expand. An official at the US Department of Energy noted that 'tree-planting will allow US energy policy to go on with business as usual out to 2015' (Lohmann 1999).

Similarly, CDM projects favour plantations and other cheap methods of reducing carbon emissions, like landfill gas capture, rather than renewable energy projects, in developing countries. One of the easiest ways to earn carbon reduction credits is to pump methane out of a waste dump. Such projects provide 'a proven technological fix, easy-to-crunch mission numbers, and prospects for rapid progress' and so are more attractive to investors than reforestation or renewable energy projects (Hawn 2005a). '[T]raditional energy efficiency or fuel switching projects, which were initially expected to represent the bulk of the CDM, account for less than 5%' (IETA 2005: 3). This is because renewable energy is more expensive for investors, even though it offers more benefits to the local community and the nation. This has caused CDM to be referred to as the 'Cheap Development Mechanism' (CDM Watch 2005: 15–6).

'Carbon neutral'

The idea that people can negate their contribution to global warming (that is, be carbon neutral) by paying for trees to be planted is a way of taking the guilt out of excessive and mindless consumerism and allowing consumerism to continue. Carbonfund.org promises individuals and businesses carbon offsets that will allow them to go on doing whatever they want with a clear conscience: 'Whether you own a hybrid or a Hummer, now anyone can reduce their climate footprint to zero' (Carbonfund.org 2005). All they have to do is pay the company the appropriate amount of money.

Similarly, by using carbon offsets, 'a utility company releasing a million tonnes of carbon a year ... can be just as "carbon-neutral" as a subsistence farming household emitting one tonne a year' (Lohmann 2001: 11). The idea of carbon neutrality thus allows the very activities that contribute to global warming to continue unabated while promoting tree plantations that very often are not environmentally beneficial (see below).

It is also a way for corporations to green their image without making any real changes. London's famous black cabs are going 'carbon neutral' in an effort to forestall likely restrictions on polluting vehicles in the central London area. The black cabs are run on diesel, which is particularly polluting – but by the business contributing funds towards forestry projects in the United Kingdom and Germany, solar projects in Sri Lanka and a small hydro power plant in Bulgaria, they can be labelled 'carbon neutral' (McCallin 2005). Various firms are also offering their customers the opportunity to be 'carbon neutral' in some of their purchases (Biello 2005).

Promoting dubious technologies

Various technologies of contested environmental benefit are being promoted as eligible for credits in the JI and CDM schemes. For example, Monsanto has argued that farmers who plant crops that are genetically engineered by Monsanto to be resistant to its herbicide Roundup will be able to reduce or even avoid ploughing their land – which will ensure that more carbon is stored in the soil. Even aluminium producers are claiming that the use of aluminium in cars should earn credits because making cars lighter reduces the amount of fuel they use, thereby reducing the amount of carbon dioxide the cars produce. This is despite the fact that aluminium is very energy intensive to manufacture (CEO 2000: 12–6).

The CDM also acts as an effective subsidy for the nuclear industry by rewarding it with carbon credits despite the known hazards associated with operating nuclear plants and storing nuclear waste. The CDM is providing an incentive for the construction of nuclear power plants in developing nations, particularly China. It is estimated that carbon credits could reduce the construction costs of such plants by 10–40 per cent (CEO 2000: 17).

Companies have even worked out a way to count logging as an emissions reduction:

> New England Electric Systems, a coal-burning utility holding company, has paid the Malaysian Innoprise Corporation (which manages the commercial exploitation of a 972,000 hectare timber concession) to carry out 'reduced-impact' logging in part of its con-

> cession. The logic to this is perverse and absurd – New England Electric can earn credits from logging if 'it causes less deforestation than would otherwise have occurred'. The Malaysian Innoprise Corporation can make money both by logging and then by replanting. (CEO 2000: 15)

One of the carbon offset projects in Minas Gerais, Brazil, involves a 23000 hectare eucalypt plantation owned by Plantar which will be used to produce charcoal for pig-iron production. Plantar argues that it deserves carbon credits for this project because without them charcoal would be uneconomical as an energy source and it would have to use imported coal, which would result in higher CO_2 emissions. Not only has the project taken up land that is needed by thousands of landless people in the state but it has perpetuated an industry – charcoal making – which is 'one of the most hazardous and poorly paid in the region' (Kill & Pearson 2003: 5).

What is more, the claim that without the credits the project would not have gone ahead because charcoal production is uneconomical is belied by the fact that another pig-iron production facility has recently been established in Brazil that will use charcoal despite not having credits to subsidise it. Thus credits are being accorded to what is in actuality a continuing and current practice, something that would have occurred anyway. Yet the World Bank expects this project to be a forerunner of more carbon credit projects like it in the future (Kill & Pearson 2003: 8).

Plantations

The idea behind carbon sinks comes from recognition of the vital role that forests play in 'regulating the earth's temperature and weather patterns by storing large quantities of carbon and water' (SinksWatch 2006). However, rather than conserve existing forests and prevent deforestation, market mechanisms focus attention on creating carbon sinks by planting trees.

Forests are much better at storing carbon than plantations: 'Plantations in the tropics for example store 20–50% less carbon in above-ground biomass than do primary forests in the same climatic zone' (Kill & Pearson 2001: 5). It can take 250 years for secondary growth in a forest to store as much carbon as the original forest. The loss of forests in countries that are not signatories to the Kyoto Protocol is not taken into consideration, so while net carbon sinks are in fact declining, the increase in one minor form of carbon sink (plantations) is allowed to justify increases in greenhouse gases in developed countries.

In contrast to forests, plantations can create 'green deserts' because they are so water intensive. Generally plantations are made up of a single species, such as a eucalypt or a pine, that grows quickly, has high fibre yields and can be easily logged. The plantations suck up all the water in an area, leaving surrounding wells dry and the land around desiccated and unable to support crops. A report funded by the UK Forestry Research Programme found that plantations often lower the water-table, draw water from the soil and drain rivers (Pearce 2005b).

Another study found that when agricultural lands in India were converted to forests there was a 16–26 per cent reduction in water yields, partly because of the increased evaporation of water from the leaves of the trees (Nicholls 2005). 'Replacing grasslands with plantations – another common practice – can be equally counterproductive. Recent studies show that the Andean Paramos [high-altitude grassland] ecosystem, for example, is more efficient than tree plantations in absorbing CO_2' (Lohmann 2000).

This focus on planting trees ignores all the other functions provided by forests composed of diverse and numerous plant species, assuming that they can be replaced by a plantation of trees of the same species. The trees are planted in rows of the same age and require heavy use of agrichemicals, including fertilisers and herbicides, that pollute remaining waterways. Such plantations reduce soil fertility, increase erosion and compaction of the soil, and increase the risk of fire. In addition, they can lead to a loss of local biodiversity because they are monocultures of non-native species and because their densely packed, uniform rows do not provide the variations of form and structure found in a forest (Kill & Pearson 2003: 3; Lohmann 1999).

While plantations are being created, natural forests are being destroyed worldwide as a result of 'inequality of land ownership, the lack of recognition of forest peoples' rights, unsustainable consumption levels of forest products in the North, the inequality in the world trading system, and the dominance of timber values in forest use' (Kill 2001: 15). If these underlying causes of deforestation are not addressed, preventing deforestation in one place may just lead to deforestation in another place.

Where agricultural activities are displaced by plantations, forests may be cleared elsewhere to grow the food that would have been grown on the land now occupied by plantations. Not only that – if carbon-credited forest protection projects cause the price of wood to rise, this will increase 'pressures for logging outside project boundaries' (Kill 2001: 12; Lohmann 1999).

Business as usual

The World Bank is a central player in the market for carbon offsets, managing carbon funds for individual countries as well as the Prototype Carbon Fund (PCF), the BioCarbon Fund and the Community Development Carbon Fund. It is also the 'chief financier of fossil fuel projects in developing countries'. Its carbon funds are worth about $1 billion over seven years – but it provided approximately $2.4 billion for fossil fuel projects in 2003 alone (CDM Watch 2005: 6).

> The Bank, however, is only one example. Globally, North-South flows of investment and governmental support through ECAs [export credit agencies] and international financial institutions favour fossil fuels, financing and entrenching them in developing country energy systems to a degree that makes the new financial flows achieved by the emerging carbon market largely irrelevant. (Lohmann 2004: 30)

Similarly, most developed nations' governments provide subsidies to the fossil fuel industry while paying lip-service to greenhouse gas emission targets. The annual global subsidies to fossil fuels between 1992 and 2002 were around $200 billion (Lohmann 2004: 30).

The companies contributing to CDM and JI projects have received hundreds of times more funding from the World Bank for fossil fuel projects during the same period, investing in these carbon funds in order to receive carbon offsets in countries where they are adding far more carbon to the atmosphere through World Bank-financed fossil fuel projects. And worse, while they get credits for the carbon-offset projects they get no debit for the carbon-adding fossil fuel projects.

Mitsubishi, for example, has four projects in Brazil which will earn it some 13 million carbon credits over 21 years. It is also investing in an oilfield project in the same country which will emit around 58 times the amount of carbon supposedly reduced by the four carbon credit projects. BP has invested $5 million in the PCF up to 2004 and received almost $1 billion from the World Bank over a decade to 2002 for fossil fuel projects. One of these projects, which is still funded by the Bank, is to open the Azerbaijan oilfields to supply oil to the USA and Western Europe (CDM Watch 2005: 7–8).

I have been unable to find examples of pollution trading schemes that have been unarguably good for the environment, although many have been good for industry in terms of money saved. The example that is most cited in the literature is the US acid rain scheme. However, although it has undoubtedly resulted in the reduction of SO_2 emissions, it has not performed as well as equivalent European legislative schemes and has created localised pollution problems.

11

THE POLLUTER PAYS AND PRECAUTIONARY PRINCIPLES APPLIED

THE POLLUTER PAYS PRINCIPLE

Internalising costs

Economic instruments such as taxes and charges are supposed to make external costs part of the polluter's decision. Laws can also force the polluter to take notice of these external costs by prescribing limits to what can be discharged or emitted. Economists argue, however, that the market is better able to find the optimal level of damage: the level that is most economically efficient. The idea that there should be a level of pollution that is above zero but is called 'optimal' is strange, and even repugnant, to many people – but it is a central assumption in the economic theory on which economic instruments are based.

If a pollution charge is equivalent to the cost of environmental damage, the theory says that the company will clean up its pollution until any further incremental reduction in pollution would cost more than the remaining charge, that is, until it is cheaper to pay the charge than reduce the pollution. This is said to be economically efficient because if the polluter spends any more, the costs (to the firm) of extra pollution control will outweigh the benefits (to those suffering the adverse affects of the pollution).

This might seem to be a less than optimal solution to the community, but economists argue that the polluter is better off than if it had paid to eliminate the pollution altogether and the community is no worse off because it is being compensated for the damage through pollution charges paid by the firm to the government. In theory, the payments made by firms in the form of charges can be used to correct the environmental damage they cause or to compensate the victims.

Figure 11.1 Economist's graph showing incremental costs and benefits of pollution control

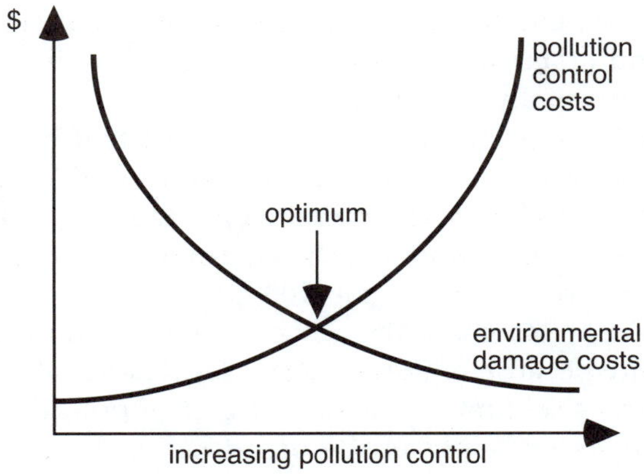

A further assumption behind the theory – that there is a point of optimal damage – is that progressively more pollution reduction is increasingly expensive (see the upward swing of the pollution control costs curve on figure 11.1) for smaller and smaller environmental gain (see the levelling-off of the other curve). This premise is based on the idea that pollution reduction is achieved by pollution control equipment being added to production processes. In contrast the aim of 'clean production' is to change production processes so that the pollution is not generated in the first place. Changes in production processes may end up saving a firm money over the long term.

Environmental taxes and charges are supposed to ensure that the price of goods includes the costs to the environment of producing them. In this way, the market is able to work out what quantities of pollutants will be produced. All this supposes that charges and taxes are in some way equivalent to the damage done, that environmental damage can be paid for, and that this is as good as, or even preferable to, avoiding the damage in the first place. This implies that the benefits that arise from the environment can be substituted for other benefits that can be bought on the market. However, environmental quality is not something that can be swapped for other goods without a loss of welfare (see chapter 8). There is also considerable doubt about whether money payments can correct environmental damage in many circumstances; and, more importantly, money collected from pollution charges is seldom used to correct environmental damage or to compensate victims.

Inadequacy of prices

In practice, governments and regulatory agencies do not attempt to relate charges or taxes to the 'external costs' of environmental damage. Additionally, environmental taxes and charges are frequently promoted by economists and others as a way of replacing other charges and taxes that firms would normally have to pay.

The UK research organisation Truscot estimated that if companies had to pay the actual cost of the economic damage caused by carbon emissions – estimated by the UK government to be some £20 per tonne – some of them would be paying around half their earnings. Overall it would cost 12 per cent of the earnings of the top 100 UK firms listed on the stock-market, the FTSE 100 (Robins 2005). This is not something governments are likely to require because of the economic (and political) ramifications.

Pollution charges seldom cover the full cost of pollution as required by the polluter pays principle in the broad sense. In the case of user charges, the difficulties involved in working out the environmental costs of natural resource extraction and use mean that water charges generally cover only the operating costs of the water authority, not the environmental costs; that waste charges generally cover only the physical costs of disposing of the wastes; and that royalties for mining are levied to provide revenue to governments rather than full compensation for resource and environmental loss (Robinson & Ryan 2002: 12–3).

Similarly, a performance bond is supposed 'to internalise the risk costs associated' with an activity such as mining or hazardous waste transport. However, the size of the bond is seldom based on a scientific assessment of the damage that might actually occur in the short or the long term (Robinson & Ryan 2002: 10).

Subsidies, bounties and tax concessions do not conform to the polluter pays principle at all, because the polluter is being subsidised rather than bearing the full cost of pollution control measures. The OECD (1989) has found that environmental subsidies tend to serve economic rather than environmental goals – most notably the provision of financial support to firms that find it expensive to meet environmental standards.

Similarly, the cost of tradeable pollution rights is determined by the market; it has no direct relationship with the cost of environmental damage. This means that polluters are not paying the actual costs of the damage they cause and that these economic instruments do not conform to the polluter pays principle. This is particularly the case when emissions credits or allowances are allocated to companies at no cost, which usually happens with emissions trading schemes. In such cases, polluters are paying only for the extra credits they need beyond those allocated, and polluters that reduce emissions below their allocations can even make money from them.

Incentives for innovation

Economists argue that the imposed costs, even if they don't internalise the real environmental costs of polluting activity, nevertheless provide an incentive for companies to reduce their pollution and thereby save money. The contention is that legal standards might ensure firms meet particular targets, but once having met them there is no incentive to go beyond them, whereas under the financial incentives provided by economic instruments, 'businesses are constantly motivated to improve their financial performance by developing technologies that allow them to reduce their output of pollutants' (Stavins & Whitehead 1992: 30).

Adding costs to a firm's operations may impose pressure on it to reduce its costs but there is no guarantee that it will do so in the area where the cost is imposed. A firm might find it easier, cheaper, or even more profitable, to apply new technology and methods in other parts of its operation or simply to pass the increased cost on to the consumer – especially in sectors where there is little price competition between firms.

A number of studies have shown that 25–30 per cent of dischargers who are subject to effluent charges do not understand the pricing system and that 'significantly different levels of payment could arise if they altered the strength/volume composition of the effluent' (Rees 1988: 184). Many of them do not have sufficient knowledge of alternative methods and costs to make optimal decisions in their own interest. Jacobs (1993: 7) gives the following example:

> In Britain a rise of 400% in sewerage charges failed to change firms' behaviour, even though it was shown that small investments in pollution control would pay back in under a year. The charging system was not understood by the firms affected; it was dealt with by the finance department, not the engineers; and the firms did not know the technological options available. A regulation requiring them to install the better technology would almost certainly have been more efficient – that is, cost less overall – than the huge price hike which would have been required to get the same changes made.

Joseph Rees (1988: 172) says that advocates of economic instruments tend to assume that 'the pollution control system is populated by economically rational entrepreneurs and regulators, operating without technical, perceptual, organisational and capital availability constraints'. This is not the situation in the real world. For example, a firm may not be able to afford the initial capital cost of changing production processes or putting in pre-treatment equipment, even if this would be cheaper in the long term than paying the charges. As Amory Lovins has pointed out, 'Although price matters, the ability to respond to price matters more' (quoted in Jacobs 1993: 7).

The degree of incentive provided will obviously depend on how large the charge or tax or subsidy is: 'If it is low, and environmental improvement is primarily achieved through major investments in plant and equipment which occur rarely, there may be little effect' (Jacobs 1993: 7). In theory, the fee or charge or price of allowances should be more than the profits made by not reducing pollution; but in practice the amounts charged are often very low. Similarly, pollution charges and user charges are usually not high enough to provide an incentive to minimise pollution or resource use (NCEE 2004: 3). This is the result of political pressure from industries not wanting to pay higher charges, and of concerns that higher charges might encourage illegal dumping and evasion of the charges.

Disincentives for innovation

Although economic instruments are supposed to encourage technological innovation, they often stifle it by allowing firms to pay for pollution rather than reduce their emissions. It is often much easier to pay a charge or buy pollution allowances than to invest in research and development that may or may not result in pollution reduction technologies that will be cheaper than the cost of the charge or allowance.

A 'trading program effectively lessens or eliminates the pollution control obligations of the sources having the greatest need for innovation, those facing high control costs', while those who can reduce their emissions for low cost don't need to innovate to gain credits to sell. Similarly, international emissions trading and offsets create 'an economic incentive to deploy existing technology abroad in lieu of innovation at home'. For example, an electricity supplier is able to install standard technology on a coal-fired power station it operates in another country rather than find renewable energy sources at home (Driesen 1998). The pressure to change production methods and energy sources to be more sustainable is reduced, thus increasing 'the risk that countries and industries that have the capacity to develop new technologies will fail to do so' (Ott & Sachs 2000:17; Richman 2003: 170–1).

Quick and easy

The market often favours the technologies that are cheapest in the short term, even though more expensive options have broader benefits and are more economical in the long term: 'Energy efficiency investments that save money for the society as a whole over a long period of time do not necessarily appear economic' to investors. Renewable energy projects, for example, 'tend to be greenfield developments [new developments] which are capital-intensive, provide low rates of return and generate relatively small volumes of credits' over a long time period. Yet these projects have 'greater environmental and social value than a project that merely captures end-of-pipe emissions' from an existing facility (Lohmann 2004: 34–5).

> The narrow focus on a tradable commodity means that a carbon market will actually frustrate environmentally superior outcomes by directing investment away from projects with the most overall benefits. By going after the cheapest reductions, the market all but ensures that investment will flow to the 'lowest quality' reductions, those that involve the least investment, least genuine technology transfer, and least sustainable development co-benefits, as all this would raise prices. (Lohmann 2004: 34)

Substantial changes to technological paradigms require institutional changes that decision-makers prefer to avoid.

> In addition, decisions to retrofit old plants or build new coal-fired power plants abroad may actually make it harder to switch to cleaner technologies once they become available. Once investors make fresh investments in older plants, they may want to keep these plants running for a long time in order to maximize the return from these sunk costs. (Driesen 1998)

In this way any technological improvements are marginal rather than wholesale, and more radical innovations are avoided.

US experience

Under the US acid rain emissions trading programme, state electricity companies have developed a pattern of buying low-sulphur coal from another state or emissions credits from another company rather than investing in new technologies such as integrated gasification-combined cycle or investing in renewable energy sources:

> The market places no value on integrated gasification-combined cycle's ability to reduce not only sulfur dioxide by an order of magnitude, but also reduce oxides of nitrogen, carbon monoxide, volatile organic compounds and heavy metals such as mercury. The polluter is interested in one – and only one – outcome: reducing emissions of sulfur dioxide to its allocated level of pollution, no more, and at the lowest possible price. (Moore 2004a: 7–8)

Under the Los Angeles Regional Clean Air Incentives Market (RECLAIM) programme, the cheap initial price of emissions credits made them more desirable than installing pollution controls. In 1997, for example, the cost of NO_x credits was less than 50 times the cost of the best available control technology to reduce nitrous oxides. Power plants, which had been responsible for 14 per cent of NO_x emissions, bought up 67 per cent of the NO_x emission credits expiring in 2000 rather than install available technologies for reducing NO_x emissions (Moore 2004b).

Under the previous legislative regime, southern California had been the leader in development of environmental technologies. The Technology Advancement Office had spent around $10 million, raised from a small portion of car registration fees, to develop new technologies such as fuel cells, low-emitting burners and turbines, ultra clean fuels and zero-emission paints. Under the RECLAIM programme, these technologies were not implemented and lost their markets (Moore 2004b).

Annual NO_x emissions were reduced by only 1305 tons between 1994 and 1998 through the implementation of pollution control equipment by companies seeking to comply with RECLAIM, compared with reductions of 9000 tons per year 'in the same time frame as a result of discretionary implementation of control equipment initiated under the rules *prior* to RECLAIM. This illustrates how emissions trading has muted the incentive to innovate' (Drury et al. 1999: 277–8). For example, the AES Alamitos electricity generating plant near Long Beach, California, had been required to install selective catalytic reduction for NO_x emissions in the early 1990s under Rule 1135, which set NO_x emission limits for power plants. When RECLAIM was introduced in 1993 the installation of this technology was abandoned, leaving two boilers with it and two without. When electricity generation increased at the plant so did NO_x emissions (Moore 2004b).

When the price of emissions credits jumped by more than 100 times in the space of a few months in 2000, polluters were caught short, with no time to install control equipment, and had to pay large amounts for credits. Companies spent some $177 million buying credits, which was far more expensive than installing the pollution control equipment that would have made buying credits unnecessary. This money went to credit brokers speculating on the market rather than to cleaning up the environment (Moore 2004b).

> In the acid rain program, for example, there is no evidence that so much as one advanced coal combustion technology has been deployed because of trading, though there is ample proof that command and control programs have induced such efforts. Similarly, the trading of leaded gasoline does not appear to have stimulated any advances in superior refining technologies. Indeed, the greatest single advance in fuel in the past 15 years, the development of environmentally engineered, or reformulated, gasoline was largely prompted by the command and control requirements of California that preceded RECLAIM. (Moore 2004b)

THE PRECAUTIONARY PRINCIPLE

Assimilative capacity

Economic instruments are based on the idea that the environment has a certain capacity to absorb waste materials without long-term damage: in other words, that the environment has an assimilative capacity. A belief in assimilative capacity arises from the way some wastes, such as organic wastes that occur naturally, decompose and break down in the environment, as long as there are not too many of them in the one place at the one time. Other materials, including some metals, may exist naturally in the environment at very low concentrations.

The philosophy behind tradeable pollution rights is based on the assumption that the environment can take a certain amount of pollution and that trading can ensure efficient allocation of that capacity to firms that need to utilise it. Tradeable pollution rights are a way of allocating ownership to the assimilative capacity of the air or water through rights to pollute it.

Assimilative capacity is based on three premises (NENT 1998: 116):

- A certain level of pollution causes no harm to the environment, or at least no irreversible harm – this is referred to as the self-healing potential of environment.
- Environments can only absorb a certain amount of pollution/wastes before there are unacceptable adverse consequences; these are then cumulative and irreversible.
- The assimilative capacity of an environment can be quantified, apportioned and utilised.

Some business groups even argue that the capacity of the environment to absorb wastes and pollution is not a scientific fact but 'will depend heavily on the level of community wealth and living standards', because people place more value on clean air and water as they become more wealthy (BCA 1991). In other words, the assimilative capacity of the environment depends on value judgments about how much pollution a community is willing to put up with.

> The unspoken assumption behind all such models is that the capacity of the environment to tolerate a certain number of renegades is something that we ought, collectively, take advantage of. We ought to make sure that all those slots are taken, we ought to allow just as many renegades as nature itself will tolerate. (Goodin 1992: 16)

The Business Council of Australia claims that Australia has excess assimilative capacity because it is not as polluted as other industrialised countries and that therefore environmental standards do not need to be so high. It argues that Australia could do the world a favour by carrying out polluting activities here 'to relieve the burden on countries already at environmental capacity' (BCA 1991: 7–8).

The assimilative capacity approach is not a precautionary approach. It assumes that a certain level of pollution is safe until proven harmful. For this reason critics of the assimilative capacity approach sometimes label it the 'permissive principle'. The precautionary principle, on the other hand, requires that if a substance is likely to harm the environment – and we can't be sure how much will do harm – we should do something about even small quantities of it.

The assimilative capacity approach is highly dependent on the ability of scientists to assess the impact of pollutants on the environment and to determine a safe level that will not irreversibly or severely damage the environment. But with some 300 000 chemicals being invented each year, and 70 000 in daily use, scientists cannot possibly keep up. Even where chemicals are tested they are only tested for toxicity, persistence and bioaccumulation, although they can have other damaging impacts, including altering salinity, physical smothering and thermal pollution. What is more, plants and animals and ecosystems interact with chemicals in such complex ways that assumptions about assimilative capacity and 'safe levels' of pollution or exposure bear little relation to reality.

The US-based Center for Progressive Regulation (CPR 2005) points out:

> So-called 'cross-pollutant' (one chemical for another) and 'cross-media' (air emissions for water discharges) trades should not occur in the absence of reliable scientific evidence that they will not worsen environmental conditions, or cause and exacerbate hot spot problems. These expansions of traditional trading can result in exchanges of markedly more benign chemicals for their far more toxic cousins, as well as the substitution of poorly characterized pollution in one medium for pollution in another medium the effects of which are better understood.

A precautionary approach would require pollutants to be progressively removed from the environment altogether through clean production techniques.

Carbon sinks

Carbon offsets are little more than a way of temporarily expanding assimilative capacity. The capacity of the planet to absorb carbon dioxide, rather than release it into the atmosphere to form the blanketing layer that causes global warming, is aided by forests. By planting trees, people hope to increase the assimilative capacity of the atmosphere to absorb carbon dioxide. The capacity of plantations to act in this way is highly uncertain, however.

Scientists are unable to accurately assess how much carbon a group of trees will store during their growth. This is, firstly, because 'Scientific understanding of the complex interactions between the biosphere (trees, ocean, and so on) and the troposphere (the lowermost part of the atmosphere) is limited' (Bachram 2004: 6). The carbon stored by growing trees varies across different species and different soil types, as well as varying with the amount of soil litter and below-ground biomass.

> Recent research in the US suggests that the flux of carbon into forests is uncertain by a factor of two or three and annual variability as high as 100 per cent. For the continental US, sink estimates range between 0.2 and 1.3 billion tonnes per year and for Europe, between 0.2 and 0.4 billion tonnes. Canadian scientists have pointed out that uncertainty in estimates of the carbon balance in their country's forests could be greater than 1,000 percent if even seemingly small factors such as increased CO_2 levels in the atmosphere are not taken into account. (Sinks Watch 2005)

In some cases, most notably in plantations located in wet areas of Finland, the loss of carbon from the soil and the draining of peatlands outweigh the gain from the growing trees. Other factors that may counteract the gains from planting trees include the removal of groundcover and the effect of plantations on erosion and soils downstream. Even preparing an area for planting of trees can release large quantities of CO_2 from the soil, and CO_2 can also be generated by the manufacture of the agrichemicals used on the plantation, and by the machinery used to clear the site (Lohmann 1999; 2001: 37).

Uncertainty of continued absorption

Another problem recognised in the 1990s by the UN's Intergovernmental Panel on Climate Change (IPCC) is that Earth's natural carbon sinks may well be at the point of saturation already. Before industrialisation, there was equilibrium in the transfer of carbon dioxide between forests and the atmosphere. The amount absorbed by photosynthesis was equal to the amount released during respiration when the plant matter broke down. When levels of CO_2 in the atmosphere increased as a result of industrialisation, the rate of photosynthesis increased and forest growth accelerated. The question is whether this can continue indefinitely.

Some experts, such as Bob Scholes from South Africa's government research agency, argue that a turning point may already have been reached, so that respiration is now increasing as a result of warmer temperatures and thus the ability of trees to absorb more CO_2 than they emit may be decreasing. In this scenario planting more trees will not help but may even hinder efforts to prevent global warming (Pearce 1999).

Sten Nilsson from the International Institute for Applied Systems Analysis (IIASA) claims that it may take 50 years to find out whether plantations and afforestation actually act as carbon sinks and to what extent. This means that nations will be using carbon sinks as a way of allowing them to put carbon dioxide into the atmosphere without there being any way of verifying that those sinks can actually absorb the extra carbon. In other words, the capacity of the environment above the ground to absorb carbon released from under the ground is limited, but we don't know how limited (Lohmann 2004: 5; Pearce 2000).

Uncertain life of trees

The second problem is that the life of those trees that are supposed to absorb carbon is uncertain. Carbon stored in oil and coal deep below the Earth's surface is locked in permanently until humans intervene. Carbon in trees is stored temporarily, while they are growing, and can be easily released through 'fire, natural decay and timber harvesting'. Plantations are fragile and monocultures are particularly vulnerable to disease and insect infestation, as well as to the usual threats of accidental fires, extreme weather events and illegal logging. In addition, global warming itself will affect the growth rate of the trees, their rate of respiration, and the likelihood of fire (Bachram 2004: 6; Kill & Pearson 2003: 2–7).

These events are often beyond the control of governments. More than half the timber exported from countries like Brazil and Indonesia comes from illegal logging. Similarly, forest fires are beyond the control of the most technically advanced nations, as can be seen in the USA and Australia. And in the event of such fires, who is liable for the lost carbon which returns to the atmosphere?

The length of time for which the carbon is stored in trees is therefore very uncertain. At best it delays for a few years a fraction of the warming that will result from greenhouse gases. Carbon offsets are thus an attempt to compensate for permanent emissions of carbon into the atmosphere by means of temporary and uncertain storage. One tonne of carbon stored in trees is not the same as one tonne of carbon stored in coal deep under the ground. A precautionary approach would favour reductions in fossil fuel use rather than relying on highly uncertain above-ground carbon sinks.

The European Commission has decided to exclude carbon sinks from Europe's emissions trading scheme (ETS) because 'they do not bring technology transfer, they are inherently temporary and reversible, and uncertainty remains about the effects of emission removal by carbon sinks' (quoted in Kill & Pearson 2003: 10). This has not prevented European companies from being involved in such projects, however.

The precautionary principle says that uncertainty should not be used as an excuse not to act to protect health and the environment. By the same token, if the actions taken are of highly uncertain effectiveness, those actions are likely to allow the original threat to health and the environment to remain. They should be subject to the precautionary principle in the same way as the original activities that pose the threat. Carbon offsets are not an adequate response to the threat posed by burning fossil fuels.

Ability to respond to new information

Economic instruments also lack the flexibility that a precautionary approach would require. Because pollution rights have economic value, once they have been allocated it is difficult to withdraw them. Thus, if new knowledge is gained about the dangers of a pollutant, to either the environment or human health, after pollution rights have been allocated, the ability of regulators to respond to, and act upon, the new knowledge will be limited.

If the established baseline level for emissions trading is found not to be the ideal ultimate level, or if new information comes to hand that means the regulator has to tighten environmental standards, the baseline level will have to be reduced. How would that affect a firm's 'banked' credits? Would the government have to buy them back? Otherwise, according to Robert Hahn and Gordon Hester, 'reductions that were once surplus would then be required, thereby effectively confiscating the property right held by the firm'. Proponents of emissions trading schemes are very much against such changes, as they add to the uncertainty of firms that may not be inclined to get involved for fear of having their banked credits devalued (Hahn & Hester 1989: 117).

A regulatory agency may want to reduce total pollutant loadings allowed in a waterway in the light of how well a trading system is working, which means reducing the value of credits or reclaiming them. This in turn means that the security and certainty of trade is compromised, and the market will not work very well unless the government promises compensation to those affected. The Golden Gate Audubon Society noted:

> Once a trading system is established it will be very difficult to go back to the polluting entities (corporations, local governments, etc.) who have been given credits and tell them those credits must be withdrawn because society is ready to go the next step to pollution-free waters. (quoted in Caton 2002)

The ability to respond to new scientific findings is a key part of the precautionary principle, which requires that measures taken to avoid or mitigate harm be provisional. This means they should be reviewed periodically so that consideration can be given to relevant new scientific information which may change the assessment of potential harm.

12

RIGHTS, EQUITY AND PARTICIPATION PRINCIPLES APPLIED

HUMAN RIGHTS PRINCIPLES

Economic instruments interfere with human rights insofar as they allow companies and nations to delay or avoid action to prevent pollution or environmental degradation that can cause death, injury, ill health and otherwise interfere with the rights of people to an environment that is conducive to their wellbeing.

Charges on natural resources which aim to motivate people to use them efficiently can prevent the poor accessing resources such as water to which they have a human right. When a user-pays policy was introduced in South Africa in 1996 for essential services such as water and electricity, water bills alone came to 30 per cent of average family incomes. According to a South African government study, 'full-cost recovery' for water and electricity services has resulted in more than 10 million people, 25 per cent of the population, having these services disconnected since 1998. Two million people have been forced out of their homes for not paying their water or electricity bills (Bond 2003; 2004).

Those who were disconnected from the water supply because they couldn't pay the charges were forced to use contaminated sources of water, causing the spread of cholera and gastrointestinal diseases. More than 140 000 people have been infected with cholera since 2000, and millions suffer diarrhoea. The government ended up having to spend millions of dollars trying to control South Africa's worst outbreak of cholera, which killed hundreds of people between 2000 and 2002 (Bond 2004; Monbiot 2004; Pauw 2003).

The human right to clean air and water can also be undermined by tradeable pollution rights which give private companies the right to use the air for pollution discharge. For example, the Clean Air Act in the USA was originally established to protect human health from air pollutants by requiring that companies install the best available pollution-control technologies. Emissions trading schemes allow companies to save money by avoiding or delaying having to install these or equivalent technologies.

Mercury, for instance, is a hazardous substance that is emitted by power plants. It can harm the nervous system, particularly that of the infant and fetus. Mercury from incinerators is controlled by regulation in the USA, and in 2000 the EPA was proposing to control mercury from power plants in the same way, hoping for a 90 per cent reduction on the 48 tons per year they emit by 2008. But in 2003 the Bush Administration decided that the cap and trade system was a better way of controlling mercury from power plants, and waived Clean Air Act regulations requiring power plants to install 'maximum achievable control technology' for mercury emissions. Power plants are now required to either reduce their emissions by 20 per cent by 2010 and 70 per cent by 2018, or buy emissions credits to cover their excess (Krugman 2004; Reuters 2005).

> Historically, courts have traditionally favored protection of life and health over protection of property. Clearly the 'right' created under these [tradeable pollution rights] programs must be substantial, because it is conferring [on] polluters a government sanctioned ability to, by definition, injure the property and health of others, whether that is the destruction of children's intelligence, the lives of middle-aged men, or the lung function of joggers ... Now, instead of an American having a right to his life, a polluter has the right to take it. It is no overstatement to say that this proposition is revolutionary. (Moore 2004a: 11)

The large amounts of money saved by emissions trading programmes – for example, \$225–\$375 million a year from the acid rain programme (Richman 2003: 146) – result directly from firms not having to make pollution reductions that they otherwise would have. Those savings have an environmental price, which is paid by those who have to breathe the polluted air and drink the polluted water.

Delays

Delays are 'implicit in trading because it requires time for markets to develop' and because polluters are typically given long periods to comply. The US acid rain programme, for example, was proposed in 1980, begun in 1993 and requires compliance by 2010. 'In contrast, Germany cut power plant emissions by 90 per cent in six years, from the first proposal in 1982 to completion in 1988' (Moore 2004a: 9).

Similarly, while the Los Angeles RECLAIM programme was in force in one part of California, a neighbouring air quality control district, Ventura, was implementing emission controls in the traditional way with legislation. Ventura power plants installed pollution controls in 1991 but it was not till 2001 that South Coast power plants were taken out of the RECLAIM trading scheme (see chapter 10) and ordered to install the same pollution control equipment (Moore 2004a: 11).

The problem with the delays associated with emissions trading is that in the meantime people die. The EPA notes that 'SO_2 and NO_x contribute to the formation of fine particles and NO_x contributes to the formation of ground-level ozone. Fine particles and ozone are associated with thousands of premature deaths and illnesses each year' (USEPA 2005: 1). In the greater Los Angeles region almost 6000 people died each year during the 1990s as a result of particulate air pollution. Millions more suffered health effects such as 'aching lungs, wheezing, coughing, headache and permanent lung tissue scarring' as a result of breathing high levels of ozone (Drury et al. 1999: 243). It can be argued that emissions trading, by preventing the implementation of the pollution control legislation that had formerly been in place, was responsible for many of these deaths.

Similarly, lead from petrol can cause heart attacks and strokes in adults and impair the intelligence of children. And while the USA took 23 years to eliminate lead from petrol using a trading programme, most other countries, including the United Kingdom, achieved the same task much more quickly (Moore 2004a: 9–11).

The typical open market trading scheme has no overall government-set cap on pollution levels, which means that air or water quality is decided by the many individual firms in the market making decisions about how to maximise their profits. In this way the driving force is cost reduction for firms, rather than public health, and the outcomes may not always be good for public health.

Hot spots

Tradeable pollution rights or emissions trading allow some firms to exceed environmental standards by buying pollution reduction credits or allowances. This may cause some neighbourhoods to get a lot more pollution than others because the companies in their area are buying up allowances rather than reducing their pollution.

For example, Rule 1610 in Los Angeles allowed a few companies to pay for reductions in emissions from vehicles across four counties in order to increase their own pollution. In this way pollutants distributed over a large region were reduced while pollutants from a number of companies concentrated in a few, mainly Latino, neighbourhoods increased.

Some companies bought 'pollution credits to avoid installing pollution control equipment – that captures toxic gases released during oil tanker loading at their marine terminals'. This created high concentrations of pollution at four Los Angeles marine terminals, increasing the risk of cancer for local residents. Three of these terminals are in neighbourhoods that are 75–90 per cent people of colour (CPR 2005; Drury et al. 1999: 252–4).

The problem with mercury trading is that mercury is heavy and tends to precipitate near its source. This means that power plants that buy up mercury emission credits put their neighbours at risk of brain damage. In May 2005, eleven US state governments sued the federal government over the trading scheme, arguing that it poses serious health risks to people living near plants which continue to emit high levels of mercury (Krugman 2004; O'Donnell 2005).

Open market emissions trading, which allows 'cross-pollutant' trading, allows companies to increase their discharges of dangerous chemicals by buying credits earned from cutting discharges of less dangerous or less reactive chemicals. This increases the health dangers for those living near the factories emitting the dangerous chemicals.

Even the trade of a non-hazardous gas like carbon dioxide can cause hot spots of pollution because it can be associated with toxic co-pollutants that increase with the increase in CO_2 emissions:

> Every combustion source also emits dozens of other co-pollutants that pose deadly health risks locally and regionally. These include cancer-causing products of incomplete combustion such as polycyclic aromatic hydrocarbons (PAHs), unburned toxic hydrocarbons, and fine particulate matter linked to excessive death rates. (Belliveau 1998)

Other pollutants are precursors to more hazardous pollutants because they contribute to the formation of those pollutants. For example, NO_x are precursors to ozone smog formation, and SO_2 is a precursor to the formation of fine particulate matter.

Similarly, water trading policies such as nutrient bubbles can create hot spots because the point sources they cover, particularly sewage treatment plants, discharge more than just nutrients. Treated effluent can include heavy metals, organochlorines and pathogens. Allowing some plants to receive less treatment than others in a bubble system can create hot spots which can threaten the health of those who swim locally as well as those who fish locally.

Perpetuating health threats

Carbon offsets can also perpetuate existing health threats. An example is the way they have extended the operations of a dangerous garbage dump in South Africa. The dump had been used for toxic waste and as a result high levels of cadmium and lead – both carcinogenic – were present in the soil. Locals, who are mainly poor and Indian, blame the dump for the high levels of leukaemia and cancerous tumours in the neighbourhood. It was supposed to have been closed in 1996 and turned into soccer fields and other recreational facilities, but its life has now been extended by a landfill gas extraction project initiated in 2002 to extract methane gas from the decomposing garbage for electricity generation (Bachram et al. 2003: 5–6).

The project is funded by the World Bank's Prototype Carbon Fund (PCF) and will earn almost 4 million emissions reduction credits for the captured methane, credits that can be sold to affluent countries (CDM Watch 2005: 11).

Climate change

The Dutch research institute RIVM calculates that through allowing emissions trading the actual reductions in greenhouse gases by 2012 will be far less than 1 per cent (cited in Bachram 2004: 2). This failure to make significant reductions will have grave consequences for millions of people around the world. A study published in the prestigious science magazine *Nature* reports that climate change is causing a dramatic increase in deaths because it is causing increased incidences of malaria, malnutrition and diarrhoea in the poorest nations (cited in Sample 2005). The World Health Organization (WHO) reported that in 2000 'more than 150,000 premature deaths were attributed to various climate change impacts' as well as 5 million illnesses. It estimates that this annual toll will double by 2030 (cited in Vidal 2005).

UN scientists have warned that the severe droughts experienced in many countries in 2005 could become a semi-permanent phenomenon as a result of climate change, and that one in six countries is short of food as a result of them (Vidal & Radford 2005). The UN has also predicted that as soon as 2010 there could be 50 million environmental 'refugees', that is, people who have been displaced from their homes by environmental problems such as drought, deforestation and soil degradation (Scheer 2005). Low-lying island states are also at risk.

The Inuit people are taking the USA to court for human rights violations because of America's contribution to climate change. The Inuit Circumpolar Conference – 'a federation of Native nations representing about 150,000 people in Canada, Greenland, Russia and the US' – is filing a petition in the Inter-American Commission on Human Rights because climate change is interfering with:

> the Inuit's ability to sustain themselves as they have traditionally done, their ability to be healthy ... their ability to maintain their unique culture, which is absolutely dependent on ice and snow; their ability to hunt and fish and harvest plant foods, their ability to have shelter and build their homes. (Gertz 2005)

Displacement of people

Plantations

The measures used to offset greenhouse gas emissions in industrialised nations are also threatening human rights. Their heavy dependence on plantations as carbon sinks interferes with the right of indigenous peoples to self-determination by taking their lands and livelihoods from them. The First International Forum of Indigenous Peoples on Climate Change (quoted in Kill 2001: 15) declared:

> Our intrinsic relation with Mother Earth obliges us to oppose the inclusion of sinks in the Clean Development Mechanism (CDM) because it reduces our sacred land and territories to mere carbon sequestration which is contrary to our cosmovision and philosophy of life. Sinks in the CDM would constitute a worldwide strategy for expropriating our lands and territories and violating our fundamental rights that would culminate in a new form of colonialism.

Those creating the plantations look for the cheapest land to do it on, which is usually in poor countries. Often it is land that is not owned by individuals but rather occupied by indigenous people without formal property rights, and it is used 'for large-scale monoculture plantations which act as an occupying force in impoverished rural communities dependent on these lands for survival'. The plantations can suck up the groundwater needed by the local people for their own crops, while the pesticides and fertilisers used on them can pollute the rivers, other water sources and the fish that are often a major source of food and livelihood for the area's people (Bachram 2004: 8).

In Uganda in the late 1990s, 8000 people were evicted from 13 villages as a result of their lands being leased by the government to a Norwegian company for a tree plantation to create carbon offsets (Bachram 2004: 8). The Tupinikim and Guarani peoples of Brazil have been displaced from some 30 villages by Aracruz Celulose, 'the biggest eucalyptus pulp producing company of Brazil and the world', as a result of its 'occupation' of 11 000 hectares of indigenous land. In Minas Gerais in Brazil, at the end of 2004, 250 people reoccupied 8000 hectares of their lands in protest at its being turned into eucalypt plantations. They had lived there for centuries and the land had provided their food, grazing, firewood, water and medicines. This area is just a small part of the 230 000 hectares of lands in the state that have been rented to eucalypt plantation companies by the state government for around 30 cents a hectare per year (AAGDM 2005).

Forests

Existing forests are also being usurped by corporations and foreign countries in the name of carbon offsets:

> Projects in countries such as Uganda and Ecuador have already led to thousands of local communities dependant on forest areas being forced off their land as private Northern corporations, backed by their governments, engage in a worldwide land-grab at wholesale prices. (Bachram et al. 2003: 16)

Where local people have been conserving old growth forests for thousands of years there is no credit, nor are measures taken that might protect their livelihoods and facilitate their sustainable forest management activities. But where foreign companies and organisations are officially put in charge of conserving the same areas, or growing trees in other areas, carbon offsets can be claimed.

Hydro-electric dams

Similarly, large hydro-electric dam projects which are displacing people in the name of carbon credits can have a devastating impact on local environments. The Nam Theun II dam in Laos, the first approved for carbon financing by the World Bank, will result in the loss of land and fisheries for tens of thousands of locals (CDM Watch 2005: 20).

THE EQUITY PRINCIPLE

Charges

Economists argue that if the money collected from pollution charges is spent on something as worthwhile as the lost environmental quality, the community is no worse off. This is a view that those who suffer from the health and environmental impacts of pollution might find hard to accept, particularly since the money is seldom spent on them and is seldom used to clean up the pollution.

Charges and taxes on individuals can have various impacts on equity. Charging people too high a price for entry into a national park, for example, may restrict the use of a community facility to the wealthier members of the community. It may also be inequitable for users of a scenic area to pay the full cost of conserving an area that is there for the benefit of the whole community as well as future generations.

In general, flat charges – that is, charges that are the same for everyone – have most impact on the poorer members of a community because the charges make up a higher proportion of their income. The impact of a fuel tax will therefore be more painful for lower income households (see table 12.1 below). Similarly, increased charges for industry are also often borne disproportionately by the poor and disadvantaged, because they are passed directly on to consumers as increased prices for goods and services, which take up a higher proportion of a poor person's income. Such charges become, in effect, a regressive tax.

Table 12.1 Proportion of budget spent on fuel in UK households

Most affluent 20%	4.2%
Poorest 20%	12.1%
Single pensioners	16.0%

Source (Robinson & Ryan 2002: 238)

Increased energy costs aimed at encouraging people to use less energy by purchasing more energy-efficient appliances such as fridges, cars and light globes may impact hardest on those who can least afford to replace such goods. Tenants are also disadvantaged, because landlords are less likely to spend money on energy-saving measures such as roof insulation or solar water heating than homeowners are, since landlords won't personally benefit from the energy savings. In the United Kingdom, affluent households are almost twice as likely to have the more energy-efficient gas central heating in place of other heating methods such as fireplaces (Tindale & Hewett 1999: 238).

A tax will only work as an incentive to change behaviour if there are alternatives available. Otherwise it only serves to penalise some sectors of the community and is inequitable. For example, a petrol tax has most impact on people who have to travel long distances to get to work and don't have access to public transport. Since it is often the poor who are forced to live in outer suburbs, because that is where the cheapest housing can be found, such a measure imposes its greatest burden on those least able to pay. People in rural areas and on the outskirts of cities are also worse off because of the longer distances they have to travel. Rural industries will also be badly hit because of the longer distances and the heavy fuel requirements of agricultural machinery.

Carbon colonialism

The Kyoto Protocol recognises that different nations have different responsibilities for reducing greenhouse gases. Nations which are at an early stage of industrial development need to be able to increase their industrial production – which also means increasing the amount of greenhouse gases they produce. The countries that have fully industrialised are responsible for 80 per cent of the greenhouse emissions added to the atmosphere since 1800, and for 65 per cent of those discharged in the mid-1990s. The USA and the EU are responsible for 45 per cent of CO_2 even though they are home to just 10 per cent of the world's population (Bachram 2004: 1; Ott & Sachs 2000: 9). This is why, despite US protestations, the Kyoto Protocol does not include limits for developing nations. Nevertheless, those nations may be subject to limits in the Protocol's second compliance period after 2010.

Emission allowances and targets

By basing greenhouse emission reduction targets on the 1990 emission levels of each country, those that were emitting the most at that time were given a greater allowance under the Kyoto Protocol. This disadvantages countries whose lower levels of economic activity at the time meant they were not emitting much at all in 1990. The 1990 baseline freezes the status quo, consolidating 'the historic overuse by Northern industry at the expense of the South', and is therefore inequitable (CEO 2001). This situation has been termed 'carbon colonialism'.

Larry Lohmann (1999) also claims that the Kyoto emission targets are inequitable:

> Any measure requiring all countries to reduce emissions by similar percentages, for example, would allow the US to go on producing roughly one-quarter of the greenhouse gases released yearly, even though it has only four per cent of the world's population. Similarly, North-South 'carbon trading' suggests that it is legitimate for rich countries or companies who already use more than their share of the world's carbon sinks and stocks to buy still more of them – using cash which has itself been accumulated partly through a history of overexploiting those sinks and stocks.

Lohmann (2004: 9–11) estimates that carbon pollution rights allocated to large industries in the United Kingdom, as part of the EU Emissions Trading Scheme, will give them the saleable rights to some 5 per cent of the world's estimated assimilative capacity for carbon. Yet he questions whether the United Kingdom has the moral right to grant such rights, given that assimilative capacity 'does not fall, geographically or otherwise, under UK legal jurisdiction, but is a capacity inherently spread around the world'. This is why he argues that the handing out of rights as part of emissions trading schemes is 'one of the largest, if not the largest, projects for creation and regressive distribution of property rights in human history'.

Clean development mechanism

Another problem is that at this early stage of emissions reductions, wealthy corporations and affluent nations are grabbing all the cheap and easy reductions: the 'low hanging fruit'. When, in a few years, poorer nations will be expected to make their own reductions, there will only be expensive options left for them to take:

> Instead of being able to meet emissions reductions quotas for the now relatively low price of installing modern pollution reduction technology, developing nations will have to forego production, invent new technologies, or attempt to purchase emissions credits from other countries. (Richman 2003: 160–2)

Alfred Mumma (cited in Richman 2003: 155–7) points out that some developing nations do not have sufficient resources to ensure that emissions trading or CDM projects are beneficial to them, nor to bargain for the best deals. For example, at the Buenos Aires conference on climate change, while the USA had an 83-person contingent, most African states were only able to send two to four people. In addition, the US and EU contingents were supported by an array of think tanks and business organisations working out what policy positions would be most favourable to their economic interests.

Differences in economic power between nations also make it difficult for poor nations to say no to deals proposed by powerful nations, like the USA, which have the power to influence World Bank lending and impose damaging trade sanctions on nations which are out of favour. The consequence of the CDM, of course, is that most of the industrial activity and growth of greenhouse gas generating activity continues to occur in the affluent countries while third world countries are supposed to soak up these extra gases.

What is more, if developing nations have to develop resources and infrastructure to be able to negotiate and monitor CDM projects, this displaces resources that might otherwise be used for development more closely tailored to the needs of local people. There is also the danger that money directed to CDM projects will come from aid budgets, so that much-needed development assistance is reduced: 'Instead of building wells, rich countries can now plant trees to "offset" their own pollution' (Bachram 2004: 3).

Share of carbon sinks

The use of plantations to create carbon offsets occupies millions of hectares of land in poor countries that are then unavailable to local people. This expands the ecological footprint of affluent nations at the expense of other nations: 'Carbon forestry proposes to lessen the atmospheric effects of the mining of fossil fuels by colonizing still other resources and exerting new pressures on local land and water rights'. This exacerbates a situation where affluent nations already use more than their fair share of the world's natural resources (Kill 2001; Lohmann 1999: 13).

The idea of tree plantations as carbon sinks also threatens intergenerational equity:

> Temporary carbon sinks credits directly breach this principle by allowing this generation to park carbon in trees and on paper to meet their reduction commitments, while leaving the responsibility for permanent reductions in greenhouse gas emissions to future generations – generations which are likely to already face far stiffer emission reductions to avert the dangers of climate change. (Kill & Pearson 2003: 7)

Market-based instruments can restrict access to environmental services that were once communally owned. The commodification and privatisation of forests, for example, can turn ecosystems which some 100 million people depend on for food, medicines, fuel, water and other services into a resource that is owned or managed by corporations for its carbon storing potential and which provides services that must be paid for (Lovera 2005).

'Carbon neutral' schemes can also be seen as inequitable in terms of resource usage:

> An organization called Future Forests offers a scheme which allows a British family of 'two parents, two children with a car' to be able to claim it is 'carbon-neutral' at a cost of a mere US$420 a year by planting 65 trees a year in Mexico or Britain.
>
> On this view, US citizens' use of 20 times more of the atmosphere than their Indian counterparts entitles them to use 20 times more other resources too: 20 times more tree plantation land, 20 times more 'carbon workers' to plant and maintain them, and so forth. In fact, it obligates them to do so.
>
> This 'ecological' resource grab is bound to exert new pressures on local land and water rights, particularly in the South, and pass on new risks to people who can ill afford to take them. (Lohmann 2000)

Economic instruments fail to recognise that not all emissions have the same social value. Some emissions come from activities essential for basic comfort and subsistence while others are generated by luxury activities.

Inequity between businesses

Just as a few nations are responsible for a large bulk of the world's carbon emissions, so do a few large transnational companies contribute more than their fair share. One study found that the largest 100 firms on the UK stockmarket directly contributed 1.6 per cent of the world's emissions:

> Just five of these companies – Shell, BP, Scottish Power, Corus and BHP Billiton – generated more than two-thirds of the FTSE 100 aggregate [and] the products sold by five UK oil and mining companies accounted for more than 10% of total global emissions from fossil fuels. (Robins 2005)

Just as the Kyoto Protocol allocates greenhouse gas targets on the basis of past emissions, so the grandfathering involved in allocating greenhouse gas emission allowances to individual firms allocates allowances or credits on the basis of a company's past emissions and clearly rewards the worst polluters by awarding them the most allowances.

Grandfathering also favours existing firms and disadvantages firms wanting to set up. In order to establish itself, a new firm must buy up enough pollution rights to cover its emissions. Existing firms may be unwilling to make room for the new company. Ironically, it is often easier and cheaper to install clean technology processes when a firm is newly established than to refit an older established firm that has outdated and polluting equipment. A government can increase the amount of rights available to give the new firm an allocation, but this will increase the overall amount of pollution.

On the other hand, auctioning allowances advantages the wealthiest companies and those most able to pass their costs on to their customers. Auctioning also means that each firm has to bear additional costs as they have to buy permits to emit gases they had previously been emitting for nothing. This is especially hard for firms that are competing with firms in other countries which do not have to bear these costs. For these reasons auctioning appears to be less acceptable to industry than grandfathering.

In Australia, tree plantations have become unpopular because of the way they are replacing farmers with absentee landlords and decimating rural communities in the process. Investors spent $3 billion between 2000 and 2005 on tree plantation schemes which will translate into some 105 000 hectares of trees planted each year. One farmer called it 'tax-subsidised social annihilation'. Another estimated that the 60 farms that have been bought up in his area by timber companies would take over $75 million 'in income from the area' (Hooper 2005).

THE PARTICIPATION PRINCIPLE

Right to know

The US EPA (2004a: 2) points out that an emissions trading programme needs to be transparent to the public to ensure that it has full public confidence. This means giving the public access to allowance data, to data on emissions discharged and on whether companies are complying. Such data also increases a company's confidence that other businesses in its field are not cheating, and adds extra scrutiny to the whole process to prevent fraud.

Emissions trading programmes are not as transparent in practice as the ideal portrayed by the EPA. It can be very difficult for local residents to find out exactly what standards a company is meeting and the extent to which it is buying up rights to exceed those standards (Drury et al. 1999: 278–9). Prices paid for emissions credits often remain secret and in some cases, such as happened in the leaded petrol trading programme, so does the ownership of credits. In other cases, such as the much vaunted acid rain programme, emissions data is made public but only some time after the emissions are made: 'It is possible to find out in 2002 the amount of pollution that came from a smoke stack in 1999 – long after a death or illness would have occurred – but not what will be emitted in 2003' (Moore 2004a: 10).

In the case of emissions trading, it has been argued that 'accountability, public participation and environmental integrity are being crushed to reduce investor uncertainty' (Climate Justice 2001). The allocation of carbon pollution rights is seldom a matter for public participation. In the United Kingdom, for example, the National Allocation Plan, rather than being subject to public scrutiny and debate, was 'more a matter of quiet negotiation between business and government, and between government departments' (Lohmann 2004: 12).

Similarly, few if any details of transactions undertaken under the joint implementation and the clean development mechanism of the Kyoto Protocol are published (IETA 2005: 15). The rules have been designed by 'the private sector and neoliberal government institutions ... with little or no public consultation or accountability'. Thousands of people protested these mechanisms outside the international negotiations in Delhi in 2002 (Bachram et al. 2003: 1).

Decision-making power to industry

As public pressure has mounted to tighten up and increase regulation, industry preference for economic instruments has increased – because industry would prefer to retain the choice of discharging wastes into the environment, even if it has to pay for the privilege. Economic instruments are less likely than legislative methods to encounter industry resistance because economic instruments accord industry greater autonomy in its pollution control decisions. In other words, the public is not consulted.

Many economic instruments allow the polluters to decide how much pollution there will be in a particular area or neighbourhood. Although a government agency may set a pollution charge or emissions cap, the decision to pollute above set standards by paying charges or buying pollution rights is made by individual firms and is not subject to public consultation. Such decisions are made on the basis of company economics, not on the basis of what is best for the community or the environment. In the end it is the polluters who decide what trade-offs should be made between economics and environmental quality, not the community.

Market-based measures grant the highest decision-making power over environmental quality to those who currently make production decisions. A market system gives power to those most able to pay. Tradeable pollution rights mean that permission to pollute above a certain level is auctioned or sold to the highest bidder.

Depoliticising the debate

Advocates of economic instruments argue that market-based instruments transform environmental conflicts from political problems to economic transactions:

> A major advantage of the market as an allocational device is that it provides a non-political solution to the social conflict raised by resource scarcity. Individuals obtain title to scarce resources through voluntary exchange and such exchange represents a solution to what would otherwise be a political issue. (Chant et al. 1990: 20)

Jeff Bennett (1991), from the conservative Australian think tank, the Institute of Public Affairs (IPA), has argued that the political process of allocation of scarce environmental resources is 'highly divisive, confrontationist and largely inefficient', because resources are misallocated and a great deal of time and money is spent on 'the largely unproductive activities of lobbying and protesting'. Instead, he argues, if the market could be used to allocate environmental resources on the basis of supply and demand, just as other choices are made (for example, between growing wool or wheat on a farm), these decisions could be removed from the political arena.

The idea of removing some aspects of environmental policy from the political arena can be attractive to certain politicians who see the 'environmental problem' as being one of potentially damaging political conflict. Currently, communities can influence governments to protect the environment through legislation by campaigning and demonstrating as well as by voting. In a system where the optimum level of environmental protection is decided 'automatically' by a market responding to prices which are supposed to have incorporated environmental costs, community influence is far more difficult.

Criminal activity or business transaction?

Businesses like the way economic instruments remove their polluting activity from the 'criminal sphere' and legitimise it. Unlike a fine that is imposed for doing something wrong, a charge or a tax indicates that the activity is official and done with approval. Economist Thomas Schelling (1983: 6–7) is quite adamant that this is how economic instruments should be viewed:

> It is typical of fees and charges ... that no moral or legal prejudice attaches to the fee itself or the action on which or for which it is paid. The behaviour is discretionary. The fee offers an option ... a fee entitles one to what one has paid for ... It is not levied in anger, it does not tarnish one's record ...

Similarly, a tradeable pollution 'right' implies that the pollution is an entitlement rather than a misdemeanour. By 'using euphemisms such as "allowance" rather than "pollution"', the stigma attached to polluting firms is reduced, 'which, in turn removes from the hands of the public one of its most effective tools, moral suasion' (Moore 2004a: 7). Drury and his colleagues (1999: 270) point out:

> Pollution trading removes the social stigma associated with pollution. Rather than treating pollution as a social ill that we should attempt to eliminate to the extent feasible, trading programs turn pollution into another commodity, to be traded when economic efficiency dictates. What is wrong with polluting, when only money for the required pollution credits stands between socially acceptable behavior and socially aberrant activity?

Economic instruments make a virtue out of the profit motive and the pursuit of self-interest whereas those arguing for a new environmental ethic take the traditional approach of trying to combat self-interest through morality. Hermann Ott and Wolfgang Sachs (2000: 17) point out:

> In essence, the opponents expect conversion of the sinner, not just payment for damages. In their eyes, it is not enough that the polluter pays; the polluter has got to change as well. 'No reparation without re-socialisation' could be their slogan.

Even more importantly, the community should have the right to decide which business activities and practices are morally acceptable and which are not, and to be able to recognise and label those that kill people as criminal.

PART V

MARKETS FOR CONSERVATION

13

QUOTAS, TRADES, OFFSETS AND BANKS

Market proponents argue that people are more likely to take care of what they own personally, and that commonly owned goods would be better looked after if they were in private hands: 'people who litter in public parks and public thoroughfares do not, in general, dump trash in their own back yards' (Seneca & Taussig 1984: 85). They argue that environmental degradation occurs because of incomplete ownership of rights to use valuable resources. These environmental resources have traditionally been owned in common by everyone (or, one might say, owned by no one individual).

Economists claim there is a strong tendency for people to overexploit and degrade common property resources – because if they don't someone else will, so they might as well get in first. Under this line of reasoning, species become endangered because no one owns them. They point to the fact that all endangered species are undomesticated, and that privately owned livestock faces no such risk of extinction. They cite the example of whales, which nobody owns. Since the supply of whales is obviously limited, those who get in first will get the most. This provides an incentive for overharvesting. Of course, overharvesting of whales has now been stopped by international treaties, but economists argue that the allocation of ownership rights is a better way to protect species.

The idea behind rights-based measures for conservation is that if people have a right to the use of particular natural resources, they will consider the longer term and manage those resources sustainably. Jeff Bennett (1991: 5) gives the example of a waterway for which legal usage rights, whether for waste disposal, recreation or fishing, are sold to the highest bidder. This, he argues, would provide an incentive for those who have paid for those rights to devise ways of protecting their environmental property.

Another rationale for creating rights to the environment is that the scarcer these rights are, and the more demand there is for them, the more they will cost. This is supposed to ensure that the rights are used as efficiently as possible. That is, if the rights to a resource such as wildlife, or water entitlements, are worth a lot of money, those who own them will not squander them. Additionally, it is assumed that those who can earn the most money from using such rights will be willing to pay the most for them and so the resource will end up being used for the highest value activity.

TRADEABLE FISHING RIGHTS

There is a tendency for commercial fishers to target commercially valuable species until the population numbers of those species decline dramatically. Efforts to prevent overfishing are generally aimed at conserving a particular species as a sustainable economic resource. This can be done by regulating inputs, such as how many boats are allowed to fish, when they are allowed to fish, or the methods that may be used. Or it can be done by regulating outputs, such as limiting the total catch for all boats or limiting the catch per boat.

Tradeable fishing rights limit who can fish and how much they can catch by allocating individual quotas, but they go one step further in encouraging the trading and marketing of these quotas. The idea is, firstly, that those who value the quotas most will buy them, which will lead to economic efficiency; and secondly, that those who own quotas will have an interest in conserving the fishery resource because they own a share of it.

However, the prime goal of tradeable fishing rights – since fishing can be limited in a number of ways – is to deal with the situation where fishing fleets have overcapitalised in relation to the size of the catch. That is, capacity has exceeded that which can be sustainably harvested: 'too many boats chasing too few fish'. It is thought that creating a market in fishing quotas will enable some fishers to leave the industry with compensation from selling their quotas and others to consolidate their share, ensuring that capacity is more in line with allowable catch. In this way the outcome will be a more efficient fleet.

Box 13.1 Some acronyms

ITQ = individual transferable quota

ITCQ = individual transferable catch quota

IFQ = individual fishing quotas

TAC = total allowable catch

TACC = total allowable commercial catch

QMS = quota management system

QMA = quota management area

New Zealand

New Zealand was one of the first countries to introduce a comprehensive system of tradeable fishing rights in 1986. At the time many of its fisheries were being severely depleted (overfished) and faced collapse as a result: 'fishing capacity had expanded well beyond that required to harvest the catch' (Bess 2005: 339). The idea of reducing everyone's catch proportionately was rejected because it would have meant that no boat would be working to its full capacity. It was thought better to have fewer boats fishing.

Each year the NZ Minister of Fisheries sets a total allowable catch (TAC), in tonnes, for each of almost 100 fish species in each quota management area, covering about 85 per cent of the commercial catch by volume and value. TACs are supposed to be based on scientific research about sustainable catches. Some of the TAC is reserved for Maori and recreational fishing and the rest – the total allowable commercial catch (TACC) – is allocated to commercial fishing. Commercial fishing requires a commercial licence and an individual transferable quota (ITQ) which entitles each fisher to a specified percentage of the TACC, which translates into a certain amount of fish of each particular species for which they hold ITQs (Bess 2005: 340; Walker 2005).

Quotas were initally allocated according to past fishing records, with those who caught most in the past getting the largest ITQs. ITQs last forever and can be used, sold, leased or given away like any other personal property. Trades are arranged through advertisements, personal contacts or brokers. No one company or individual can own more than a specified percentage of the TACC for a species in a particular management area. That percentage varies from 10 to 45 per cent for different species (SFN 2003).

Australia

Regulations on southern bluefin tuna in Australia were replaced by individual transferable catch quotas (ITCQs) in 1984, ostensibly as a conservation measure. The government set the total allowable catch, and the rights to shares of that catch, or quotas, were allocated on the basis of boat value and catch history of each boat. Quotas could be traded or leased. The predicted result of this new system was 'a reduction of fishing effort per unit of fish catch' (Campbell et al. 2000: 110–3).

Following introduction of the ITCQ system almost two thirds of the boats with a quota over 5 tonnes sold their quotas and left the fishery, including most of the NSW fleet and the Western Australian fleet. At the same time the quotas owned by South Australians increased from 66 to 84 per cent and the value of the overall Australian catch increased despite the declining TAC: 'The change to an individual quota system changed the incentive structure to one where operators could concentrate on minimising the cost of taking their catch, and on maximising the value of their quota' (Campbell et al. 2000: 113).

In 1989 the Australian government decided that tradeable fishing rights were the best way to manage fisheries (Campbell et al. 2000: 109). Fisheries governed by the federal government which employ ITCQs include the southern bluefin tuna fishery, the south-eastern fisheries and the Macquarie Island fishery. There are also transferable quota systems for some state fisheries.

United States

In the early 1990s three individual fishing quota (IFQ) programmes were established in the USA. Their primary purpose was to prevent overcapitalisation in the commercial fishing industry and thereby increase its economic efficiency. Open access to fisheries had led to a race to catch the fish, which led to increasing investment in equipment to out-fish other boats, as well as increasing safety risks. It also led to a glut of fish early in the season, causing prices to fall, and a surplus of frozen fish later in the season, when the fish were gone or the TAC taken (Buck 1995).

IFQs allowed some fishers to sell out, thus reducing the size of the fishing fleet. The aim was for those who remained in the industry to take their time catching their quota, which meant they wouldn't have to overcapitalise their boats and could work with fewer crew. They also had more control over fish prices. IFQs were not supposed to be considered permanent but their 'substantial capital value' – the hundreds of millions of dollars invested in them – means that it would not be politically feasible for the government to revoke them, even though the legislation allows this (Buck 1995).

In 1996 a six-year moratorium was placed on further IFQ programmes being introduced. That moratorium has now expired and the current Bush Administration is very much in favour of reinstating them. New legislation, aimed at doubling the number of such programmes by 2010, would replace legislation that requires 'all fisheries to be restored to healthy levels in 10 years' by limiting when fish can be caught (Bell 2005).

Other nations

Individual fishing quotas were introduced in Iceland as a temporary measure after a series of reports from the Icelandic Marine Research Institute about the imminent collapse of cod stocks (Hannibalsson 1995). Although there had been some limited capacity to transfer quotas earlier, it was not till 1990 that ITQ systems were formally established in Iceland with the Fisheries Management Act. Quotas were separable from fishing boats and 'provided a basis for a quota "stock market" which continuously redistributes fishing rights between vessel owners, communities and regions'. As elsewhere, the numbers of vessels decreased dramatically but the fleet's overall capacity increased because of increased engine power and greater catch capacity per vessel (Eythorsson 2000: 486–7).

ITQ programmes have been established in a number of other countries, including Canada, Spain, Italy, the Netherlands and South Africa (Buck 1995; Laxe 2005). The United Kingdom is proposing an ITQ system to replace its system of fixed quota allocations (FQA), which are usually allocated to fishing producer organisations (POs). POs may in turn allocate quotas to individual vessels, which can be traded, but this is an informal arrangement and lacks the security that fishing people would like (Hatcher & Read 2001; SFP 2004).

WATER TRADING

Trading is used in Chile, Mexico, Peru, the USA and Australia to control and allocate water use. It requires the separation of water rights from land title so that water rights can be separately traded. Legislation to facilitate water markets has also been introduced in Spain. In the United Kingdom the Water Act 2003 facilitates water rights trading (Arriaza et al. 2002; EA 2005c).

Water allowance trading in Australia

In 1994 the Council of Australian Governments (COAG) put together a Water Reform Framework to deal with 'concern about the state of many of Australia's river systems', which required each state to separate water and land titles and enable water trading to occur. Ten years later, in 2004, a National Water Initiative was agreed to by most state governments. It included four objectives:

- more secure water access entitlements
- protection of environmental assets
- expansion of water trading between districts and states
- water conservation in cities. (DAFF 2005a)

A National Water Commission was established to achieve these objectives. Today the water market in Australia involves the annual trade of some 1000 GL (1000 billion litres) of water and is thought to be worth from $200 to $300 million a year. Trades can be temporary or permanent. In New South Wales temporary water entitlements cost $50–$100 per megalitre (ML) and the cost of a permanent general security entitlement is between $550 and $3000 per ML (Martin 2005; Wahlquist 2005a).

The 'primary objective of water allocation within rural Australia is the promotion of economic growth'. The idea is that water trading will enable those who can make the most money out of the water to buy it and for those who make less money out of it to sell it, rather than use it on 'low value' crops. It is also hoped that having paid so much for the water, users will have an incentive to improve water efficiency through the use of different practices and new technologies. During a drought some farmers may find that it is more economical to sell their reduced water entitlement than to try to grow crops. Also, urban areas may need to buy water from irrigators during such times, as has happened in Adelaide and Perth (ENRC 2001: ch 7; Wahlquist 2005a).

Australian states

In Victoria, water rights were separated from land title and made transferable in 1989, even before the COAG 'reforms': 'water is now an asset with a dollar value' (ENRC 2001: ch 4). The government has since set up the Watermove exchange to facilitate trade and establish a weekly price based on offers from buyers and sellers. Trades may also be private arrangements or undertaken through a broker or stock and station agent. There is also a national Internet water exchange, Waterexchange, which covers trades in regulated and unregulated water and in groundwater. Trading is mainly between agricultural irrigators. The government is required to review allocations every 15 years to take account of issues like climate change (Hodge 2005d).

In the Wimmera-Mallee area in Victoria, a 'Sales-for-Savings' programme began in 1989. Water use in the catchment is capped but new allocations can be made if developers pay the authority to undertake 'works (such as piping or lining of channels) that lead to water savings through reductions in evaporation and/or seepage'. The water saved by these works is then allocated to the developer (ENRC 2001: ch 4).

In South Australia, water rights are separated into water-holding allocations and water-taking allocations. Water-holding allocations are based on a share of the total allocation – based on available flow at the time – and have been allocated on the basis of land ownership. These are tradeable, but have to be converted to water-taking allocations before the water can be taken from the waterway. Conversion requires a permit that involves a hydrogeological assessment of the water diversion (DWLBC 2003).

The Murray-Darling river system

Water use from the Murray-Darling river system, which covers four states – Queensland, New South Wales, Victoria and South Australia – and the Australian Capital Territory, is subject to a cap and trade system. The Murray-Darling Basin covers over 1 million square kilometres and includes around 70 per cent of Australia's irrigated land – used for vineyards, fruit, dairy, livestock, cereals and rice, and even cotton. Because of extremely variable rainfall, the ratio of maximum annual flow to mean annual flow in the Darling River, 'which drains three-quarters of NSW', is 11 000:1 compared to 3–15:1 for rivers in Europe and the Americas. Farmers try to deal with this large variability by storing water on their properties. This variability has 'encouraged over-allocation of irrigation water [in times of low flow], leading to problems of unreliable supplies, low residual flows and conflict between upstream and downstream users'. Land clearing and irrigation, which account for most of the diversions from the river, have led to land degradation, salinity of land and river, poor water quality and loss of biodiversity (Brennan & Scoccimarro 1999: 72; Crase et al. 2000: 314–5; Quiggan 2001: 68, 75).

In 1995 a moratorium on new diversions of water from the Murray-Darling Basin was imposed and in 1997 the amount of water that could be diverted from the river system was capped. The cap varies according to climatic and hydrologic conditions. There are periodic auctions of water rights that can then be traded (NCEE 2004: 31; Quiggan 2001: 75).

Security of entitlement

In New South Wales water rights have been over-allocated. In the Murray-Darling Basin, if all rights were exercised they would exceed the maximum capacity of the catchment. The state government therefore introduced the *Water Management Bill* in 2000, which defines water rights in a way that is supposed to protect the river. The two main categories of water entitlements – general security and high security – provide different levels of certainty depending on water flow. A third category is only relevant in situations of high flow.

General security entitlements, which make up some 90 per cent of entitlements, vary according to the level of river flow. In August each year the government authority announces what percentage of each entitlement can be diverted from the river. This may be adjusted upward, depending on subsequent rainfall (Crase et al. 2000: 305; Quiggan 2001: 88). In the midst of drought in 2002, general security allocations were cut to 10 per cent of entitlements, which caused the cost of temporary allowances to increase from $10 to $250 per ML (Wahlquist 2005b).

High security water entitlements give the holders guaranteed access to their full entitlements 'in all but the most severe droughts'. They are granted to urban water suppliers and to electricity companies, and can be bought by farmers growing grapes and fruit trees. These entitlements cost around double the cost of general security licences (Crase et al. 2000: 305; Quiggan 2001: 88; Wahlquist 2005b).

US water banks

In the USA, water banks are a fairly recent development. Most of the western states have them, although only about half have been set up under specialised legislation. Their aim is to ensure that water is used for the highest value purposes. The banks act as an intermediary or broker between buyers and sellers (Clifford et al. 2004; Evans 2004: 1). The aims of water banks include:

- creating reliability in water supply during dry years
- creating seasonal water reliability
- ensuring a future water supply for people, farms, and fish
- promoting water conservation by encouraging water-right holders to conserve and deposit water rights into the bank
- acting as a market mechanism
- resolving issues of inequity between groundwater and surface-water users
- ensuring compliance with intrastate agreements of instream flow. (Clifford et al. 2004: 3)

The term 'bank' is used both for the institution which runs the water market and for the physical storage of water, which may be in the form of reservoirs on the surface or underground storage in aquifers. Groundwater banking is a particularly recent phenomenon and doesn't yet occur much. It involves injecting excess surface water into the ground during times of plenty and extracting it again during times of drought (Clifford et al. 2004: 5).

SALINITY TRADING AND OFFSETS

Salinity is a particular problem in Australia because irrigation and the clearing of native trees with deep roots have caused the groundwater level (watertable) to rise in many regions. 'As the groundwaters rise, naturally occurring salts (principally sodium chloride) are dissolved and brought towards the surface, where the water evaporates leaving high concentrations of salt' (Quiggan 2001: 71).

In 2000 it was estimated that 5 per cent of all cultivated land in Australia was affected by dryland salinity and that this was likely to rise to 22 per cent in the next few decades if nothing was done about it. Dryland salinity makes land unproductive, at a cost of some $46 million per year in the Murray-Darling Basin alone. It has also reduced the number of bird species in agricultural areas by half (COAG 2000: 5; Quiggan 2001: 84). Brian Fisher (2001), Executive Director of the Australian Bureau of Agricultural and Resource Economics (ABARE), warns:

> Within 20 years, Adelaide's drinking water, which comes from the Murray, will fail World Health Organization salinity standards on two days out of five. The biological integrity of 7000 wetlands is threatened by salinity, and the Australian Bureau of Agricultural and Resource Economics (ABARE) estimates that the cost to farming associated with falling water quality will be hundreds of millions of dollars.

Offset credits

In 1992 an interstate market in salt emission permits was established for the Murray-Darling Basin: 'States earn credits by funding the construction of salt interception schemes or other methods of reducing river salinity and use credits by constructing drainage or allowing other actions which increase salinity' (Brennan & Scoccimarro 1999: 75).

A salinity offset scheme is also being trialled by the NSW EPA in three different regions where point source polluters are being required 'to offset their emissions by investing in works that reduce salinity from diffuse sources'. Salinity offset trading is being trialled in Queensland, and salinity credit trading is being applied to dryland salinity in Victoria (NMBIPP 2005).

In one pilot programme in New South Wales, salinity 'credits can be earned for investments that limit the entry of salt into the river system. The tradable credits are used to offset debits for drainage into the system' (NCEE 2004: 30). Landowners in the upper Macquarie Valley are earning extra income from tree plantations on their land planted by Forests NSW. The plantations earn 'salinity control credits' that are sold to Macquarie River Food and Fibre, which operates downstream and suffers the salinity impacts of upstream clearing. Forests NSW retains title to the timber and carbon (Sundstrom 2000; Wahlquist 2000).

Cap and trade

A system of tradeable salinity credits was introduced into the NSW Hunter River Valley in 2002. Saline discharges into the river are not allowed during times of low river flow but salinity permits can be traded and used during times of high river flow. One thousand permits or credits are issued at any time, which allow the holder to discharge 0.1 per cent of total allowable discharge, which is determined by the NSW Environmental Protection Authority (EPA). Permits are auctioned off every two years and last for 10 years. During times of flood there are no restrictions on discharge and permits are not necessary. Holders include coal-mining facilities and power stations (Ecosystem Marketplace 2005; Hawn 2005c).

Various pilot projects for cap and trade schemes to control salinity are being trialled in New South Wales and on the lower Murray River in South Australia (NMBIPP 2005).

MITIGATION BANKING

Wetland mitigation banks

It was not until the 1980s that government authorities in the USA fully realised the value of wetlands, by which time more than half the country's wetlands had been destroyed by agriculture and development. Regulations were put in place to prevent any degradation or filling of wetlands without a permit, and in 1989 the first President Bush introduced a policy of 'no net loss' of wetlands. Authorities such as the US Corps of Engineers, which were able to permit wetlands loss, required a developer to avoid and minimise discharge of materials into a wetland,

and if this couldn't be avoided the Corps could issue a permit on the condition that the developer restored, created or enhanced wetlands elsewhere to compensate for the loss. In this way it was hoped that the 'no net loss' goal would not interfere with development and economic growth (BEST et al. 2001: 1–2).

Developers, however, found the requirement for compensatory mitigation burdensome and expensive. Early attempts by individual developers at mitigation through restoration and enhancement of wetlands elsewhere had been generally unsuccessful because of 'poor site selection, improper or insufficient monitoring and evaluation, lack of wetland persistence, poor hydrological design, sparse vegetative cover, inadequate management, and insufficient wildlife utilization ... delays in construction and lack of maintenance' (Zinn 1997).

Mitigation banking was proposed as a way of making development cheaper and easier for those not expert in wetland management. The regulatory authorities believed that 'mitigation banks' might be more successful than previous mitigation efforts because they would be professionally designed, more easily supervised, and employ economies of scale.

'Mitigation banks' were areas of wetland that were being preserved, restored, enhanced or created (see box 13.2). Bank owners sold credits to developers needing a permit to destroy or degrade a wetland somewhere else. In other words, the damage developers were causing in one area was supposed to be offset by the conservation occurring at a mitigation bank in another area.

The way a mitigation bank might work is this. An entrepreneur buys 500 acres of wetland at \$1000 per acre, and spends \$2000 per acre to restore and maintain it – a total upfront investment of \$1.5 million. The entrepreneur then sells credits for each acre of land to developers needing to mitigate the damage they are doing on wetlands elsewhere. Each credit costs \$8000 and a developer might need to buy several to gain a permit to develop their own land (Zinn 1997):

> After several clients have purchased credits, the costs of setting up the bank may be repaid. The bank sponsor may become the long-term manager of the site after credits are sold and the bank site is a fully functioning wetland, or it may sell the property to another owner, such as a conservation group, who assumes long-term responsibility for maintaining the site.

The amount of land required for mitigation is not necessarily equal to the amount of wetland being destroyed. Often a larger area has to be preserved, restored or enhanced than is being destroyed to make up for the fact that no new wetland is being created to replace the destroyed wetland, and so the total amount of wetland is being reduced.

Box 13.2 Methods of compensatory mitigation for wetlands

Restoration: Re-establishment of wetland and/or other aquatic resource characteristics and function(s) at a site where they have ceased to exist, or exist in substantially degraded state.

Creation: The establishment of a wetland or other aquatic resource where one did not formerly exist.

Enhancement: Activities conducted in existing wetlands or other aquatic resources that increase one or more aquatic functions.

Preservation: The protection of ecologically important wetlands or other aquatic resources in perpetuity through the implementation of appropriate legal and physical mechanisms. Preservation may include protection of upland areas adjacent to wetlands as necessary to ensure protection and/or enhancement of the aquatic ecosystem.

Source (USEPA 1995)

In 1990 the Department of Army and the EPA signed a Memorandum of Agreement that gave official endorsement to mitigation banks. The Fish and Wildlife Service (FWS) also helped to establish a system of wetland mitigation banks in the early 1990s (ELI 2002c; FWS 2004). California introduced legislation in 1993 for wetland mitigation banks to compensate for wetlands destroyed by developers in urban areas (CRA 1995a). Federal guidelines issued in 1995 defined mitigation banking:

> [M]itigation banking means the restoration, creation, enhancement and, in exceptional circumstances, preservation of wetlands and/or other aquatic resources expressly for the purpose of providing compensatory mitigation in advance of authorized impacts to similar resources. (EPA 1995)

Many of the early mitigation banks were established by government authorities such as state departments of transport wanting to compensate for wetlands lost to roads and highways. Today wetland mitigation banks are a 'mainstream option' in the USA, and there are more than 500 banks in more than 40 states. They range in size from 6 acres to 24 000 acres, with most being over 100 acres. Most are commercial enterprises owned by private entrepreneurs. Wetland credits cost between $5000 and $250 000 per acre (ELI 2002c; Wilkinson et al. 2002: 5).

Stream mitigation banks

In 2000 the first stream mitigation bank was formed in the USA. It covered a 2.6 mile section of Fox Creek in Missouri, and the owner earned stream mitigation credits by planting vegetation along its banks. By 2005 there were around 25 stream mitigation banks, ranging in size from 15 000 to 150 000 linear feet (Gillespie 2005). They work in the same way as wetland mitigation banks, in that a developer can destroy a stretch of river by paying a stream mitigation bank to restore a section of a waterway somewhere else.

Conservation banks

Conservation banks extend the idea of wetland mitigation banks to other conservation areas, with the aim of protecting endangered species. The US Endangered Species Act 1973 aimed to avoid development that threatened endangered species. The Act prevented anyone from 'taking' a listed animal species; 'taking' included not only deliberate hunting and trapping but also habitat modification (Mills 2004: 523–5).

In 1983 the Act was amended to allow developers or landowners to obtain an 'incidental take' permit from the US Fish and Wildlife Service which enabled them to undertake habitat modifications. To obtain a permit they must present a habitat conservation plan (HCP) that shows how they will minimise damage to habitat and compensate for any impact on the species. This may be through acquiring land elsewhere that can support the species. In 1994 a further policy change guaranteed those who undertook an HCP that if new species were found on their land, they would not have to protect them (Fox 2005; Mills 2004: 526-7).

These changes were made because of claims that some landholders were going to great lengths to ensure that endangered species were not found on their land, so that they would not need a permit to develop it, build on it or farm it: 'Damaging shrubs, stomping on seedlings, disposing of nests, and removing trees are all regular activities in some quarters' (Fox 2005).

Conservation banking enables a private entrepreneur or a public authority or a partnership of both to buy and manage an area of land that is habitat to a listed endangered or threatened species, then sell credit for that land to developers who want to 'destroy, degrade, or adversely alter' the habitat of endangered species elsewhere (CRA 1995a). Credits may be equivalent to:

1. an acre of habitat for a particular species;
2. the amount of habitat required to support a breeding pair;
3. a wetland unit along with its supporting uplands; or
4. some other measure of habitat or its value to the listed species. (FWS 2004)

The idea of introducing markets in conservation is to make conservation profitable so that private landowners will want to save species rather than destroy them, because they can make some money from them: 'the more effective the species recovery on the property, the more a landowner can charge for the corresponding conservation bank credits' (Mills 2004: 537).

> From an economic perspective, banking is advantageous because it allows a private landowner to transform a former legal liability (i.e., the species) into a financial asset (i.e., the credit) ... From a conservation perspective ... banking may not result in an increase in quantity of suitable habitat for a particular species, but it may result in higher quality habitat being conserved for an individual species. (Fox & Nino-Murcia 2005: 997)

California was the first state to introduce conservation banking, in 1995, in cooperation with federal agencies, including the FWS. In 2003 the federal government issued guidelines to promote conservation banks nationwide (FWS 2004).

It is argued that conservation banking is a better system than project-by-project mitigation, which requires developers to preserve a part of the land they were developing (on site) or to find their own compensating preservation area somewhere else (off site). Such a process was expensive for the developer and thought not to be good for the environment as it resulted in the preservation of small, isolated, fragmented areas. A conservation bank would ensure preservation of a larger area, which would not only ensure economies of scale in terms of management and greater ease of administration in terms of government oversight, but also a more viable habitat for larger populations of species (CRA 1995a; FWS 2004).

Such schemes are attractive to economists and business because they seem to harness the forces of the market by turning 'the protection of habitat' into 'an economic asset' that can be bought and sold (CRA 1995a). Developers are happy because they are able to develop land that is home to endangered species or has other ecological values just by buying credits from the banks. One of the first private businesses to promote conservation banking was the Bank of America (1999). Conservation banking enabled land it had repossessed to become more valuable.

By 2005 there were 76 conservation banks, 35 of them established under an official agreement approved by the FWS. The 35 official banks covered 40 000 acres (16 000 hectares), of which 91 per cent was financially motivated, that is, for-profit; the remaining 9 per cent was conservation motivated (Fox & Nino-Murcia 2005: 996). Anyone can establish a conservation bank provided the land has been determined by 'an authorized wildlife agency' to have 'substantial regional habitat value, be in need of preservation and/or restoration, and be worthy of permanent protection' (CRA 1995a).

In order to work out how many credits are available from a particular area and how much they are worth, an environmental baseline is negotiated between the owner of the land (the bank manager), the regulatory authority and the developer seeking to buy credits:

> This baseline will be used to establish credits for a number of categories requiring resource management, including, but not limited to, the following:
>
> a. Resource Preservation (the preservation of specified resources through acquisition or other appropriate means);
>
> b. Resource Enhancement (the enhancement of a degraded resource);
>
> c. Resource Restoration (the restoration of a resource to its historical condition);
>
> d. Resource Creation (the creation of a specified resource condition where none existed before. (CRA 1995b)

The first such agreement was brokered between the California government, the Bank of America, the Nature Conservancy (an environmental NGO) and the US Department of the Interior.

To become a conservation bank the land must be permanently protected through a conservation easement on the land title, or through some other legal mechanism. Conservation easements prohibit certain types of developments on the land, regardless of changes in ownership, and may include restrictions on what type of activity can take place there. They are generally monitored by public agencies, land trusts or government-authorised conservation groups. The land may still be used for farming, ranching and timber harvesting, provided that the listed endangered species are not put at risk. There may be limits on the number of livestock kept on the land, or prohibitions on the use of off-road vehicles and the construction of roads and buildings (FWS 2004).

A conservation bank also requires a management plan and some sort of permanent funding, such as a large sum of money deposited in a bank account that provides enough interest to perpetually fund the management of the land without using up the capital.

> A management plan may include removing trash on a regular basis; mending and replacing fencing; monitoring the listed species or habitat conditions; controlling exotic, invasive species that interfere with the naturally functioning ecosystem; conducting prescribed burns; and other activities to maintain the habitat. (FWS 2004)

Australian biodiversity banking

In New South Wales, Australia, where over 1000 species are under threat, a system of biodiversity banking has been proposed for coastal areas, where development pressures are greatest. Regions will be classified as 'green-light', 'amber-light' or 'red-light' as part of a regional conservation plan. In green-light areas that are determined to have 'low biodiversity values', development will be fast-tracked with no requirements to protect threatened species. In red-light areas that have high biodiversity values, new development that may destroy the habitat of endangered species will not be allowed (DEC 2005: 3-6).

It is in the amber-light areas that biodiversity banking will be applied. Where an area is to be developed an assessment will be made by the regulator as to how many biodiversity credits will be required to offset the damage the development is likely to do. The developer can then decide to 'reconfigure the project to eliminate' the damage; undertake an offsetting conservation project, or buy biodiversity credits from a biodiversity bank manager or 'approved conservation broker' (DEC 2005: 8).

The biodiversity bank is created by a 'scheme manager' negotiating with existing landholders to improve the biodiversity values of their land. This might be done by paying landholders to set aside some of their land for conservation with a covenant or agreement. The scheme manager might pay the landowner to manage the land 'through controlling weeds and feral animals, excluding stock and undertaking revegetation'. This would generate biodiversity credits that the scheme manager could sell to developers and brokers. The scheme manager might be an entrepreneur looking to make a profit from the credits or a not-for-profit organisation interested in conservation (DEC 2005: 7–8).

In this way the bank's properties need not be large aggregates as in the case of conservation banking in the USA, but may be isolated and fragmented. As with US conservation banks, the aim is to make conservation of land profitable to private owners. The scheme is being trialled for two years in the Lower Hunter Valley and Far North Coast.

Tradeable fishing quotas, water allowance trading, salinity trading and offsets, mitigation, conservation and biodiversity banks and auctions, as well as tradeable development rights, are all market-based policies which have environmental protection as either a primary or subsidiary goal. Chapter 14 considers how well they comply with the sustainability principle. Chapter 15 examines these policies in the light of the precautionary principle, the equity principle and the participation principle.

Further Reading

'Biodiversity Certification and Banking in Coastal and Growth Areas', Department of Environment and Conservation (NSW), Sydney, July 2005, <http://www.environment.nsw.gov.au/resources/biodiversitybankingweb.pdf>

Board of Environmental Studies and Toxicology et al., *Compensating for Wetland Losses under the Clean Water Act*, National Academy Press, Washington DC, 2001, <http://www.nap.edu/books/0309074320/html/>

Buck, Eugene H (1995) 'Individual Transferable Quotas in Fishery Management', *Congressional Research Service* 95 (849), 25 September, <http://www.ncseonline.org/NLE/CRSreports/Marine/mar-1.cfm?&CFID=7981623&CFTOKEN=73755620>

Environment & Natural Resources Committee, 'Inquiry into the Allocation of Water Resources for Agricultural and Environmental Purposes', Parliament of Victoria, Melbourne, November 2001, ch 7, <http://www.parliament.vic.gov.au/enrc/inquiries/old/enrc/water_alloc/report/>

Fox, Jessica & Anamaria Nino-Murcia (2005) 'Status of Species Conservation Banking in the United States', *Conservation Biology* 19 (4), August, pp. 996–1007.

Robinson, Jackie & Sean Ryan (2002) 'A Review of Economic Instruments for Environmental Management in Queensland', CRC for Coastal Zone, Estuary and Waterway Management, 2002, <http://www.coastal.crc.org.au/pdf/economic_instruments.pdf>

Special issue on fisheries of *The Ecologist*, 25(2–3), March–June 1995.

14

THE SUSTAINABILITY PRINCIPLE AND CONSERVATION MARKETS

FISHERIES TRADING

Tradeable fishing quotas are often introduced to increase the economic efficiency of the industry rather than to ensure the ecological sustainability of the fishery. As Fernando González Laxe (2005: 4) notes in the journal *Marine Policy*: 'the individual transferable quota is an economic tool used to guarantee the economic efficiency in a fishery; that is, it is not a tool to guarantee either the biological sustainability or the social equity', so we should not be surprised if an individual transferable quota (ITQ) system does not protect fish species or result in social equity.

In some cases, such as the rock lobster fishery in Tasmania, Australia, biological sustainability is not even a secondary goal. The population of rock lobsters was not endangered when the ITQ system was introduced, as population levels were adequately protected by regulations about the size of lobsters caught, achieved by having pots with appropriately sized escape gaps for smaller lobsters. However, the race to catch the lobsters resulted in 'economic overfishing'; that is, in 'excess' effort being expended. The 'rhetoric of conservation' was used to justify the introduction of an ITQ system which enabled quota owners to reduce crew size and other expenditure to catch lobsters in the most economically efficient way (Phillips et al. 2002: 462).

Outcomes

In many places, transferable fishing quotas have not prevented the decline of commercial fishing species. According to the Australian Department of Agriculture, Fisheries and Forestry (DAFF 2005b), the southern bluefin tuna fishery, which has been managed by a tradeable fishing quota system for 20 years, is overfished, spawning stock are severely depleted, and 'current catches severely limit probability of rebuilding'.

The same kind of outcome has resulted from an ITQ system in Iceland, where Ólafur Hannibalsson (1995), a deputy MP, noted in the mid-1990s:

> There is no doubt about the fact that by initiating the quota system, authorities hoped to protect the fish stocks, and in particular the cod. The result, however, has turned out to be the opposite. According to the MRI [Icelandic Marine Research Institute], the cod stock has been on a steady decline in the past years, and unless the fishing fleet is drastically reduced, there may be a 50% chance of a Newfoundland-like collapse of the Icelandic cod stock within the next three years.

The decline of particular fish species can have significant impacts on ecological sustainability as they are part of a complex marine habitat which is in turn part of a wider food chain. When the Norwegian spring-spawning herring and the Barents Sea capelin populations went into decline, the north-eastern Arctic cod lost an important source of food and went into decline. This in turn led to 'crowds of underfed seals' coming into Norwegian coastal waters 'and thousands of dead seabirds' drifting ashore (Hagler 1995: 78).

The orange roughy fishery in New Zealand was often cited as a case study of the success of tradeable fishing quotas, but it has turned out to be a failure. It is now thought that these fish live for some 100 years and that it may take 30 years for them to mature and reproduce. Because this was not known, the total allowable catch was set far too high. By 2000 '[t]wo roughy fisheries have collapsed, and most are now at 10% of their original populations' (Walker 2005).

Such miscalculation about the sustainable level of fishing could occur under any regulatory system, but the market system ensured that the industry was motivated by short-term economic concerns to resist severe cutbacks in the TAC when they were proposed in response to falling populations in the early 1990s.

Profit vs conservation

Although the New Zealand scientists recommended that the orange roughy total allowable commercial catch be substantially cut, to 3400–5900 tonnes in 1993, the minister responsible left it at 14 000 tonnes because of pressure from fishing lobbyists. In 2000 the catch was even higher, at over 15 000 tonnes. Rather than seeing the need to protect their quotas by ensuring the long-term sustainability of the orange roughy fishery, it seems that quota owners are more interested in 'fishing as much as they can and then moving on to another fishery' (Duncan 1995: 99; Walker 2005). Leith Duncan (1995: 99) noted that 'catches have to stay high to pay off debts incurred' by fishing infrastructure investment 'and to maintain profitability; these immediate incentives override any long-term concern for ecological sustainability. As orange roughy collapses deep sea dory is being promoted'.

The race to fish, characteristic of an open fishery with a limited season or a total allowable catch, is not necessarily eliminated in an ITQ fishery. There may still be a race at the beginning of the season when population numbers are highest and fish easiest to catch. Moreover, 'anxiety and uncertainty about the future can cause ITQ share owners to become just as oriented to short-term profits, as opposed to long-term sustainability, as open-access fishermen' (Buck 1995).

Quota owners who are participating in the fishing effort may feel that they will be in the best position to know when the fishery is about to collapse and be able to sell their quota at that time to someone who doesn't know any better. Investors who own quotas may well be more interested in quick returns on their investment than in lower long-term returns. Certainly the fishing crews and contract fishers have no added incentive to conserve the fishing resource in an ITQ system.

Moreover, while public authorities which manage fisheries have an interest in the future of public resources, private owners are concerned firstly with present needs. As quotas are increasingly held by larger fishing companies and non-fishing companies (see next chapter), repayment of debt becomes a larger factor in decision making. The shift from owner-operators to shore-based companies and transient fishers who have leased quotas also means that fishing practices change, because the experienced fishing people, who 'have first hand experience with the health of the catch' are no longer calling the shots (Macinko & Bromley 2002: 26; Walker 2005).

When tradeable quota systems are being proposed there is an incentive for existing fishers to catch as much as possible and report they are catching more than they actually are, so that when quotas are allocated, based on their past catches, they will get a larger quota. This is referred to as 'speculative fishing-for-history'. This not only impacts directly on the sustainability of the fisheries but distorts the figures used by fisheries managers to estimate what catches are sustainable. Also, vessels that might have been retired are kept on in the hope of getting saleable quotas (Buck 1995; Macinko & Bromley 2002: 18). In New Zealand, fishers also put greater effort into catching species of fish not in the quota management system (QMS) in anticipation of their inclusion (Bess 2005: 341).

Perpetuating bad practices

Tradeable fishing quota systems focus on efficiency and completely neglect technological inputs and their negative impact, both on the target species and on non-target species and the wider marine environment. According to the Swedish National Board of Fisheries, overfishing is 'the product of both the efficiency of the finding and catching technologies and of the amount used … a 4% increase in efficiency per year would cause a doubling of the fishing mortality rate in 18 years if the fishing effort remained constant' (Swedish National Board of Fisheries 1995).

The aim of tradeable fishing quotas is to make the fleet more economically efficient. The idea that a smaller, more efficient fleet will reduce overfishing is faulty, however.

> Which boats are too numerous? The three million canoes, skiffs and workboats that catch most of the world's foodfish and provide a living for about 20 million fishers and their families? Or the few thousand highly-capitalized ships of the industrial fishing corporations whose disproportionate share of the world's catch is destined as much for factory-produced fishmeal (used as animal feed) as it is for human consumption? (*The Ecologist* 1995)

Some argue that by reinforcing and accelerating the shift of fishing from a small-scale subsistence activity to a globalised, corporate-dominated industry, tradeable fishing quotas are also reinforcing the very causes of overfishing: 'the enclosure of local fishing grounds; the creation of global markets for fish; and the build-up of industrial fishing fleets' (Fairlie et al. 1995: 46). What happens in practice is that the smaller, 'inefficient' boats are priced out of the market but those that remain more than make up for this reduction with their extra boat size, power and technology. The technologies they use can also be far more damaging to the environment.

In the US surf clam tradeable quota system 'the number of boats in the fishery fell from 133 to 48, while the remaining boats tripled their catch'. There was no gain for fish conservation (Parravano & Crockett 2000). Hannibalsson (1995) described similar developments in Iceland in the mid-1990s: 'The fleet is larger than ever, measured in tonnage, engine power – and foreign debt. It has to be operated at maximum effort in order to be able to meet financial obligations'.

The larger boats favoured by tradeable fishing quota systems 'fish more intensively, having potentially greater effect on stock levels and on sensitive areas such as coral reefs' (Walker 2005). Fishers who use line and hook have been progressively eliminated while there are more and more large vessels which tend to drag heavy fishing gear across the ocean floor, killing crustaceans, uprooting aquatic plants, 'eroding plants and benthic life, levelling the ground and destroying shelter for the young – in short, transforming the bottom of the sea into a lifeless desert' (Hannibalsson 1995).

Tradeable fishing quotas can also cause a displacement effect: when fishers are forced out of one fishery they often move into another. In the case of the southern bluefin tuna fishery in Australia, when the ITQ system was introduced the number of boats seeking bluefin tuna was reduced by 70 per cent in two years, but many of the boats that once sought the tuna moved to other fisheries, some of which were already being overfished (Duncan 1995: 103).

By-catch

A major problem with fisheries trading is that the quota refers to fish that are caught and brought to shore for sale. Significant quantities of fish are discarded, however, because they are too small or too big or of inferior quality or exceed quota. Often the by-catch and discards exceed the actual fish landed. The discarded fish may be very important to the food chain of endangered fish and to 'biological community structure in marine systems' (Hagler 1995: 76).

When fishing is commercialised in an ITQ system industrial fishing gear tends to be adopted, including commercial trawl nets which 'can catch anything from a shrimp to a whale' as well as 'swordfish, sharks, birds and marine mammals' such as dolphins (Hagler 1995: 77).

> For instance, draggers are equipped with electronic sensor devices that allow them to home in on a dense body of fish and virtually annihilate it. In theory, immature fish can escape through the mesh of dragger nets; in practice, when fish are densely congregated, the meshes rapidly clog up and everything is hauled up, big or small. Hundreds of millions of immature dead and dying fish have been dumped by draggers in Canadian waters in the past 15 years. (Matthews 1995: 88)

In Australia, only about 90 of the 300 fish species caught in trawl nets 'are commercially valuable leaving 37–58% of the catch to be discarded' (Robinson & Ryan 2002: 25). This unintended catch is inevitable since the fishers cannot determine what will be caught in their nets, on their lines or in their traps. Almost all the discarded fish die, yet they are not counted in the quota even though they are lost to the environment. What is more, 'Unrecorded fish mortality can affect the stock that year and create a cycle of setting total allowable catches on incorrect data' (Walker 2005).

The by-catch problem is exacerbated under a tradeable quota system because it leads to a practice called 'high grading'. In order to get the most value from their quota, fishing people don't only throw away those fish that have no sale value and those for which they have no quota, but also the smaller and less valuable fish for which they do have a quota. In this way they maximise the value of their catch and their quota. In Canada, for example, the size of sablefish caught, and kept, increased after an ITQ programme was introduced (Buck 1995; Walker 2005).

In the Pacific, according to the Alaska Marine Conservation Council, the failure to take account of by-catch in the total allowable catch for rockfish was 'a cause among others that drove the groundfish populations precipitously down' (AMCC 2005). In New Zealand there is even speculation that valuable species such as rock lobsters have been kept in the ocean after they have been caught in the expectation of price increases. If they die in the meantime, they are not counted as part of a fisher's quota (Walker 2005).

In some fisheries a quota system is 'notoriously ineffective'. An attempt at introducing an ITQ system in Peru failed because 'the anchovy shoal in vast, easily catchable quantities, and vessels were obliged to discard enormous amounts of dead fish if they stuck to their quota' (Duncan 1995: 103).

Monitoring and enforcement

Fishing quota trading systems provide an incentive to cheat. With open fishing, under-reporting of an individual catch benefits all fishers as it takes longer to reach the official total allowable catch. But in an individual quota system, under-reporting an individual catch directly and immediately profits an individual fisher, as do poaching and exceeding one's quota. The incentives to cheat are therefore much higher. Yet most ITQ systems rely on dockside monitoring because extra monitoring, such as providing onboard observers, is very expensive (Buck 1995).

Illegal ways of exceeding one's quota include 'fishing out of season and selling fish on the black market, which are widespread in many, if not most, industrialized fisheries. The quantities involved can be quite considerable' (Duncan 1995: 101). There are also cases of catch misreporting, for example where a valuable quota species such as cod is reported as another species such as saithe (Hannibalsson 1995).

The idea that ownership of fishing rights would ensure that quota owners would police each other is negated by the shift of ownership from owner-operators to investors who pay others to fish for them. Contract fishers have much less incentive to report illegal fishing by others, particularly if they are doing it themselves (Phillips et al. 2002: 465). On top of this, poaching of fish has increased because those dispossessed by not having a quota and those feeling their allocated quota is unfair feel justified in taking what they believe they deserve (Duncan 1995: 102).

The increase of fishing vessels that process the fish at sea, which is occurring under ITQ systems, also 'provides an opportunity to bend the fisheries management rules'. Some commentators have pointed to the way such vessels manage to get a higher yield per catch than land-based factories as evidence that some cheating is occurring. Onboard monitoring of these trawlers is often sporadic and ineffective. Large trawlers have also been caught landing some of their catch in other countries, for example Icelandic trawlers taking fish to Germany and Britain (Hannibalsson 1995).

WATER ALLOWANCE TRADING

Changing flow conditions

Water allowance trading is primarily aimed at economic benefits, with environmental benefits a secondary consideration. In fact, water allowance trading can have an adverse impact on the environment. Irrigators tend to release water in the summer when 'riparian ecosystems require low flows', and they alter the 'frequency and magnitude' of spring floods, which can also have significant adverse impacts on ecosystems and biodiversity (Brennan & Scoccimarro 1999: 74).

> Trading of water rights can alter timing of flows in streams at different locations along the river. This can affect ecosystems and diverters of water lower in the river. If water is traded across wide geographical distances, trading could affect the route the water takes. It could also lead to different uses with different impacts on ecosystems and communities. (ENRC 2001: ch 7)

However temporary trades in water, which make up the vast majority of water trading, generally do not require any sort of environmental clearance (Fullerton 2001: 164).

The trading of water allowances also means that, in some places, additional areas of land are irrigated, which can have environmental consequences. In Australia, for example, it can lead to increased salinity of the soil because the extra water raises the level of the underground watertable, which is saline. Most of the water traded in a pilot interstate water market has gone to South Australia from New South Wales and Victoria, causing salinity problems in South Australia (Wahlquist 2002).

The National Water Initiative (NWC 2005) seeks to expand water markets across 'the widest possible geographic scope' in Australia and not to restrict it to particular catchment areas. This can be done by piping water from one catchment to another. However, this ignores the fact that 'some in-stream uses [such as fishing, boating and swimming] are location-specific and depend on the volume of flow in the river at that location'. There can also be environmental impacts when water is shifted from one catchment to another, including the introduction of alien fish viruses and increased salinity (Brennan & Scoccimarro 1999; NWC 2005).

Outcomes

Despite having a cap and trade system for water allocation since 1997, Australia's Murray River is dying. More than 75 per cent of the river system's water is still diverted before the river reaches the sea, which has caused serious environmental problems, especially at the mouth of the river, where there has seldom been any river flow since 2001. As a result the river mouth has become hypersaline because of the ingress of seawater. Over 300 000 red gums which had survived on the lower Murray for 300 years, in the face of natural droughts, have died as a result of this human-induced perennial drought. The cycles of floods so essential to river health no longer occur. Additionally, the 'internationally recognised Coorong wetlands at the Murray mouth may not survive' (Fullerton 2003; Hodge 2005c).

A parliamentary inquiry in Victoria 'was made aware of failures of water markets, as presently operating, to provide water for recreational and social purposes as well as commercial fishing'. These water uses are common purposes, which don't actually consume the water, but require it to be there rather than withdrawn by those who have licences. Water quantity also affects water quality for downstream water users. The inquiry concluded that 'Market trading, by itself, is inadequate to meet environmental needs' (ENRC 2001: ch 7).

Water allowance trading often involves the trade of water licenses that had previously not been used or only partly used, that is, sleeper (or 'dozer') licences or rights. In the first few years of trading on the Murray River most of the trades were for such rights. An audit in 1995 found that 'only 63% of allocated water was being fully used', so that trading actually resulted in more use of water rather than less because those who bought sleeper rights used them. As a result a cap on water use had to be introduced. If governments seek to cancel sleeper licences in order to protect ecosystems, there is likely to be a rush to use them before they are lost because they now have financial value (ENRC 2001: ch 7; Krijnen 2004: 4; Olszewska 2001).

Profit vs conservation

In any water trading system there is an ongoing conflict between the needs of irrigators and the needs of the environment. Irrigators demand certainty about the amount of water they will have so that they can plan ahead and safely invest in irrigation infrastructure. But rainfall varies, and any certainty provided to irrigators creates problems for ecosystems, particularly in times of drought when the surplus water is not available.

The economic goals of a functioning water market also seem to conflict with the goals of a healthy ecosystem. An overallocated river system threatens the environment, but if there are not enough spare water entitlements there will be no trade. This occurred in Queensland's Mareeba-Dimbulah Irrigation Area where water allocations varied according to rainfall, and allocation holders were unwilling to trade because they might need their spare water allocations in times of drought, or for alternative crops (Robinson & Ryan 2002: 24).

In order to protect the environment governments have to vary entitlements according to environmental requirements and as new information comes to hand or community attitudes to the environment change. This is called 'clawback'. Water allowances are sometimes based on a proportional share of available water so that they decrease in times of low water flow and regulators can take account of environmental needs when deciding the total amount that can be withdrawn. Farmers generally oppose such systems because they cannot know how much water will be available in future. Even where entitlements are proportional, governments are wary of reducing the total water allocation too much because of irrigator opposition (*Ecos* 2003: 24; ENRC 2001: ch7).

In the case of the Murray River, for example, the logical thing to do is to reduce entitlements to a level that is compatible with a healthy river ecosystem. However, this is politically undesirable because of the strong opposition of irrigators. In fact, Australian governments go out of their way to please irrigators. In 2003 the federal government moved, as part of its National Water Initiative, to increase the security of irrigators' water entitlements (Krijnen 2004: 6). In 2005 the NSW government was accused of 'plundering water set aside to preserve one of the Murray River's most important wetland forests to top up irrigators' allowances' (Hodge 2005a).

Economists argue that any reduction of entitlements 'undermines the market process and prevents permanent water entitlements moving to their highest-value use' (Crase et al. 2000: 314). Government clawback is not only unpopular with commercial water users but can lead to lawsuits opposing the measures and to claims for compensation from those whose water allocations are thereby reduced. Such compensation or buyback could easily make water markets the most expensive way of meeting environmental objectives, particularly to the taxpayer, rather than the most cost effective.

Nevertheless, many people think that governments should buy water to ensure that ecosystems are protected. Irrigators, in particular, would prefer those caring for the environment to have to buy water on the market when it was needed, presumably so they would have a chance to outbid them or otherwise reap enough from sales of their own water entitlements to compensate for not growing crops (Crase et al. 2000; NSW Farmers 2004) – but most people object to paying for a resource that the public already owns.

In Victoria, the environment is not given a priority right to water under the *Water Act*, 1989, which means that the government must negotiate reductions with stakeholders, invest in water-saving measures, purchase water on the market or charge water taxes on trades, in order to obtain more water for the environment. Only the direct purchase of water provides any certainty that the required amount of water will be left in the rivers, and that can be very expensive, a fact which can severely test government resolve to protect the environment.

Perpetuating bad practices

While water trading seeks to ensure that the highest value crops are grown, there is no guarantee that those crops will be the most environmentally beneficial. They may require more chemicals to grow than lower-value crops, and therefore be worse for the environment in the long run. Nor does water trading ensure that less water-dependent crops are grown. There has been a shift in Australia from wheat growing to cotton growing because cotton is a more profitable crop. This has serious ramifications for the environment, since cotton is much more dependent on water and agricultural chemicals than wheat. Moreover, the concentration of water usage in particular areas where cotton is grown completely disrupts the natural river flows (Fullerton 2001: 160).

As water prices have increased, farmers have built dams on their property to capture and store the rain: 'In Victoria alone, there are said to be about 90,000 dams, and for every meg [ML] held in the dam, between one and three are lost to the system in evaporation'. This means that less water is available to rivers despite caps on total water diversions. In New South Wales the government attempted to deal with this problem by allowing farmers to keep only 10 per cent of the rain that fell on their land for free, leading to claims that the government was privatising the rain (Fullerton 2001: 155).

The other problem is that when farmers have to pay more for their water they do not necessarily use less. Rather, they work out ways to get their water to cover greater areas of crops, that is, expanding the area of irrigation for the same amount of water. What is more, about half the water used with inefficient methods like flood irrigation returns to the river through groundwater and surface run-off. With an efficient method like drip irrigation, only around 15 per cent returns to the river. Thus increased water efficiency does not necessarily benefit water flows in the rivers but rather increases the area under production and therefore the farmer's profits (*Ecos* 2003: 26; ENRC 2001: ch 7).

Monitoring and enforcement

Lack of monitoring is also a problem with water allowance markets. In Australia, a national water market is going ahead 'without accurate meters or accounting systems', so that it is impossible for authorities to ensure that water users are complying with their licences (not cheating). The authorities spent many months working out water property rights but left the issue of measuring and accounting to the last minute (Hodge 2005b).

Another problem is water poaching, which has become more of a temptation as the price of water has increased. Given the choice between taking more water than is allowed, or risking the failure of a crop and the possibility of losing the farm, many are going to take more water (Fullerton 2001: 172). 'Calls are now being made for the creation of a water police force to monitor water extractions', but this is being opposed by farmers (Krijnen 2004: 4; NSW Farmers 2004).

MITIGATION BANKING

Mitigation and conservation banking are aimed at maintaining the environmental status quo while economic growth and development occur, and at minimising costs rather than maximising environmental benefits. Gains made to the environment in one area allow degradation in another area rather than benefiting the overall environment.

Outcomes

Mitigation banking seems like a way of being able to have development and environmental protection at the same time. It 'promised a way to have your K-mart and your wetland, too … Your highway will disrupt the habitat of an endangered bird? No sweat, just move the bird to a new ecosystem built conveniently out of the way'. The problem is that it doesn't work (Roberts 1993: 1890).

In 2001 a National Research Council study (BEST et al. 2001: 3) found that mitigation was not preventing loss of wetlands. Between 1993 and 2000 alone, 24 000 acres (9700 hectares) of wetlands in the USA were permitted to be filled on the condition that 42 000 acres (17 000 hectares) of mitigation take place. However, these mitigation projects were sometimes not undertaken and those that were often did not meet permit conditions:

> ... in many cases, even though permit conditions may have been satisfied, required compensation actions were poorly designed or carelessly implemented. In other cases, the location of the mitigation site within the watershed could not provide the necessary hydrological conditions and hence the desired plant and animal communities, including buffers and uplands, necessary to achieve the desired wetland functions.
>
> At some sites, compliance criteria were being met, but the hydrological variability that is a defining feature of a wetland had not been established ... Compliance criteria sometimes specified plant species that the site conditions could not support or required plantings that were unnecessary or inappropriate. (BEST et al. 2001: 6)

So although the ratio of destroyed wetlands to compensatory wetlands is around 100:178, only 134 of each 178 hectares actually goes ahead as a mitigation project and only 77–104 hectares comply with the criteria set by the Corps of Engineers. Of these, 'only about 19 ha would be judged functionally equivalent to appropriate reference sites'. So despite wetland mitigation, there is significant net loss of wetland function (Zedler 2004: 94).

Another study by the Washington State Department of Ecology (Johnson et al. 2002) found that only three compensatory wetland-mitigation projects out of 24 (at 31 sites) were fully successful (see figure 14.1).

Figure 14.1 Success of 24 wetland offset projects

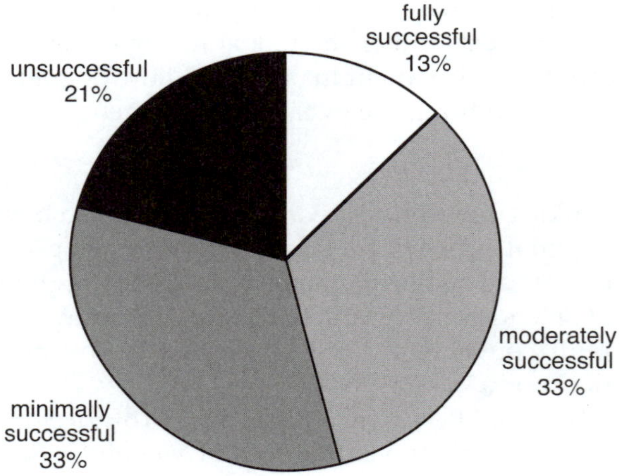

Source (Johnson et al. 2002: ix)

In the case of conservation banks, no study has been done into whether they work or not. This is a crucial question given that there are over 1200 endangered and threatened species in the USA alone (Fox & Nino-Murcia 2005: 1005–6).

The claim by advocates of mitigation and conservation banking that the larger areas of mitigation made possible by mitigation banks – as opposed to mitigation by individual developers – are more environmentally beneficial is called into question by environmental groups. The US-based Sierra Club (2005) argues that such assertions are not supported by science: 'bigger is not always better when it comes to many species of plants and animals'.

Net losses

The problem with preservation as a compensatory mechanism is that no new wetland is created, so that allowing the destruction of one wetland in return for the preservation of another means a net loss of wetland. According to the 1995 official guidelines, preservation is only supposed to be used as compensatory mitigation in exceptional circumstances, but the 2001 guidelines clear the way for preservation to be used on its own for mitigation banks (ELI 2002c). The US Environmental Law Institute (ELI 2002a) found preservation to be commonly used by mitigation banks. Forty-four per cent of mitigation banks that provided ELI with information included preservation as part of their offerings, and 5 per cent only did preservation.

Restoration or enhancement may also result in net loss of wetlands. If a 5-hectare wetland is destroyed and a mitigation bank restores a 10-hectare existing wetland – by getting rid of an invasive species with the use of herbicides, for example – has there been a gain of 5 hectares or a loss of 5 hectares? Joy Zedler (2004: 95), professor of botany and Aldo Leopold Chair in Restoration Ecology at the University of Wisconsin, argues:

> Even if the mitigator modifies the mitigation site's topography and installs native species, there would still be a net loss in wetland area ... Some functions performed by the 5 ha that are filled and the 10 ha that are treated with herbicide might be lost. Only if the 10 ha that were remodelled could be made functional enough to make up for all the processes of the 5 ha fill site and the 10 ha before remodelling could wetland functions be sustained by this trade-off.

In the case of conservation banks, 94 per cent are based on preservation of habitat so there is inevitably a loss in total habitat (Fox & Nino-Murcia 2005: 1005). Even if conservation banking credits are based on the number of species protected, if some of an endangered species are incidentally killed in the process of development and the developer pays for the conservation of the same number elsewhere, there will still be a net loss of members of that species.

In the case of the biodiversity banks in New South Wales, the habitat for one species may be destroyed in return for the 'management' of existing habitat for another species somewhere else. Although the policy is supposed to end the 'tyranny of small decisions' that lead to 'a downward spiral of continuing incremental biodiversity loss' (DEC 2005: 6), it seems that it will contribute to it. New habitat is not being created and habitat on private land is only being conserved at the expense of habitat elsewhere.

Regional needs

Because wetlands perform functions for a particular location it is preferable that existing wetlands be maintained and that where mitigation occurs it be close by so that the same functions are maintained in the same area. Those functions (see box 14.1) cannot be replaced by having them performed elsewhere, sometimes at a considerable distance. Yet mitigation banks are sometimes not even in the same watershed as the wetland being destroyed (Fleischer 2005; Zinn 1997).

The 2001 Regulatory Guidance from the US Corps of Engineers does not require mitigation to be close to where the damage is done. In fact, it even 'promotes mitigation of wetland impacts with non-wetland habitats' in some areas (ELI 2002c). Similarly, although the guidelines for conservation banks express a preference for them to be sited adjacent to existing habitat, less than half of them are (Fox & Nino-Murcia 2005: 1005).

Box 14.1 Functions performed by wetlands

- water purification
- flood storage, conveyance and abatement
- sediment trapping
- wildlife habitat
  - wide variety of plants and animals
  - rare and endangered species
  - migratory birds
  - commercially valuable fish
- groundwater recharge
- groundwater discharge
- pollution control, including nutrient and waste retention
- diminish droughts
- stabilise shorelines and prevent erosion
- recreation
- aesthetic values

Sources (BEST et al 2001: 1; ELI 2002b: 7; Zinn 1997)

Although mitigation banks are praised because they can be coordinated with regional environmental plans, this seldom happens. The ELI found that 'less than one percent of all banking instruments specifically reference consistency with a watershed management plan' and only two states require mitigation banks to 'be planned in a watershed context'. Most US states do not even have formal siting criteria for mitigation banks (ELI 2002a). Sites are selected on the basis of availability and price rather than ecological importance or regional significance. Rather than mitigation sites being defined by regional watershed plans – that is, 'watershed needs and functioning' determining 'the positioning and design or mitigation projects' – mitigation determines the configuration of watersheds (Zedler 2004: 97).

Profit vs conservation

Problems associated with creating, enhancing and restoring wetlands habitats or streams are exacerbated by the fact that mitigation banks are usually driven by profit, rather than scientific or environmental goals, and owners are seldom willing to spend the time and money trying to get it right (ELI 2002a; Roberts 1993). The conflict between economic and environmental goals inherent in profit-motivated mitigation banks leads to compromises and short cuts:

> Studies that have evaluated mitigation projects have shown that the type of habitat to be created or restored is often determined not on the basis of the ecological need or the habitat lost, but on the basis of cost, ease of construction, aesthetics, and provision of non-habitat functions. (Rowinski 1993)

An early study in the USA found that 'the only wetland type that is increasing in acreage in the country – is open water pond with a fringe of wetland vegetation' because that is the type that is easiest and cheapest to create. This type of wetland mitigation is allowed even in places where it does not naturally occur (Roberts 1993; Zedler 2004: 95). Other common types of wetland favoured by mitigation banks include shrub, marsh or tidal wetlands because they 'require less planning, management, and expense than other types of wetlands, such as bottomland hardwood forests' or those with peat soils that rely on groundwater or rainfall. This means that some types of wetlands are being increasingly lost as a result of mitigation banking (Zinn 1997).

Similarly, stream mitigation banks favour the restoration of rural streams, even though developers tend to destroy urban streams. Urban streams are more expensive to restore and because they are subject to rapid-flow urban run-off are also more difficult to maintain. Larger rivers also cost more to restore because they are wider and cover a greater area, have a larger floodplain, and are in areas of higher population density:

> These conditions have led to a situation where, like brook trout and other sensitive fish species, stream mitigation bankers appear to be migrating to the headwaters where they are more apt to find the last refugia of natural hydrology, far from the hazards of potential landowner conflict and the devastating advance of suburbia. (Gillespie 2005)

Conservation and mitigation banks actually tend to facilitate the creation of barren areas. Because rural land is cheaper than urban or suburban land, conservation efforts tend to be concentrated in rural areas while urban areas become more developed. This means that urban areas progressively lose every pocket of nature (Mills 2004: 544).

If trades are confined to areas of similar ecosystem types to avoid the problems resulting from working out equivalencies, trades become too restricted and the market will not work: 'A robust market with a large trading volume would require little or no market restriction and a simple currency to allow for low transaction costs' (Mills 2004: 548). This is a clear example of how the compromises necessary to ensure a viable market are often made at the expense of the environment.

Monitoring and enforcement

Certification, verification and monitoring are particular problems for conservation markets because of the difficulty of measuring biodiversity. Thus, wetland offsets have historically been defined in terms of acreage rather than function and 'the area of *wetland type* is often used as a proxy for wetland functions'. Most wetland mitigation banks still define credits according to acreage (ELI 2002a; Meadows 2005).

The use of simple measurements like acreage for wetlands or linear measurements for streams has 'the major advantage of keeping trades simple, reducing transaction costs, and ensuring that all parties understand the transaction that is taking place'. Simple measurements are necessary to ensure that markets work. Comprehensive measurements that take account of various biological criteria such as 'habitat quality, species, conservation values and benefits' are expensive to work out and raise more questions than they answer in terms of equivalencies for trading purposes (Mills 2004: 547).

Wetland mitigation banks are seldom monitored for the full time it takes for either restored or created wetlands to reach complete functional performance, which may be 20 years or more. 'Habitat for swamp dwelling animals that require a closed tree canopy could take decades to develop, unless mature trees are already present or are planted' (SWS 2005). The ELI found that enforcement of compliance conditions is poor in the USA. What monitoring takes place is often fairly superficial and does not include assessment of function.

Fourteen per cent of wetland banks do not even have specified monitoring and maintenance provisions; 'over a third of the instruments for wetland mitigation banks fail to specify required performance standards'; and 'only a little over half of the banks with performance standards incorporate hydrologic criteria and very few include standards for water quality, soils, wildlife habitat, or other criteria ...' Functional assessment is even rarer. Often all that is required is a specified level of plant cover, even though the existence and survival of the right vegetation is not sufficient to indicate whether the wetland is functioning as it should (ELI 2002a; SWS 2005; Wilkinson et al. 2002: 6; Zedler 2004: 95).

Perpetuating bad practices

Mitigation banks facilitate poor development practices because they allow developers to destroy and degrade wetlands and endangered species habitats simply by paying for conservation elsewhere. The Sierra Club (2005) points out that: 'Mitigation banks are likely to facilitate developments in existing wetlands by promising restorations that may never be successfully completed and will not replace, much less increase, wetland functions'. The concern is that with such an option increasingly available, the pressure on developers to pick appropriate development sites and avoid or minimise the environmental damage they cause will be reduced (Zinn 1997).

In the case of the proposed NSW biodiversity bank, the choice of avoidance or compensation is to be left to the developer within the amber-light areas. PENGO (2002: 2), the coalition of peak Australian environmental groups, argues that offset schemes 'use habitat destruction or pollution of the environment as a "driver" for environmental conservation and improvement'. They 'do not accept that this will lead to positive environmental protection and the reversal of environmental degradation'.

PENGO (2002: 5–10) notes that landowners have a duty of care to manage vegetation on their land and the fact that they do this should not be traded off against 'further land degradation'. This may well provide an incentive for landowners to let the conservation value of their land be degraded – through lack of care and poor management – so as to be eligible for claiming payment for undertaking normal, accepted land management practices as offsets for damage elsewhere. Similarly, conservation actions that are supposed to be core business for local governments – such as catchment maintenance, improvement and rectification – may be used as offsets for environmental damage elsewhere.

In Western Australia, where environmental offsets – but not mitigation banks – have been used as an environmental management tool since the 1980s, the Environmental Protection Authority (WAEPA 2005: 1) has critically observed that environmental offsets are perceived as 'being used to make otherwise "unacceptable" adverse environmental impacts "acceptable" within government':

> [The EPA] is aware that some environmental offsets, proposed in the guise of sustainability tools, are sometimes over-riding the protection and conservation of our State's most valuable environmental assets. Over time, the cumulative effects of this type of decision-making would contribute to a gradual decline in both the quality and quantity of the State's priority environmental assets. The EPA is of the view that this approach is neither sustainable nor focused on protecting the environment.

15

THE EQUITY, PARTICIPATION AND PRECAUTIONARY PRINCIPLES APPLIED

THE EQUITY PRINCIPLE AND TRADEABLE FISHING QUOTAS

Allocation

The allocation of fishing quotas is usually made on the basis of the past catch history of fishing vessels and awarded to the owners of those vessels. The aim of doing it this way is to 'preserve the status quo of a fishery and to gain the support of the industry' (Bess 2005: 340). But this 'allocation by grandfathering' means that those who caught the most fish, and were least sustainable in their fishing practices, are rewarded with the largest quotas.

Grandfathering is a great source of inequity, because quotas are usually given free and quickly become very valuable, so that those who are granted quotas get a windfall benefit.

> Currently, there are no standards on how allocations might be done fairly and equitably. For example, regardless of one's record in the Alaska halibut and sablefish fishery, vessel owners who did not fish between 1988 and 1990 were ineligible to receive initial IFQ [individual fishing quota] shares. Conversely, someone who last fished in or retired after 1988 would have received (or their estate would have received) quota shares, while someone who entered the fishery in 1991 would receive none. (Buck 1995)

The US group Taxpayers for Common Sense (TCS 2002a) claims that:

> Once handed out, the quotas amount to a winning lotto ticket that can be sold to the highest bidder … In the Alaska Halibut program, for instance, many fishermen became instant millionaires when they sold their quota shares to other, less fortunate fishermen who had not received quotas.

In the meantime, others involved in the fishing industry suffer, including the fishers who don't own a share of a fishing vessel: crew, onshore fishing industry workers, and the community that supports the industry.

Groups like TCS (2002b) argue that since fisheries are a public resource, it is taxpayers who should benefit from the resource, not private individuals and companies: 'In some cases, the IFQ recipients don't even fish. Instead, they charge others to use their free quotas, making a profit that rightfully belongs to taxpayers'. TCS points out that the government has to pay for the administrative and enforcement costs of the trading programme as well as spending over $1 billion each year 'sustaining the fisheries'.

Similarly, in Iceland, where quota owners are renting their quotas to those who want to fish, many fishers are effectively paying taxes to quota owners rather than the government. These quota owners are referred to as 'Lords-of-the-Sea' (Hannibalsson 1995).

Access

Traditionally, fishing has been an industry of small-scale operators. This description of the US fishing industry in the 1970s is typical: 'The fishing industry is highly fragmented. Fishermen consist, for the most part, of small independent fishing vessel operators, more than 90% of which employ less than five people' (Macinko & Bromley 2002: 26). Under individual transferable quota (ITQ) systems, all that has changed.

In New Zealand, more than 2000 part-time fishers, including many Maori fishers living in rural areas and seasonal workers who fished to supplement their meagre incomes, were not given quotas because they were not defined as commercial fishers and thus were excluded from fishing. This violated the Treaty of Waitangi – an agreement between the government and the Maori people on which the nation was founded – that gave the Maori people rights to fisheries resources. In 1992 Maori fishers were allocated 10 per cent of the ITQ for species already in the system and 20 per cent of the ITQ for species brought into the system after that date (Bess 2005: 341; Duncan 1995: 102–3).

Small 'commercial' fishers in New Zealand received quotas that were too small to be commercially viable. The price of quotas quickly rose, 'with just a few tonnes worth many thousands of dollars'. It meant that small fishers either had to buy expensive quotas in the hope that their catch would earn enough profit to pay back the investment – a risky proposition – or sell their quotas and leave the business. Many could not raise the money and were forced to sell their quotas, with their boats becoming virtually worthless. As a result the small independent fishers have all but disappeared (SFN 2003; Walker 2005).

> The 1980s management procedure was, firstly, to commodify access to the fish species most under threat, in the form of catch 'quota'; and then to award these rights to the major commercial operators as a free gift, pro rata according to their documented histories. The small-scale and 'informal' operators, and the local people who thought they enjoyed an environmental domain as a collective heritage and source of sustenance, were told that they do not 'own' it at all. Effectively, ownership (all commercial catch rights) were awarded to the large commercial operators. (Duncan 1995: 102)

Concentration

Grandfathering also makes it more difficult for new fishers to come into a fishery because they have the extra cost of buying quotas. Those with best access to low-interest capital are able to buy up quotas: 'Thus, corporate investors, rather than more efficient fishermen, are likely to purchase available ITQ shares'. Fish processors or wholesalers who buy up quotas are able to 'exert substantial control over the industry'. For example, by 1995 the largest holders of quahog and surf clam quotas in the USA were the National Westminster Bank of Jersey and transnational accounting firm KPMG (Buck 1995). According to Taxpayers for Common Sense: 'More than $80 million worth of fish were given away to 180 individuals and companies, now 51% of the quotas are owned by just 5 companies' (TCS 2002b).

Although some countries restrict the amount of the total allowable catch of a species that individuals or companies can own in a particular area, concentration of ownership still occurs. It is easy enough 'to create ad hoc subsidiaries for quota-holding purposes' (Greer 1995: 100). In New Zealand, for example, 'quotas have rapidly transferred into the hands of fewer and fewer companies and individuals and the process is still ongoing', despite legal limits to the extent of ownership of quotas (SFN 2003; Walker 2005).

> Many companies also put themselves in the favourable (and illegal) position of controlling even more quota in each area than the QMS [quota management system] rules allowed. Some conspired and made secret deals with each other, while others bought up extra quota through the use of subsidiary companies. (SFN 2003)

As a result 'shore based fishing companies control almost the entire New Zealand fish catching sector' (SFN 2003). By 1995 three companies owned more than 60 per cent of the quota. In Australia, quotas in the southern bluefin tuna fishery were concentrated in the hands of South Australian corporations (Duncan 1995: 102–3).

Small inshore fishing boats decreased in numbers in Iceland as elsewhere, while there was a growth in large trawlers with processing facilities on board: 'There has been a substantial concentration of quota shares within the larger, vertically integrated companies since the introduction of ITQs', so that by 1999 the five largest quota owners controlled 25 per cent of the total allowable catch and more than half the TAC was owned by the 20 largest companies (Eythorsson 2000: 487–8).

> Along with a general liberalisation of the economic policy in Iceland, there is a trend towards an ideological shift within the industry, leaving behind the idea that fisheries and fish processing should be locally embedded in fisheries communities. Many fisheries companies have joined the Icelandic stock-market, and ownership is in many cases not linked to any particular community. Investors without fisheries background are now well represented among the owners of quota holding companies. (Eythorsson 2000: 488)

Employment

A reduction in vessel numbers and employment has been observed in many fisheries around the world which have been subjected to tradeable quota systems, including the southern bluefin tuna fishery in Australia (vessels down 70 per cent in two years); the halibut fishery in British Columbia, Canada (employment down 32 per cent); and the surf clam and ocean quahog fishery in the USA (employment down 30 per cent in four years) (Greer 1995: 100; Guyader & Thébaud 2001: 107).

In addition, the reduced demand for experienced crew can keep wages down and increase working hours, particularly when the industry is dominated by large corporations. For example, in the surf clam and quahog fishery remaining crew work longer hours for less wages, and in the British Columbia halibut industry the remaining workers have to work longer hours and more days for the same pay. Those who lost their jobs generally received no compensation, unlike the boat owners who could sell their quotas if they left the industry (Buck 1995; Duncan 1995: 102; Guyader & Thébaud 2001: 107–8).

Similarly, in Iceland, 'where fisheries contribute 70 per cent of exports and employ 12 per cent of the working population, severe layoffs in fisheries since quota markets have been implemented have prompted great concern' (Walker 2005). Wages have been halved in some cases because there are so few other employment choices. Fishing crews went on strike several times during the 1990s in an unsuccessful attempt to rectify this state of affairs (Eythorsson 2000: 488; Guyader & Thébaud 2001: 108).

Quota owners often pass on the cost of buying quotas to their crews rather than to consumers in order to remain competitive. In other words, wages are reduced to take account of the cost of the quotas and contract crews are paid for the price of the fish minus the cost of the quota (Eythorsson 2000: 488; Guyader & Thébaud 2001). In Iceland:

> Vessel owners expect the fishermen to share in the cost of buying additional quotas, and in fact, they do so by reducing the fishermen's pay. There are even examples of owners who have sold their own quota, pocketing the profit, and then had the fishermen share with them the cost of buying a quota to replace the one they sold. (Hannibalsson 1995)

The ITQ system has also thwarted the career path from crew to boat owner. In Tasmania, for example, the market value of lobster pots went from $10 000 in 1997 to over $25 000 in 2002, so that a full 40-pot licence was worth over $1 million, taking it beyond the reach of a worker's savings:

> There is a trend toward increased ownership of quota units by non-fishing investors and increased ownership by non-Tasmanians. The high cost of quota units has now made it almost impossible for fish-workers without capital to work their way up from deck-hand to skipper, to eventually acquiring access rights and becoming owner-operators, the path followed by many in the past. The separation between capital and labour is becoming increasingly entrenched. Ownership of property in the form of quota units is increasingly providing power over dependent suppliers of contract labour. (Phillips et al. 2002: 465)

Fishing communities

The impact on local fishing communities of concentration in the industry and loss of employment has been massive. Each fishing job is thought to be responsible for three more jobs in the community, and each dollar earned through fishing earns three more in the community (Duncan 1995: 102). Fishing has also become a far more centralised activity as a result of this concentration, causing rural unemployment. In New Zealand:

> Crews are recruited from city offices and cheap labour comes from overseas. Administrative structures are rationalised and landings have become concentrated in ever fewer ports. Rural slipways and harbours have lost the vast majority of their commercial trade while rural engineers, net and pot makers, and other fishing industry suppliers have all diversified and shrunk, or shut down altogether. (SFN 2003)

Icelandic fishing has traditionally been 'a strictly regulated industry with units of production embedded within local communities' (Eythorsson 2000: 490). But it is those local communities that have suffered from the introduction of tradeable fishing quotas. Remote villages with populations of less than 500 people, which were dependent on fishing for their livelihood, have tended to lose more quota than larger villages and towns as a result of vessel owners selling their quotas or moving elsewhere. The shift of fish-processing to onboard processing facilities or to other regions and even other countries has exacerbated this problem (Duncan 1995: 103): 'The livelihood of the coastline fishing communities depends entirely upon the fish being landed and processed there'. In such small communities there is little else to employ villagers or provide an income, and the 'drastic event of losing the right to fish has a strong demoralising effect' (Eythorsson 2000: 489; Hannibalsson 1995).

The allocation of quotas to fishing boat owners 'does not recognise the traditional composite role of all parties in creating an historic catch record' (Buck 1995). While the boat owners get compensation for selling their quotas, their crews and the communities which supported them get nothing in return for their financial investments in homes and community infrastructure, or for their emotional and cultural investment in the communal life of the village. In Iceland, 'The quota owner has assets that allow for a comfortable retirement in Reykjavik or by the Mediterranean, while his neighbour has lost both his livelihood and his lifetime savings placed in a house which is now impossible to sell.' (Eythorsson 2000: 489)

In 1998 the Supreme Court of Iceland found that the handout of exclusive and permanent rights to publicly owned fisheries to people who happened to own fishing vessels at the time of the 1990 Fisheries Act was not in the best interests of the public nor the best way to conserve fisheries resources. It ruled that the Act was unconstitutional because the Icelandic constitution incorporated the principle of equality. However, only two years later, the same court ruled that the allocation of quotas was constitutional because quotas were not defined as private property in the Act (Eythorsson 2000: 490).

The ITQ system has generated more controversy in Iceland than anywhere else as a result of the large inequities it has created in a nation very largely dependent on fishing. Most people are critical of the system and a single-issue anti-ITQ political party even got two candidates elected to parliament in 1999 (Eythorsson 2000: 490).

In the Tasmanian rock lobster industry, quota trading was introduced to make fishing more efficient and therefore more profitable for boat owners – but this came at the expense of crew, regional economies and social equity: 'Tasmania could have a large fleet maximising employment and lifestyle opportunities, each limited to a low annual catch, or a more "efficient" smaller fleet producing more economic surplus' (Phillips et al. 2002: 464).

The new quota owners 'are increasingly influenced by financial interest, rather than by identification with the values of industry traditions and sympathy with the concerns and interests of fishworkers' which often characterised the previous owner-operators (Phillips et al. 2002: 465). The wealth of the new quota owners, who are often not based in fishing communities, is spent in other towns and cities.

In South Africa the new tradeable fishing quota management system has provided access to new commercial entrants and allowed many more black people into the industry, but traditional fishers have been marginalised. Traditional subsistence fishers are generally organised in a communal way 'where fishers are fishing co-operatively as a part of longstanding cultural tradition'. This does not fit with the individual rights paradigm, which is designed to enhance economic efficiency rather than equity or sustainability, and many small-scale fishers have lost access to their livelihood (van Sittert et al. 2005; Sowman 2005: 11–12).

> In the case of a capital-intensive fishery it may be most appropriate to adopt an individual rights system. On the other hand, in a coastal fishing community, where there is geographic clarity of the community, cohesiveness and a level of organisation amongst the fishers, a collective rights approach may be more appropriate. In such situations, fishers usually have an interest in the longterm sustainability of the resource, and through community moral pressure and the creation of appropriate management institutions and support from government, could create collective incentive for resource stewardship and effective compliance. (Sowman 2005: 11)

THE EQUITY PRINCIPLE AND WATER TRADING

Speculation

Speculation and price manipulation can cause the market price of water to be volatile and to escalate dramatically during times of shortage. This is not only a problem for farmers who need the water for their crops but also for urban users and the environment if governments have to buy extra water. The South Australian government recognises that 'speculation is a feature of every market and the water market is no exception' (DWLBC 2003).

Ralph Nader's advocacy group Public Citizen argues that in the USA, water 'plutocrats ... seek to "game" public water projects – much as Enron "gamed" energy deregulation ... setting up insider water trading systems' so that 'profit rather than need dictates the destiny of California's water' (Gibler 2003: 1). In the United Kingdom, the Office of Water Services claims that 'a company establishing a dominant position' in the water market 'would not in itself infringe the Competition Act' but if such a company restricted the right of others to extract water, the regulator could step in and direct it to provide access (DEFRA 2005).

Some governments have tried to put in place safeguards against speculation. In Victoria there are limits on how much water 'non-water users' are able to own, intended to prevent 'water barons' becoming established. However, that only limits speculation by those who don't use water themselves, and there are ways of getting around the safeguards (Anderson & Newton 2004; DSE 2005). For example, people are buying land to position themselves as water-users 'and then just deserting the land and keeping the water'. Arable land is now going to waste as people use it just to get water rights for speculation purposes. Don Blackmore from the Murray-Darling Basin Commission says, 'I can take you to a block where there are six farmers in the same region and they don't put a drop of water on their property. They sit down and dryland farm and they just wait for the stock market to suit them' (Fullerton 2003).

In the meantime those who need the water for their farms can't outbid the big players who are often not farmers at all. Real estate agent Neil Camm, for example, has found that water trading is more profitable than real estate trading and with an annual turnover of 100 000 megalitres claims to be Australia's biggest water trader. His company, National Waterbank Ltd, was established for the purpose of raising money to buy up water licences (Fullerton 2001: 166; Lewis 2003).

In 2003, the largest private owner of water in Australia lived in Argentina. The investigative television programme *Four Corners* reported that his company had rights to some 157 000 megalitres a year (Fullerton 2003). Thomas Krijnen (2004: 4) has written, in the journal *Natural Resource Management*, of:

> the expected rise in the number of 'water barons' – people who buy up water allocations and trade in them much as they would trade in any other commodity on the stock market. The fear is that, motivated by a straightforward desire for profit, they will create artificial markets, manipulate supply and raise the cost thus pricing genuine irrigators, who would otherwise be viable, out of the market.

Between 1999 and 2003 the price of water in Australia increased by 27 times and many blame this on speculators. 'Water rights are being touted as the next big investment after housing, according to a board member of the Reserve Bank, and there is speculation that the boom in the price of irrigation rights could harm the nation's farming industry as speculators try to profit from the water shortage' (*EnviroInfo* 2003). More radical critics argue:

> given the desperate shortage of river water in general, the agribusinesses may find the trade in water more profitable than the production of crops. If so, the government will simply have burdened the nation with a layer of totally unproductive middle men with a stranglehold on our most precious natural resource – a resource which should rightfully belong to the people and be managed by government. (*The Guardian* 2004)

Efficiency vs equity

Water allowance trading aims to ensure that water is allocated 'efficiently':

> According to classical market economics, economically efficient allocation of resources is achieved by competition between consumers for products they want ... In this case 'efficiency' is defined as allocation that produces the greatest net benefit to society – not necessarily the most equitable sharing of resources, nor one that maximises production. (ENRC 2001: ch 7)

In reality, those who can pay the most for water are not necessarily those who produce the crops or the products that are most important to the community. Those with best access to capital have best access to water, and often producers of luxury crops such as wine grapes are better able to pay for water than those farmers producing staples such as milk, cereals and vegetables, which the community depends on (ENRC 2001: ch 7). This means that the price of basic food items will increase, something that impacts most heavily on the poor, for whom food represents a greater proportion of their living expenses.

What is more, the idea that a water market will ensure that water is used for the most valuable product ignores the way that the market value of different crops changes: 'What is considered high value one day, may be in overproduction or may be overtaken by technology shortly thereafter' (Fullerton 2001: 159). In fact, by 2005 there was a glut of wine grapes in Australia, causing their price to fall and leaving growers with increasing water costs and declining profits.

Another problem occurs when a large number of farmers in a district sell their water rights permanently to get the cash to leave their farms. Not only are the abandoned farms left as magnets for weeds and feral animals and as eyesores on the landscape, but the cost of maintaining shared irrigation infrastructure is left to the few farmers who stay. This 'Swiss cheese effect' has been felt in parts of Australia such as Rochester West in northern Victoria, where half the farms have closed down. In the nearby Goulburn-Murray Rivers district, half the water has been sold to other areas. This impacts on employment as the shops and businesses that once serviced the local area close down also (Carruthers 2005).

THE PARTICIPATION PRINCIPLE

Loss of control of public resources

Markets for conservation reduce public participation in the same way that tradeable pollution rights schemes do. By granting private ownership to fish species and waterways and conservation areas, much of the decision making is shifted to the private sector. The introduction of tradeable fishing rights is often viewed by the community as the privatisation of a public resource, with the transfer of power, control and benefits away from the community. Similarly, there is a tendency for the public to view water as a community resource; in the USA private rights to water and privately-owned water banks are widely seen as a loss of a community resource and of democratic control over it (Clifford et al. 2004).

In Iceland the introduction of ITQs means that the trading of fishing quotas can now occur without consultation with the unions, the local community or the ministry, as had previously been required. The 'practice of working out the fisheries management policy by broad debates and consensus in the Fisheries Assembly and by preparing new legislation by task forces with broad representation from different stakeholder groups' has been discarded as quota owners and the vessel owners association have become more powerful (Eythorsson 2000: 486–90).

In California, even though the state Constitution holds water to be a public good, private interests seem to be profiting from water marketing at the expense of the public (Gibler 2003: 1).

> In a new era of buying and selling water, there may be no bigger stockpile than the Kern Water Bank. It was conceived in the mid-1980s by the state Department of Water Resources as a way to store water in the aquifer in wet years so that it can be pumped out in dry years.
>
> Today, though, the massive underground pool is controlled by one corporate farmer, wealthy Los Angeles businessman Stewart Resnick, who owns Paramount Farming Co., the Franklin Mint, and Teleflora, a flowers-by-wire service.
>
> The Kern Bank, which was intended to help balance out the state's water supply to cities, farms and fish, has instead allowed Paramount Farming to double its acres of nuts and fruits since 1994. (Arax 2003)

Increase in power of vested interests

The creation of markets in environmental resources often encourages a concentration of ownership and vested interests that wields considerable political power. The system of tradeable fishing rights which has granted quota owners great wealth and power in the industry has also created a strong vested interest that lobbies government to prevent changes that threaten those interests. In the Tasmanian fishing industry, '[a] new management environment is emerging with greater involvement of lobbyists, lawyers, accountants, and brokers of fishing entitlements ... There is an ongoing push by the industry to further "liberalise" the market for quota units in order to increase their value' (Phillips et al. 2002: 465).

The more concentrated the industry the more influence it will wield over the politicians setting the total allowable catch (TAC). In Iceland, for example, quota owners 'include wealthy, well-connected, and influential individuals in Icelandic society who have every reason to fight tooth and nail to protect their newly-found treasure' (Hannibalsson 1995). In New Zealand the TAC is supposed to be based on scientific research showing what is sustainable, but in reality the TACs for most species 'have shown no variation whatsoever during recent years', indicating a political unwillingness to reduce them in the face of pressure from the fishing industry (SFN 2003).

Restriction of information and participation

Finally, the conversion of environmental decision-making into a series of commercial transactions tends to exclude the public and restrict the amount of information about these transactions that is available to the public. For example, the 'public has very little access to information' on mitigation banking. There are no standardised descriptions of wetland types and the rules for different banks vary so it is difficult to compare banks or evaluate them (ELI 2002a). Data on their ecological performance is even more difficult to come by. Additionally, there is often no process for public comment on proposed mitigation banks (BEST et al. 2001; Wilkinson et al. 2002: 17). NGOs 'feel they have little or no ability to influence the process on decisions regarding location, design, or service area designation' (Fleischer 2005).

Similarly the transformation of community fishing into a global industry has removed decisions about fishing from the community to the boardrooms of large corporations. The introduction of transferable quotas has enabled quota owners to take their quotas out of the community, or sell them to city-based fishing companies, without any consultation with those affected.

THE PRECAUTIONARY PRINCIPLE

Fisheries

Fishing involves the risks that catch levels will cause fish populations to collapse and that by catching one species other species may be adversely affected. The magnitudes of these risks are unknown because of scientific and management uncertainties. The ability of scientists to calculate just how many fish can be caught without jeopardising fish populations is limited:

> Scientific uncertainties arise because ecosystems are complex and dynamic, and subject to long-term change as well as chaotic and chance events. These factors contribute to uncertainty in predicting stock recruitment, the responses of fish stocks to changing fishing effort, or the interactions between fisheries and other aspects of the environment. (JNCC 2005)

It is difficult to assess existing population numbers, let alone how far they can safely be reduced. One fisher claimed that assessing fish numbers 'is like counting sheep from a helicopter on a cloudy day' (Walker 2005). Assessing populations of fish species is 'an imprecise and difficult task' because there are considerable variations over time, due not only to overfishing but also to climatic variation and ecological effects. This means that estimates can be 20–30 per cent inaccurate. What is more, estimates made by fishing people are often quite different from those made by scientists (DEFRA 2003: 18).

Fish recovery

The managers of fisheries, and designers of ITQ systems, assume that when fish numbers start to decline, it is just a matter of reducing the allowable catch and stocks will rebound to former levels. However, the evidence for this is mixed. In some cases population numbers do recover, although not necessarily to their full healthy state. For example, after stocks of Peruvian anchovy collapsed in the early 1970s they recovered to 60 per cent of their former numbers by the 1990s. But English salmon have never recovered from overfishing in the nineteenth century, nor have herring stocks in the North Sea recovered since a moratorium was put in place in the late 1970s. 'In other words, no one really knows to what extent fish stocks can recover from overfishing' (Hagler 1995: 74).

Yet on the basis of the assumption that stocks do recover, scientists work out a maximum sustainable yield (MSY), which is the maximum amount of fish that can be caught in any one season that will still enable fish numbers to recover to the level they started at:

> Essentially, MSY is a form of brinkmanship in which fishery managers attempt, as a matter of principle, to extract maximum yields from a natural resource, on the assumption that, if they get it wrong one year, they will be able to get it right the next. (Hagler 1995: 75)

MSY calculations usually do not take account of the time it may take a long-lived fish like the cod or the orange roughy to re-establish their numbers. Nor do they take account of species interactions, migration patterns, marine pollution, or the destruction of fish breeding grounds such as coral reefs and seagrass beds often caused by fishing trawlers (Hagler 1995: 75).

The MSY estimated by scientists is typically less than half the natural level of the population. A precautionary approach, on the other hand, would require that 'fisheries stocks must be maintained at levels of abundance which are not substantially below their range of natural fluctuation'. It would also ensure that some areas of habitat would be off limits for trawlers and especially for fishing gear that comes in contact with the sea bottom (Earle 1995: 70).

Management response

On top of the scientific uncertainties are the management uncertainties – how will different regulatory policies change fishing behaviour and will fishers comply with the policies? A precautionary approach requires fisheries managers to be able to adapt to new information quickly. If it is found that fish numbers are declining to unsustainable levels, controls need to be implemented quickly to reverse the situation. This is difficult with a system of individual transferable fishing rights.

It can take an ITQ management system some time to react and adjust total allowable catches, mainly because of the opposition from vested interests created through the allocation and trading of quotas (DEFRA 2003: 18). In New Zealand 'the final decision on TACs seems to owe more to the lobbying of the powerful fishing industry than to the best science available or the concerns of conservationists'. What is more, the TAC is often exceeded because of loopholes in the rules that allow fishers to have their unfilled quotas for one year carried over to the next, or make 'surrender payments' for excess (Duncan 1995: 99–101).

In Australia, where 17 out of 74 commercial fish species are overfished, government is having to buy fishers out at a cost of $220 million, which includes $149 million to buy back their licences (Darby 2005).

Incidental damage

A further uncertainty in scientific assessments of sustainable catches arises from the way they are based on officially recorded fish landings – which do not take account of by-catch, discarded fish and misreported landings. As we saw in the previous chapter, ITQ systems provide an incentive to cheat and misreport their catches, and by-catch can be significant: 'Scientists now receive more figures than ever before, but those figures are less reliable than ever' (Hannibalsson 1995).

Discards and by-catch may be very significant to an ecosystem. But because scientists know little about how fish species interact and because they focus on population numbers of specific commercial species, they do not take account of by-catch in their estimates of maximum sustainable yield. A precautionary approach would be more interested in overall fish mortality than in ensuring that a fleet was economically efficient and profitable and so counting only the fish caught for legal sale (JNCC 2005).

The incidental damage caused by modern fishing technology is also neglected by tradeable fishing quota systems. The impacts of trawlers on the marine environment, for example, are well documented. The precautionary principle requires that new fishing equipment and technologies be evaluated before being permitted to operate (Earle 1995: 70).

Water trading

Rivers and waterways require certain water flows at particular times to ensure the ecological health of the ecosystems of which they are part. Water trading is based on the assumption that rivers have the capacity to deal with a certain amount of water extraction without long-term ill effect. It is that capacity, like the assumed assimilative capacity of the air and water to take pollutants, that water trading seeks to allocate.

This is not a precautionary approach. It assumes that the amount of water that can be extracted without long-term ecological consequences can be accurately determined. However, as with other trading schemes, the capacity of a river system to deal with extraction of water is highly uncertain. It varies considerably with changes in climate, particularly in a country like Australia, where droughts are common.

Proponents of water trading argue that the environment can be protected by the appointment of environmental managers, who can manage an allocation for the environment, selling water during droughts at high prices and buying it back for the environment at low prices during flood times. It is argued that this would simulate actual environmental conditions – but it is doubtful whether any such manager would have the experience and knowledge to predict with any certainty when the environment needed water – and how much – and when it did not (Brennan & Scoccimarro 1999: 79). Nor would the periods of need necessarily coincide with periods of lower prices.

As with fisheries, a precautionary approach requires water managers to be able to adapt to new information quickly. By giving water allowances the status of rights, it becomes difficult for the authorities to reduce allocations in the face of extraordinary weather conditions or new evidence that river flows need to be increased for ecological reasons. The existence of entitlements shifts the burden of proof back to the government, rather than requiring water users to carry it as the precautionary principle would require (Robinson & Ryan 2002: 23).

Mitigation, stream and conservation banks

Mitigation banks are like carbon sinks in that they are supposed to offset damage done elsewhere and expand the ability of the environment to assimilate damage by replacing functions that are being destroyed. However, like the science of carbon sinks, the science of mitigation banks is highly uncertain, particularly when scientists try to recreate ecosystems such as wetlands.

Recreating nature

It is only by creating new wetlands that degraded or destroyed wetlands can be truly replaced without overall loss. However, wetland creation is most likely to result in failure, according to the Society of Wetland

Scientists. This is because of the difficulty of recreating, from its components, a fully functioning ecosystem that has evolved over thousands of years and includes 'animal and plant communities that reflect precise relationships between wet and dry conditions'. Environmental scientists agree that wetland creation is experimental at best and claim that 'a priceless original is too often bargained away for a cheap counterfeit' (Roberts 1993; SWS 2005; Zinn 1997).

> Perhaps the biggest gap is in the understanding of the interaction of soil, surface water, and groundwater on which the ecosystem depends. Getting it right, says Zedler, is a 'crap shoot.' And while it's easy to figure out which plants to bring in, where to put them – specifically, at what elevation – is not so clear. Planting them a few inches too high or too low, in relation to the tidal regime, can spell death to a newly introduced plant population. (Roberts 1993)

The enhancement and restoration of conservation areas is also problematic, particularly in situations where 'enhancement' involves the introduction of new species and plants which may do more harm than good. Additionally, a replacement wetland in another location seldom replaces the functions of the wetland being destroyed, because the functions that served depended on its location in the watershed and on the surrounding water uses.

Similarly, stream mitigation is of uncertain value because 'the dynamism and scale associated with streams often make it difficult to identify and rectify disturbances to their biological, chemical and hydrological functions'. This problem is exacerbated by the problems associated with equivalency and replacement value, that is, in deciding whether one stretch of water is equivalent to another. For example, 'a road construction project could affect 1,000 linear feet of a stream you'd need a canoe to cross, and for mitigation, the state highway department could purchase credits for 1,000 linear feet of a restored mountain brook that your child might jump across' (Gillespie 2005).

The assumption that humans can 'recreate ecological functions' and 'move them around the landscape, and yet not lose a part of our environment that we might not yet fully understand' is a dangerous one. Steve Moyer from Trout Unlimited, which is dedicated to protecting and restoring trout and salmon habitat, argues that some projects that impact on streams should never be permitted. Mitigation banking enables authorities to approve such projects in the false confidence that they can be replaced by an artificially maintained stream somewhere else (Gillespie 2005).

In the event of failure

Mitigation banking is supposed to overcome the problem of wetlands destruction by achieving the mitigation in advance of selling the credits, but often this does not happen. It can take several years for the success or failure of a wetland to be known, and commercial ventures cannot wait. The Environmental Law Institute (ELI) found that in the USA 92 per cent of mitigation banks sell credits before the wetlands have become fully functional and 42 per cent of credits are sold before any performance criteria have been achieved (ELI 2002a).

If a mitigation bank fails, not only is the original wetland lost but also the one that was supposed to replace it. Mitigation banks are subject not only to ecological failure but also to economic failure where they are owned by private entrepreneurs. Businesses go out of business all the time but mitigation banks are supposed to last forever. While most mitigation banks have contingency plans for such events, around one in four do not: 'only 31 percent of the banks with contingency plans specify potential enforcement mechanisms' (ELI 2002a). This is an important consideration, for even though 91 per cent of conservation banks are motivated by financial goals, many are not making a profit (see figure 15.1).

Figure 15.1 Economic success of conservation banks

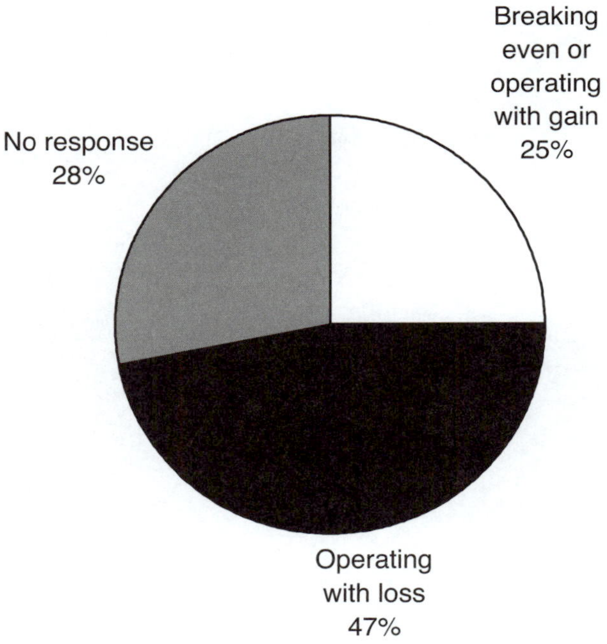

Source (Fox and Nino-Murcia 2005: 1004)

The Western Australian EPA suggests that a larger area of ecological value needs to be offset than that being destroyed to cover the risk that the offset area will fail to provide the environmental benefits expected. Making an area larger does not necessarily improve the chances of success, however. The EPA suggests in that case that the '[r]isks of failure could be reduced through, for example, putting offsets in more than one location' (WAEPA 2005: 10). 'The decision of whether to permit the destruction of a wetland', argues wetland scientist Mary Kentula, should 'be based on whether we can afford to lose that system', not on whether we think we might be able to replace it (quoted in Roberts 1993).

The uncertainty about whether mitigation will adequately replace wetlands lost through development means that regulatory authorities are supposed to insist on avoidance and minimisation of damage to existing wetlands wherever possible before considering mitigation as an alternative. 'Minimization might include redesigning or scaling back aspects of a proposal, or limiting proposed modifications to a portion of the project site' (Zinn 1997). Environmentalists, however, are concerned that having the easy option of mitigation banks available will mean that regulatory authorities will not take the precautionary approach, which is to avoid or minimise damage to sensitive ecosystems.

16

CONCLUSION

Can the problems associated with economic instruments and market-based environmental policies – that is, economics-based environmental policies – be fixed? Is it just a matter of making adjustments to take account of important environmental and social principles, or are these policies inherently faulty and incompatible with those principles? It seems likely that the problems outlined in this book are not a series of ad-hoc, incidental side-effects of policies that have yet to be perfected. They are too many and too wide ranging, and have too many commonalities across the range of policies. Their common features are no accident – they demonstrate that the fundamental goals and assumptions underlying economics-based policies are at odds with the environmental and social principles concerned communities and governments around the world are seeking to achieve.

As discussed in the introduction, economics-based environmental policies were promoted by business at a time when public consciousness of environmental problems was high and demands for stricter regulation were growing. Business saw these policies as a way of avoiding the costs of stricter regulation and of maintaining autonomy over manufacturing and development decisions. They were also seen as a way of enabling industrial growth and economic development to continue in areas that were already polluted and degraded.

Economics-based environmental policies were thus primarily designed to achieve economic efficiency, facilitate economic growth, and allow businesses to decide how they would meet environmental expectations. Governments, particularly in English-speaking countries, believed that economics-based policies would allow them to set an environmental goal and let the market decide how it would be met.

The problem is that a great deal rides on exactly how an environmental goal is met. It can be met in a way that takes account of broadly-held ethical, environmental and social principles or it can be met in a way that only takes account of the total economic costs and benefits. Economics-based environmental policies give priority to economic efficiency above all else. Principles that cannot be quantified in monetary terms and that are not compatible with business priorities are ignored.

When economic efficiency becomes the overriding concern a situation develops where business rights are given priority over human rights. Human rights are supposed to be inalienable, which means they cannot be taken away, sold or given away. Yet economics-based environmental policies do just that. Access to environmental resources such as clean air and water, and to a healthy environment, become just more figures in the calculus of economics-based decisions. Whether it is government economists working out a cost–benefit analysis or industry economists working out whether to buy emission credits or reduce pollution, human rights become tradeable elements that can be taken away and sold.

The economic efficiency focus of economics-based environmental policies means that the inequitable distribution of impacts that result is disregarded. Pollution is shifted around nations and offsets created around the world with little concern for the rights of those impacted or displaced. At best their plight will be recorded as a cost element in an economic analysis that weighs gains in wealth for individual companies against the injury and suffering of members of the community, as if such things are equivalent and interchangeable. The loss of environmental amenity, even the lives of future generations, is heavily discounted to reflect present monetary preferences.

Economics-based environmental policies perpetuate existing social and power relations. The wealthy are able to buy up entitlements, pay the highest charges, and exert most control over natural resources. The worst environmental burdens are further concentrated into areas that have poor populations and low property values, and the polluters in their midst are permitted to go on polluting through payments – for charges, credits and allowances – which seldom provide any compensation for the community that is affected.

It matters how environmental goals are met. If they are met by providing ways to make environmental protection profitable then the community pays the price of those profits rather than polluters paying to prevent or clean up their pollution. While the polluters make profits out of shifting pollution and conservation areas around the landscape, poor communities suffer health effects, pay proportionately higher charges, and lose access to resources and environmental amenity. And those who profit increase their economic and political power and ensure that the system that benefits them will not change.

Economics-based environmental policies are designed to incorporate nature into the economic system rather than the economic system being designed to fit nature's constraints. Nature is commodified so that it can be bought and sold, so that it is subject to the market laws of supply and demand. But this assumes that parcels of nature can be bargained away like so many pork bellies without serious consequence.

While commodities in the marketplace are interchangeable and replaceable, and supply can be increased when demand increases, this is not the case with parts of the environment. Many aspects of the environment cannot be 'manufactured' like other commodities. Once lost they are lost forever; and this means environmental losses are cumulative. Over time the cumulative degradation can threaten human health and wellbeing in a way that cannot be compensated for by the wealth which markets can sometimes create.

Economics-based environmental policies make assumptions about the capacity of the environment to deal with human impacts: it can take a certain amount of pollution; it can absorb a certain amount of carbon; it can recover from a certain amount of fishing; it can deal with a certain amount of water diversion; functions that have been lost can be recreated. In each case, the ability of the environment to rebound is highly uncertain. Yet its capacity to rebound is allocated in the form of relatively secure entitlements – rights and permits – which use up that unknown capacity in a way that allows little scope for adjustment as new information comes to hand.

Where an activity is likely to seriously or irreversibly harm the environment, highly uncertain assumptions about the capacity of the environment to rebound, or the ability of humans to reverse the damage, do not diminish the need for the activity to be avoided or minimised in the first place. Similarly, highly uncertain offset activities undertaken elsewhere do not diminish the need for the precautionary principle to be applied and the original activities to be avoided or curtailed.

It would be far more environmentally beneficial to design processes and products that are ecologically sustainable than to attempt to find ways to repair and replace lost environmental amenity and functions that are essential to life and wellbeing. Yet the priority currently given to short-term economic efficiency and economic growth stunts such endeavours by encouraging and facilitating the continuation of environmentally damaging practices.

The advantage of markets is supposed to be that supply and demand are automatically balanced over time, which thus removes the need for government planning. However, environmental markets are highly dependent on government oversight and monitoring to prevent fraud and cheating, and this can be very expensive. If monitoring is done properly, costs escalate and economic efficiency is undermined. Therefore the policing of markets is seldom done properly.

A major attraction of economics-based environmental policies – to business leaders, bureaucrats and politicians – is clearly that they reduce political debate. Public debates over values, ethics, morals, social goals and priorities are reduced to debates about costs and benefits, as measured by economists. Sometimes even these severely limited economic debates are bypassed, because economics-based policies increasingly turn environmental decisions into private and commercial decisions.

Baselines and caps and total allowable catches are decided by government experts and adjusted under pressure from vested interests. It is the polluters, farmers, fishers and developers – not the community as a whole – who decide where the pollution should be; where the water should go; where the conservation should take place; what technologies should be used. And such decisions become business transactions rather than public decisions subject to public scrutiny. At the same time, the exercise of degrading the environment becomes an entitlement rather than an offence, and the ability of concerned citizens and environmentalists to shame and control an environmentally-damaging company disappears.

It matters how environmental goals are met because some methods will be more successful than others. Economics-based environmental policies are an indirect and ultimately ineffective method of achieving environmental goals. They are aimed at altering the conditions in which decisions are made rather than directly prescribing decisions. But regulators cannot be sure that the changed conditions will bring about the desired decisions.

If the precautionary principle requires that a threat of unacceptable harm be avoided, economic instruments do not offer sufficient confidence that the necessary level of protection will be put in place.

BIBLIOGRAPHY

AAGDM: Alert Against the Green Desert Movement (2005) Indigenous peoples of Brazil fight to take back their land from plantations, *Carbon Trade Watch*, 5 March.

Aarhus Convention (1998) Convention on Access to Information, Public Participation in Decision-Making and Access to Justice in Environmental Matters, United Nations Economic Commission for Europe, <http://www.unece.org/env/pp/>

Abelson, P (1979) *Cost Benefit Analysis and Environmental Problems*, Saxon House, London.

ACHPR (1981) African Charter on Human and Peoples' Rights, Human Rights and Constitutional Rights, <http://www.hrcr.org/docs/Banjul/afrhr2.html>

Ackerman, F & L Heinzerling (2004) *Priceless: On Knowing the Price of Everything and the Value of Nothing*, The New Press, New York.

Ackerman, F & R Massey (2002) *Prospering with Precaution: Employment, Economics, and the Precautionary Principle*, Precautionary Principle Project, Tufts University, August.

ACTU & UMFA (1992) Employment impacts in the achievement of ecologically sustainable development: a canvassing of the issues, Paper presented at the 9th ECO '92 public forum, University of Sydney, 31 Jan–1 Feb.

Adams, J (1996) Cost–benefit analysis: the problem, not the solution, *The Ecologist*, 26(1): 2–4.

AMCC (2005) Reauthorization of the Magnusson-Stevens Fishery Conservation and Management Act, Alaska Marine Conservation Council, viewed 16 December 2005, <http://www.akmarine.org/ourwork/msa.shtml>

Anderson, G & A Newton (2004) *Victorian Government's White Paper on Water*, Allens Arthur Robinson, Melbourne, June.

Anderson, MR (1996) Human rights approaches to environmental protection: an overview. In AE Boyle & MR Anderson (eds) *Human Rights Approaches to Environmental Protection*, Clarendon Press, Oxford, pp. 1–23.

Anderson, T & D Leal (1991) *Free Market Environmentalism*, Pacific Research Institute for Public Policy, San Francisco.

Andorno, R (2004) The precautionary principle: a new legal standard for the technological age, *Journal of International Biotechnology Law*(1): 11–9.

Arax, M (2003) Massive farm owned by L.A. man uses water bank conceived for state needs, *Los Angeles Times*, 19 December.

Arriaza, M, JA Gomex-Limon & M Upton (2002) Local water markets for irrigation in southern Spain, *The Australian Journal of Agricultural and Resource Economics*, 46(1): 21ff.

Article 19 (1999) *The Public's Right to Know: Principles on Freedom of Information Legislation*, Article 19, London, June.

Atkinson, S & TH Tietenberg (1991) Market failure in incentive based regulation: the case of emissions trading, *Journal of Environmental Economics and Management*, 21: 17–31.

Atkisson, A & J Davis (2001) Donella Meadows, lead author of 'The Limits to Growth', has died, *Ecological Economics*, 38: 165–6.

ATO (1999) *A Guide to Tax Incentives for Landcare*, Australian Taxation Office, Canberra.

Ayres, RU (1996) Limits to the growth paradigm, *Ecological Economics*, 19: 117–34.

Bachram, H (2004) Climate fraud and carbon colonialism: the new trade in greenhouse gases, *Capitalism Nature Socialism*, 15(4): 1–16.

Bachram, H, J. Bekker, L. Clayden, C. Hotz, & A. Ma'anit (2003) The sky is not the limit: the emerging market in greenhouse gases, *Carbon Trade Watch*, Amsterdam, January.

Bailey, P (2005) The creation of the Universal Declaration of Human Rights, Universal Rights Network, viewed 25 April 2005, <http://www.universalrights.net/main/creation.htm >

Baillie, JEM, C Hilton-Taylor & SN Stuart (eds) (2004) A global species assessment, IUCN – The World Conservation Union, Gland, Switzerland and Cambridge, UK.

Bank of America (1999) Conservation banking, Bank of America, 9 February, <http://www.bofa.com/community/env_p7.html>

Barbour, I (1980) *Technology, Environment and Human Values*, Praeger, New York.

Barkley, P & D Seckler (1972) *Economic Growth and Environmental Decay: The Solution Becomes the Problem*, Harcourt Brace Jovanovich, New York.

Barney, GO (2000) The whole world in our hands, *San Francisco Gate*, 31 December.

Barry, B (1999) Justice between generations: power and knowledge. In MJ Smith (ed.) *Thinking through the Environment*, The Open University, London and New York, pp. 80–8.

BCA (1991) *Achieving Sustainable Development: A Practical Framework*, Business Council of Australia, Melbourne, July.

Beckham, N (1991) Trees: finding their true value, *Australian Horticulture*, August, p. 16.

Beder, S (1996) *The Nature of Sustainable Development*, 2nd edn, Scribe Publications, Melbourne, Australia.

Bell, T (2005) Bush calling for private fisheries, *Portland Press Herald*, 20 September.

Belliveau, M (1998) Smoke and mirrors: will global pollution trading save the climate or promote injustice and fraud? *CorpWatch*, 1 October 1998.

Bennett, J (1991) Economics and the resolution of environmental questions, Paper presented at the Launch of Reconciling Economics with the Environment, Sydney, 3 September.

Bess, R (2005) Expanding New Zealand's quota management system, *Marine Policy*, 29: 339–47.

BEST: Board on Environmental Studies and Toxicology et al (2001) *Compensating for Wetland Losses under the Clean Water Act*, National Academy Press, Washington DC.

Biello, D (2002) Trading under attack, *Environmental Finance*, May.

—— (2005) Climate friendly fuels, *Ecosystem Marketplace*, May.

BirdLife International, WWF European Policy Office, EEB & FOE Europe (2001) *Consultation of Interested Parties on a Working Document on the Prevention and Restoration of Significant Environmental Damage (Environmental Liability)*, European Commission, Luxembourg.

Bocking, S (2004) Put your foot in it: it's time to review the usefulness of the 'ecological footprint', *Alternatives Journal*, 30(2): 32–3.

Bodansky, D (1994) The precautionary principle in US environmental law. In T O'Riordan & J Cameron (eds) *Interpreting the Precautionary Principle*, Earthscan, London, pp. 203–28.

Bond, P (2003) The new apartheid, *New Internationalist*, April, pp. 24.

—— (2004) ANC privatizations fail to deliver in South Africa, *CorpWatch*, 18 August.

Bosselmann, K (2005) Human rights and the environment: redefining fundamental principles? University of Melbourne, viewed 9 April 2005, <http://www.arbld.unimelb.edu.au/envjust/papers/allpapers/bosselmann/home.htm>

Boulding, KE (1966) The economics of the coming spaceship Earth. In M Allaby (ed.) *Thinking Green: An Anthology of Essential Ecological Writing*, Barrie & Jenkins, 1989, London, pp. 133–7.

Bowers, J (1990) *Economics of the Environment: The Conservationists' Response to the Pearce Report*, British Association of Nature Conservationists, Telford, Shropshire.

Boyle, A (1996) The role of international human rights law in the protection of the environment. In AE Boyle & MR Anderson (eds) *Human Rights Approaches to Environmental Protection*, Clarendon Press, Oxford, pp. 43–69.

Brennan, D & M Scoccimarro (1999) Issues in defining property rights to improve Australian water markets, *The Australian Journal of Agricultural and Resource Economics*, 43(1): 69–89.

Brickman, R, S Jasanoff & T Ilgen (1985) *Controlling Chemicals: The Politics of Regulation in Europe and the United States*, Cornell University Press, Ithaca, New York.

Buck, EH (1995) Individual transferable quotas in fishery management, *Congressional Research Service*, 95(849).

Bullard, R (1992) The politics of race and pollution: an interview with Robert Bullard, *Multinational Monitor*, June, pp. 21–5.

Bustillo, M & D Rosenzweig (2004) Smog credit trader held in fraud case, *Los Angeles Times*, 17 June.

Buttigieg, BJ & M Fernando (2003) The Supreme Court of Canada endorses the concept of 'polluter pays' – but what does it mean? Miller Thomson LLP, Toronto, November.

Callahan, D (1999) What obligations do we have to future generations? In MJ Smith (ed.) *Thinking through the Environment*, The Open University, London & New York, pp. 71–7.

Cameron, J (1999) The precautionary principle: core meaning, constitutional framework and procedures for implementation. In R Harding & E Fisher (eds) *Perspectives on the Precautionary Principle*, Federation Press, Sydney, pp. 29–58.

Cameron, J & R MacKenzie (1996) Access to environmental justice and procedural rights in international institutions. In AE Boyle & MR Anderson (eds) *Human Rights Approaches to Environmental Protection*, Clarendon Press, Oxford, pp. 129–52.

Campbell, D, D Brown & T Battaglene (2000) Individual transferable catch quotas: Australian experience in the southern bluefin tuna fishery, *Marine Policy*, 24: 109–17.

Carbonfund.org (2005) Reduce your climate footprint to zero with Carbonfund.org, *CSRwire*, 23 June.

Carruthers, F (2005) The flow-on effect, *Australian Financial Review*, 1 July, p. 81.

Case, D (2005) Liberté! égalité! Environment? French constitution gets a dash of green, *Grist Magazine*, 14 July.

Cato Institute (1995) *Natural Resource Studies: Energy and the Environment*, 1995, <http://www.cato.org/>

Caton, P-A (2002) Developing an effluent trading program to address nutrient pollution in the Providence and Seekonk Rivers, Masters thesis, Brown University, Providence, RI.

Cawthorne, A (2005) Kenya forest evictions leave thousands in penury, *Planet Ark*, 15 July.

CCPR (1966) International Covenant on Civil and Political Rights, Office of the High

Commissioner for Human Rights <http://www.unhchr.ch/html/menu3/b/a_ccpr.htm>
CCX (2005) Chicago Climate Exchange, <http://www.chicagoclimatex.com/>
CDM Watch (2005) The World Bank and the carbon market: rhetoric and reality, April.
CEDHA (2002a) *A New Development Strategy for the Americas*, Center for Human Rights and Environment, C{rdoba, Argentina, March 2002.
—— (2002b) *Human Rights, Health and Environmental Protection: Linkages in Law and Practice*, Center for Human Rights and Environment, C{rdoba, Argentina, 2002.
CEO (2000) *Greenhouse Market Mania*, Corporate Europe Observatory, Amsterdam, November.
—— (2001) 'Saving' the Kyoto Protocol means ending market mania, *CorpWatch*, 16 July.
CEPA (1994) National Pollutant Inventory: Public Discussion Paper, Commonwealth Environment Protection Agency, Canberra, February.
CESCR (1966) International Covenant on Economic, Social and Cultural Rights, Office of the High Commissioner for Human Rights, <http://www.unhchr.ch/html/menu3/b/a_cescr.htm>
Chambers, N, C Simmons & M Wackernagel (2000) *Sharing Nature's Interest: Ecological Footprints as an Indicator of Sustainability*, Earthscan, London.
Chant, J, D McFetridge & D Smith (1990) The economics of the conserver society. In W Block (ed.) *Economics and the Environment: A Reconciliation*, Fraser Institute, Vancouver, p. 332.
Charte de l'environnement (2005) National Assembly, France, <http://www.assemblee-nationale.fr/12/dossiers/charte_environnement.asp>
Chatterjee, P (2005) The carbon brokers, *CorpWatch*, 18 February.
CHRI (2005) What is the right to information? Commonwealth Human Rights Initiative, viewed 27 May 2005, <http://www.humanrightsinitiative.org/programs/ai/rti/rti/what.htm>
Churchill, RR (1996) Environmental rights in existing human rights treaties. In AE Boyle & MR Anderson (eds) *Human Rights Approaches to Environmental Protection*, Clarendon Press, Oxford, pp. 89–108.
Clean Air Action Corporation (2002) *US Experience with Emissions Trading*, International Institute for Sustainable Development, Winnipeg, Canada, 22 January.
Clean Water Fund, Minerals Policy Centre, OMB Watch, UK Public Research Interest Group & Working Group on Community Right to Know (2001) Ignorance is toxic bliss: the secret war on our right-to-know, *TerraKnowledge Network*, April 2001.
Clifford, P, C Landry & A Larsen-Hayden (2004) *Analysis of Water Banks in the Western States*, Washington State Department of Ecology and WestWater Research, July.
Climate Justice (2001) Climate justice or corporate agenda? *CorpWatch*, 5 November.
COAG (2000) *A National Action Plan for Salinity and Water Quality*, Council of Australian Governments, Canberra.
Coffey, C & J Newcombe (2001) *The Polluter Pays Principle and Fisheries: The Role of Taxes and Charges*, Institute for European Environmental Policy, London.
COMEST (2005) *The Precautionary Principle*, World Commission on the Ethics of Scientific Knowledge and Technology, UNESCO, Paris, March.
Commission for the Future (1990) A sustainable future for Australia. In WCED, *Our Common Future*, Oxford University Press, Melbourne.
Commonwealth Government of Australia (1990) *Ecologically Sustainable Development: A Commonwealth Discussion Paper*, AGPS, Canberra.
Cooper, P & A Hart (1992) The Legitimacy of Applying Cost–Benefit Analysis to Environmental Planning, *People and Physical Environment Research*(41–42): 19–30.
Corner House, The (1999) *The Cost–Benefit Analysis Dilemma: Strategies and Alternatives*, The Corner House, Dorset, UK, 8–10 October.
Costle, D (1981) The decision-makers' dilemma, *Technology Review*, July, pp. 10–1.

Council of Europe (1950) European Convention on Human Rights, <http://www.hri.org/docs/ECHR50.html>

Cousteau Society (2005) Rights for Future Generations, viewed 10 July 2005, <http://www.cousteau.org/en/cousteau_world/our_programs/future_generations.php>

CPR (2005a) Emissions Trading: 'Market-Based' Regulatory Tools, Center for Progressive Regulation, viewed 24 July 2005, <http://www.progressiveregulation.org/perspectives/emissions.html>

—— (2005b) The Precautionary Principle, Center for Progressive Regulation, viewed 24 July 2005, <http://www.progressiveregulation.org/perspectives/precaution.html>

—— (2005c) The Public's Right to Know, Center for Progressive Regulation, viewed 24 July 2005, <http://www.progressiveregulation.org/perspectives/right.html>

CRA (1995a) *Market Created for Habitat Improvements*, California Resources Agency, 7 April 2005.

—— (1995b) *Official Policy on Conservation Banks*, California Resources Agency and California Environmental Protection Agency, 7 April.

Crase, L, L O'Reilly & B Dollery (2000) Water markets as a vehicle for water reform: the case of New South Wales, *The Australian Journal of Agricultural and Resource Economics*, 44(2): 299–321.

DAFF (2005a) National Water Initiative, Department of Agriculture, Fisheries and Forestry, viewed 21 October 2005, <http://www.affa.gov.au>

—— (2005b) Southern Bluefin Tuna Fishery, Department of Agriculture, Fisheries and Forestry, viewed 18 March 2005, <http://www.affa.gov.au>

Daly, HE (ed.) (1973) *Towards a Steady-state Economy*, WH Freeman, San Francisco.

Daly, HE & JBJ Cobb (1989) *For the Common Good: Redirecting the Economy toward Community, the Environment, and a Sustainable Future*, Beacon Press, Boston.

Darby, A (2005) Struggling fishermen off the hook as deal reached on rescue package, *Sydney Morning Herald*, 24 November, p. 6.

de Sadeleer, N (2002) *Environmental Principles: From Political Slogans to Legal Rules*, Oxford University Press, Oxford.

DEC (2005) *Biodiversity Certification and Banking in Coastal and Growth Areas*, Department of Environment and Conservation (NSW), Sydney, July.

DEFRA (2003) *UK Fisheries Industry: Current Situation Analysis*, Department for Environment, Food and Rural Affairs, UK, 19 June.

—— (2005) *Tuning Water Taking*, Department for Environment, Food and Rural Affairs, UK.

Deville, A & R Harding (1997) *Applying the Precautionary Principle*, Federation Press, Sydney.

Devraj, R (2004) 'Polluter pays' principle may yet gain ground, *Global Information Network*, 25 March.

DHAE (1984) *A National Conservation Strategy for Australia*, Department of Home Affairs and Environment, Canberra.

Dias, A (2000) *Human Rights, Environment and Development: With Special Emphasis on Corporate Accountability*, United Nations Development Program, 2000.

Dickie, P (2005) Australia's first carbon fund nears initial close, Ecosystem Marketplace, viewed 14 August 2005, <http://ecosystemmarketplace.net>

Doern, GB & T Conway (1994) *The Greening of Canada: Federal Institutions and Decisions*, University of Toronto Press, Toronto.

Dommen, E (1993) The four principles for environmental policy and sustainable development: an overview. In E Dommen (ed.) *Fair Principles for Sustainable Development: Essays on Environmental Policy and Developing Countries*, Edward Elgar, Aldershot, Hants, pp. 7–32.

Douglas-Scott, S (1996) Environmental rights in the European Union: participatory democracy or democratic deficit? In AE Boyle & MR Anderson (eds) *Human*

Rights Approaches to Environmental Protection, Clarendon Press, Oxford, pp. 109–28.

Dovers, SR & JW Handmer (1999) Ignorance, sustainability, and the precautionary principle. In R Harding & E Fisher (eds) *Perspectives on the Precautionary Principle*, Federation Press, Sydney, pp. 167–89.

Draft Principles on Human Rights and the Environment (1994), E/CN.4/Sub.2/1994/9, Annex I, University of Minnesota Human Rights Library,<http://www1.umn.edu/humanrts/instree/1994-dec.htm>

DRD (1986) Declaration on the Right to Development, Office of the High Commissioner for Human Rights, <http://www.unhchr.ch/html/menu3/b/74.htm>

Driesen, DM (1998) Free lunch or cheap fix? The emissions trading idea and the Climate Change Convention, *Boston College Environmental Affairs Law Review*, Fall.

—— (2005) *Is Cost–benefit Analysis Neutral?* Center for Progressive Reform, Riderwood, MD, June.

Drury, RT, ME Belliveau, JS Kuhn & S Bansal (1999) Pollution trading and environmental justice: Los Angeles' failed experiment in air quality policy, *Duke Environmental Law and Policy Forum*, 9(2): 231–90.

DSE (2005) *Securing Water for Farms*, Department of Sustainability and Environment, Victoria, May.

Duncan, L (1995) Closed competition: fish quotas in New Zealand, *The Ecologist*, 25(2–3): 97–104.

DWLBC (2003) *Water Trading in the South East: Benefits & Common Misconceptions*, Department of Water, Land and Biodiversity Conservation and the South East Catchment Water Management Board, July.

EA (2003) *Summary of the Responses to the Discussion Document on the Feasibility of a Trading Scheme for NOx and* SO_2 *Emissions from Large Combustion Plants*, UK Environment Agency, May.

EA (2005a) EPER, the European Pollutant Emission Register, UK Environment Agency, viewed 23 December 2005, <http://www.environment-agency.gov.uk>

—— (2005b) Pollution Inventory Home Page, UK Environment Agency, viewed 23 December 2005, <http://www.environment-agency.gov.uk>

—— (2005c) Water Resources, UK Environment Agency, viewed 26 October 2005, <http://www.environment-agency.gov.uk>

Earle, M (1995) The precautionary approach to fisheries, *The Ecologist*, 25(2–3): 70.

EC (2000a) *Communication from the Commission on the Precautionary Principle*, Commission of the European Communities, Brussels, 2 February.

—— (2000b) *White Paper on Environmental Liability*, European Commission, Luxembourg, 9 February.

—— (2003) *Directive 2002/96/EC of the European Parliament and of the Council of 27 January 2003 on Waste Electrical and Electronic Equipment (WEEE)*, European Commission, Luxembourg.

—— (2003b) *Directive 2003/4/EC of the European Parliament and of the Council of 28 January 2003 on Public Access to Environmental Information*, European Commission, Luxembourg.

—— (2004) Directive 2004/35/CE of the European Parliament and of the Council of 21 April 2004 on Environmental Liability with Regard to the Prevention of Environmental Damage, *Official Journal of the European Union* L143, 2004, 56–75.

The Ecologist (1995) Editorial/Introduction, 25(2–3): 42–5.

Ecosystem Marketplace (2005) Water Markets, The Katoomba Group, viewed 14 August 2005, <http://ecosystemmarketplace.net>

ECOTEC – UK (2001) *Ecological Footprinting*, European Parliament Directorate General for Research, Luxembourg, March.

Edie News (2005), Londoners leave huge footprints, May.

Editors of *The Ecologist* (1972) *A Blueprint for Survival*, Penguin, Harmondsworth.

Ehrenfeld, D (1988) Why put a value on biodiversity? In EO Wilson (ed.) *Biodiversity*,

National Academy Press, Washington DC, pp. 212–16.
Ehrlich, PR & JP Holdren (1971) Impact of population growth, *Science*, 171: 1212–17.
Eilperin, J (2005) Forests' recreational value is scaled back, *Washington Post*, 15 August, p. A03.
Ekins, P (1992) 'Limits to growth' and 'sustainable development': grappling with ecological realities, *Ecological Economics*, 8: 269–88.
ELI (2002a) *Banks and Fees Study: Study Methodology and Summary Findings*, Environmental Law Institute, Washington, DC.
—— (2002b) *Banks and Fees: The Status of Off-site Wetland Mitigation in the United States*, Environmental Law Institute, Washington DC.
—— (2002c) *The Federal Context for Wetland Mitigation Banking*, Environmental Law Institute, Washington, DC.
England, RW (2000) Natural capital and the theory of economic growth, *Ecological Economics*, 34(3): 425–31.
ENRC: Environment & Natural Resources Committee (2001) *Inquiry into the Allocation of Water Resources for Agricultural and Environmental Purposes*, Parliament of Victoria, Melbourne, November.
Environment Australia (1999) *Contaminated Sites*, Department of Environment and Heritage (DEH), Australian Government, 1999.
Environment Canada (2001) *A Canadian Perspective on the Precautionary Approach/Principle*, Economic Issues Branch, Hull, Quebec, September.
EPER (2005) Welcome to EPER! The European Pollutant Emission Register, viewed 23 December 2005, <http://eper.eea.eu.int/eper/>
ESD Working Group Chairs (1992) *Intersectoral Issues Report*, AGPS, Canberra.
ESD Working Groups (1991) *Final Report: Mining*, AGPS, Canberra.
Evans, KL (2004) *Water Banking: A General Description and Policy Issues*, Environmental Quality Council, Montana State Legislature, Helena, 10 February.
Eythorsson, E (2000) A decade of ITQ-management in Icelandic fisheries: consolidation without consensus, *Marine Policy*, 24: 483–92.
Faeth, P (2000) *Fertile Ground: Nutrient Trading's Potential to Cost-effectively Improve Water Quality*, World Resources Institute (WRI), Washington DC.
Fairlie, S, M Hagler & B O'Riordan (1995) The politics of overfishing, *The Ecologist*, 25(2–3): 46–73.
Falk, J, G Hampton, A Hodgkinson, K Parker & A Rorris (1993) *Social Equity and the Urban Environment*, Commonwealth Environment Protection Agency, Canberra.
Farrier, D (1999) Factoring biodiversity conservation into decision-making processes. In R Harding & E Fisher (eds) *Perspectives on the Precautionary Principle*, Federation Press, Sydney, pp. 99–121.
Featherstone, L (2005) E-raced: EPA says race, income shouldn't be environmental-justice factors, *Grist Magazine*, 1 August.
Ferrara, S & J Mesquita (2003) *Supreme Court of Canada Upholds a Minister's Application of the Polluter-Pays Principle*, Gowling Lafleur Henderson LLP, Toronto, October.
Fichthorn, N & A Wood (2002) Preserving the SO_2 market, *Environmental Finance*, September, p. 28.
Fisher, B (2001) Fix water costs, then fix salinity, *Business Review Weekly*, 3 August.
Fisher, EC (1999) The precautionary principle as a legal standard for public decision-making. In R Harding & E Fisher (eds) *Perspectives on the Precautionary Principle*, Federation Press, Sydney, pp. 83–98.
Fleischer, D (2005) Wetland mitigation banking: environmentalists express concerns, The Katoomba Group, viewed 25 April 2005, <http://ecosystemmarketplace.net>
FOE Canada (2005) Top court slams door on polluter pays principle, *Friends of the Earth*, Canada, 21 January.
Fox, J (2005) Conservation banking: moving beyond California, Ecosystem Marketplace, viewed 14 August 2005, <http://ecosystemmarketplace.net>
Fox, J & A Nino-Murcia (2005) Status of species conservation banking in the United

States, *Conservation Biology*, 19(4): 996–1007.

Frew, W (2005) Green millions squandered, *Sydney Morning Herald*, 14 September, pp. 1, 11.

Fullerton, T (2001) *Watershed: Deciding Our Water Future*, ABC Books, Sydney.

—— (2003) Sold down the river, *Four Corners*, ABC TV, 14 July.

FWS (2004) *Conservation Banking: Incentives for Stewardship*, US Fish & Wildlife Service, Arlington, VA, September.

Gertz, E (2005) The snow must go on: Inuit fight climate change with human-rights claim against US, *Grist Magazine*, 26 July.

Gibler, J (2003) Water heist: how corporations are cashing in on California's water, *Public Citizen*, Oakland, CA, December.

Gillespie, B, D Eva & R Johnston (1982) Carcinogenic risk assessment in the USA and UK: the case of aldrin/dieldrin. In B Barnes & D Edge (eds) *Science in Context*, MIT Press, Cambridge, pp. 303–35.

Gillespie, N (2005) Stream mitigation banking, Ecosystem Marketplace, viewed 14 August 2005, <http://ecosystemmarketplace.net>

Gleeson, K (2005) Worldwide influence of the Universal Declaration of Human Rights and the International Bill of Rights, Universal Rights Network, viewed 25 April 2005, <http://www.universalrights.net/main/world.htm>

Gleick, P (1999) The human right to water, *Water Policy*, 1(5): 487–503.

Golding, MP (1999) Obligations to future generations. In MJ Smith (ed.) *Thinking through the Environment*, The Open University, London & New York, pp. 64–70.

Goodin, R (1992) The ethics of selling environmental indulgences, Paper presented at the Australasian Philosophical Association Annual Conference, University of Queensland, July.

Goodstein, ES (1997) *A New Look at Environmental Protection and Competitiveness*, Economic Policy Institute, Washington DC.

—— (1999) *The Trade-off Myth: Fact and Fiction about Jobs and the Environment*, Island Press, Washington DC.

Gosden, R (2000) Schismatic mind: controversies over the cause of the symptom of schizophrenia, PhD thesis, University of Wollongong.

—— (2001) *Punishing the Patient: How Psychiatrists Misunderstand and Mistreat Schizophrenia*, Scribe, Melbourne.

Greer, J (1995) On course to a corporate fishery, *The Ecologist*, 25(2–3): 100.

Gunningham, N & A Cornwall (1994) *Toxics and the Community: Legislating the Right to Know*, Australian Centre for Environmental Law, Canberra.

Gunningham, N & D Sinclair (2002) *Leaders and Laggards: Next-Generation Environmental Regulation*, Greenleaf Publishing, Sheffield, UK.

Guyader, O & O Thébaud (2001) Distributional issues in the operation of rights-based fisheries management systems, *Marine Policy*, 25: 103–12.

Haggerty, M & SA Welcomer (2003) Superfund: the ascendance of enabling myths, *Journal of Economic Issues*, 37(2): 451ff.

Hagler, M (1995) Deforestation of the deep: fishing and the state of the oceans, *The Ecologist*, 25(2–3): 74–9.

Hahn, R & G Hester (1989) Where did all the markets go? An analysis of EPA's emissions trading program, *Yale Journal of Regulation*, 6: 109–53.

Hancock, J (2003) *Environmental Human Rights: Power, Ethics and Law*, Ashgate, Aldershot, UK.

Hannibalsson, Ó (1995) The dark side of the quota system, North Atlantic Islands Programme, viewed 8 July 2001, <http://www.upei.ca/islandstudies/naip/dark.htm>

Hardin, G (1977) Ethical implications of carrying capacity, Die Off Web Site, viewed 15 March 2006, <http://dieoff.org/page96.htm>

—— (1986) Cultural carrying capacity: a biological approach to human problems, Die Off Web Site, viewed 15 March 2006, <http://dieoff.org/page46.htm>

Harding, R & E Fisher (eds) (1999) *Perspectives on the Precautionary Principle*, Federation Press, Sydney.

Harramoës, P et al. (eds) (2001) *Late Lessons from Early Warnings: The Precautionary Principle 1896–2000*, European Environment Agency, Copenhagen.

Harris, S (1991) Ecologically Sustainable Development: Implications for the Policy Process, Paper presented at the Royal Australian Institute of Public Administration Conference on Ecologically Sustainable Development, Canberra, 9 December.

Harrison, EB (1993) *Going Green: How to Communicate Your Company's Environmental Commitment*, Business One Irwin, Homewood, IL.

Hatcher, A & A Read (2001) Fishing rights and structural changes in the UK fishing industry. In R Shotton (ed.) *Case Studies in the Effects of Transferable Fishing Rights on Fleet Capacity and Concentration of Quota Ownership*, FAO, Rome.

Hawn, A (2005a) Horses for courses: voluntary vs. CDM carbon projects in Mexico, Ecosystem Marketplace, viewed 22 June 2005, <http://ecosystemmarketplace.net>

—— (2005b) Nutrient trading and dead zones – can they wake each other up? Ecosystem Marketplace, viewed 14 August 2005, <http://ecosystemmarketplace.net>

Hencke, D (2000a) £1bn waste scandal as green tax flops, *Guardian*, 5 April.

—— (2000b) Landfill regulator under fees cloud, *Guardian*, 21 August.

—— (2000c) Tide of polluted landfill 'beyond control', *Guardian*, 6 April.

—— (2001) MPs doubt fitness of landfill tax regulator, *Guardian*, 20 April.

Hodge, A (2005a) Murray 'plundered' in states' water grab, *The Australian*, 6 July, p. 5.

—— (2005b) No accounting for water torture, *The Australian*, 4 July, p. 4.

—— (2005c) Plan for national water trading market, *The Australian*, 1 October, p. 9.

—— (2005d) Cartels pull plug on state water trades, *The Australian*, 5 October, p. 3.

Hodges, H (1997) *Falling Prices: Cost of Complying with Environmental Regulations Almost Always Less than Advertised*, Economic Policy Institute, Washington DC, November.

Holland, A (1999) Sustainability: should we start from here? In A Dobson (ed.) *Fairness and Futurity: Essays on Environmental Sustainability and Social Justice*, Oxford University Press, Oxford, pp. 46–68.

Hooper, N (2005) Trouble grows on trees in timberland, *Australian Financial Review*, 8 October, p. 22.

Hopkins, D (2005a) Africa being turned into digital dump for west's toxic waste, *Edie News*, 26 October.

—— (2005c) Forget the forests, the future is carbon neutral, *Edie News*, 13 September.

—— (2005b) Nigeria orders end to gas flaring, *Edie News*, 17 November.

HRSCEC: House of Representatives Standing Committee on Environment and Conservation (1987) *Fiscal Measures and the Achievement of Environmental Objectives*, AGPS, Canberra.

Humphreys, D (1999) Forest policy: justice within and between generations. In MJ Smith (ed.) *Thinking through the Environment*, Open University, London, pp. 109–21.

ICC (1990) *The Business Charter for Sustainable Development*, International Chamber of Commerce, 1990.

IETA (2005) *State and Trends of the Carbon Market 2005*, International Emissions Trading Association, Washington DC, May.

IIIEE (1998) *Extended Producer Responsibility as a Policy Instrument*, International Institute for Industrial Environmental Economics, 1998.

ILEX Energy Consulting (2005) *The Environmental Effectiveness of the EU ETS: Analysis of Caps*, World Wide Fund for Nature, October.

ILO (1991) Convention (No. 169) Concerning Indigenous and Tribal Peoples in Independent Countries, Office of the High Commissioner for Human Rights, <http://www.unhchr.ch/html/menu3/b/62.htm>

ILSR (2005) The concepts of extended producer responsibility and product stewardship, Institute for Local Self-Reliance, viewed 7 September 2005, <http://www.ilsr.org/recycling/epr/concepts>

Imhoff, ML, L Bounoua, T Ricketts, C Loucks, R Harriss & WT Lawrence (2004) Global patterns in human consumption of net primary production, *Nature*, 429: 870–73.

Information Commissioner (2005) *Environmental Information Regulations Factsheet*, Wilmslow, England.

IRTK (2003) *International Right to Know: Empowering Communities through Corporate Transparency*, AFL-CIO, Amnesty International USA, EarthRights International, Friends of the Earth, Global Exchange, Oxfam America, Sierra Club & Working Group on Community Right to Know.

ISEE (1994) *Investing in Natural Capital: The Ecological Approach to Sustainability*, International Society for Ecological Economics and Island Press, Washington DC.

IUCN, UNEP and WWF (1980) *World Conservation Strategy*, International Union for Conservation of Nature and Natural Resources, the UN Environment Programme, and the World Wildlife Fund.

Iyer, V (2000) Freedom of information: principles for legislation, Bytes for all.org, viewed 15 March 2006, <http://www.bytesforall.org/Egovernance/html/freedom_info.htm>

Jacobs, M (1993) Economic instruments: objectives or tools? Paper presented at the 1993 Environmental Economics Conference, Canberra, November.

Jacobson, J (1990) Holding back the sea. In L Brown, A Durning, C Flavin, H French, J Jacobson, M Lowe, S Postel, M Renner, L Starke, J Young (eds) *State of the World 1990*, Allen & Unwin, Sydney.

Jago, H (1969) Introducing Water Pollution Bill, NSW Legislative Assembly, 12 March 1969.

James, D (1997) *Environmental Incentives: Australian Experience with Economic Instruments for Environmental Management*, Department of Environment and Heritage, Canberra.

—— (1999) Economics concepts and the precautionary principle and implementation of safe minimum standards. In R Harding & E Fisher (eds) *Perspectives on the Precautionary Principle*, The Federation Press, Sydney, pp. 154–62.

Jellinek, S (1980) On the inevitability of being wrong, *Technology Review*, August-September, pp. 8–9.

JNCC (2005) Fisheries management: sustainability and the precautionary principle, Joint Nature Conservation Committee, viewed 14 November 2005, <http://www.jncc.gov.uk/page-2520>

Johnson, P, DL Mock, A McMillan, L Driscoll & T Hruby (2002) *Washington State Wetland Mitigation Evaluation Study. Phase 2: Evaluating Success*, Washington State Department of Ecology, Lacey, WA, January.

Juhasz, F (1993) Guiding principles for sustainable development in the developing countries. In E Dommen (ed.) *Fair Principles for Sustainable Development: Essays on Environmental Policy and Developing Countries*, Edward Elgar, Aldershot, Hants, pp. 33–59.

JWPTE: Joint Working Party on Trade and Environment (2002) *The Polluter-Pays Principle as It Relates to International Trade*, OECD, Paris, 23 December.

Kahn, H, W Brown & L Martel (1989) Putting growth in perspective. In M Allaby (ed.) *Thinking Green: An Anthology of Essential Ecological Writing*, Barrie & Jenkins, London, pp.

Keats, K (2005) Will the combustion plant directive ignite trading? *Environmental Finance*, April, pp. 20–1.

Kelman, S (1994) Cost–benefit analysis: an ethical critique. In D Westphal & F Westphal (eds) *Planet in Peril: Essays in Environmental Ethics*, Harcourt Brace, Fort Worth, TX, pp. 137–48.

Kill, J (2001) *Sinks in the Kyoto Protocol: A Dirty Deal for Forests, Forest Peoples and the*

Climate, FERN, Brussels, July.
Kill, J & B Pearson (2003) *Forest Fraud: Say NO to Fake Carbon Credits*, FERN and Sinks Watch, Gloucestershire, UK, November.
Kinsman, J (2002) Emissions trading, the economy and the environment, *Environmental Finance*, October, pp. 26–7.
Korsah-Brown, D (2002) Environment, human rights and mining conflicts in Ghana. In L Zarsky (ed.) *Human Rights & the Environment: Conflicts and Norms in a Globalizing World*, Earthscan, London, pp. 79–95.
Krijnen, T (2004) Tradeable water entitlements in the Murray–Darling Basin, *Natural Resource Management*, 7(1): 2–7.
Krugman, P (2004) The mercury scandal, *New York Times*, 6 April.
Ksentini, FZ (1994) *Final Report: Review of Further Developments in Fields with which the Sub-Commission has been Concerned: Human Rights and the Environment*, Commission on Human Rights, 6 July.
Laxe, FG (2005) Transferability of fishing rights: the Spanish case, *Marine Policy*, in press.
Lease, K (2002) *The Republic of Korea: Deposit Refund System*, Institute for Local Self-Reliance, Washington DC, 25 January.
Lenzen, M & SA Murray (2001) A modified ecological footprint method and its application to Australia, *Ecological Economics*, 37: 229–55.
Leonardo Academy (2005) Emissions trading basics, viewed 1 June 2005, <http://www.leonardoacademy.org/Resources/moreinfo.htm>
Lewis, D (2003) Rivers of gold, *Sydney Morning Herald*, 25 August, p. 12.
Linehan, C (2003) *Corporate Veil Pierced to Give Effect to 'Polluter Pays' Principle*, William Fry Solicitors, Dublin, 22 April.
Lohmann, L (1991) Dismal green science, *The Ecologist*, 21(5): 194.
—— (1997) Cost–benefit analysis: whose interest, whose rationality? The Corner House, viewed 10 March 2005, <http://www.thecornerhouse.org.uk/item.shtml?x=52011>
—— (1999) The Dyson effect: carbon 'offset' forestry and the privatization of the atmosphere, *The Corner House Briefing* (15).
—— (2000) *The Carbon Shop: Planting New Problems*, World Rainforest Movement, Montevideo, Uruguay, December.
—— (2001) Democracy or carbocracy? Intellectual corruption and the future of the climate debate, *The Corner House Briefing*, October.
—— (2004) *Inquiry into the International Challenge of Climate Change: UK Leadership in the G8 and EU*, The Corner House, SinksWatch, Carbon Trade Watch, 29 October.
Lovera, S (2005) Guest editorial: environmental markets impoverish the poor, Ecosystem Marketplace, viewed 15 March 2006, <http://ecosystemmarketplace.net/>
Low, N & B Gleeson (1998) *Justice, Society and Nature: An Exploration of Political Ecology*, Routledge, London.
Lynch, C (1998) Case study with American Electric Power, *Amicus*, Winter.
MacGarvin, M (1994) Precaution, science and the sin of hubris. In T O'Riordan & J Cameron (eds) *Interpreting the Precautionary Principle*, Earthscan, London, pp. 69–101.
Macinko, S & DW Bromley (2002) *Who Owns America's Fisheries?* Island Press, Washington DC.
MacKay, F (2002) The rights of indigenous peoples in international law. In L Zarsky (ed.) *Human Rights and the Environment: Conflicts and Norms in a Globalizing World*, Earthscan, London, pp. 9–30.
MacNeill, J (1989) Strategies for sustainable economic development, *Scientific American*, September, pp. 105–13.
Maddox, J (1972) *The Doomsday Syndrome*, MacMillan, London.
Marriott, P (2005) Australia urged to review stance on carbon trading, *Planet Ark*, 17 October.

Martin, R (2005) Green gold, *Catapult*, ABC Radio, 1 February.
Massey, R & F Ackerman (2003) *Costs of Preventable Illness: The Price We Pay for Pollution*, Global Development and Environment Institute, Tufts University, Medford, MA, September.
Matthews, DR (1995) Commons versus open access: the collapse of Canada's east coast fishery, *The Ecologist*, 25(2–3): 86–96.
McCallin, J (2005) London gets carbon-neutral cabs, Ecosystem Marketplace, viewed 31 May 2005, <http://ecosystemmarketplace.net>
McCallin, J (2005) Neutralizing the G8's carbon, Ecosystem Marketplace, viewed 6 July 2005, <http://ecosystemmarketplace.net>
McIntosh, P (1990) Most prepared to put environment ahead of growth, *Sydney Morning Herald*, 15 June.
McLaren, D, O Cottray, M Taylor, S Pipes & S Bullock (1999) *The Geographic Relation between Household Income and Polluting Factories*, Friends of the Earth Trust, UK, April.
McNeely, J, K Miller, W Reid, R Mittermeier & T Wemer (1990) *Conserving the World's Biodiversity*, IUCN, WRI, CI, WWF and the World Bank, Gland, Switzerland.
Meadows, DH, DL Meadows, J Randers & WW Behrens (1972) *The Limits to Growth: A Report for the Club of Rome's Project on the Predicament of Mankind*, Pan, London.
Meadows, R (2005) Wetland mitigation banking, Ecosystem Marketplace, viewed 14 August 2005, <http://ecosystemmarketplace.net>
Merrills, JG (1996) Environmental protection and human rights: conceptual aspects. In AE Boyle and MR Anderson (eds) *Human Rights Approaches to Environmental Protection*, Clarendon Press, Oxford, pp. 25–41.
Mills, CS (2004) Incentives and the ESA: can conservation banking live up to potential? *Duke Environmental Law and Policy*, 14: 523–65.
Mishan, EJ (1967) *The Costs of Economic Growth*, Penguin, Harmondsworth, Middlesex.
Monbiot, G (2004) Africa exploitation on tap, *The Guardian*, 20 October.
Moore, CA (2004a) Marketing failure: the experience with air pollution trading in the United States, *Health and Clean Air Newsletter*, Sacramento, CA, 3 February.
—— (2004b) Southern California's failed experiment with air pollution trading, *Health and Clean Air Newsletter*, Sacramento, CA, 26 January.
Myers, N, A Rabe & K Silberman (2005) *Act on Early Warnings*, The Louisville Charter for Safer Chemicals, May.
NAEI (2005) Emissions of air pollution in the UK, National Atmospheric Emissions Inventory, viewed 23 December 2005, <http://www.naei.org.uk/>
National Heritage Trust (2004) *Managing Our Natural Resources: Can Markets Help?* Australian Government, 26 August.
NCEE (2004) *International Experiences with Economic Incentives for Protecting the Environment*, National Center for Environmental Economics, US Environmental Protection Agency, Washington DC, November.
NENT (1997) *The Precautionary Principle: Between Research and Politics*, National Research Ethical Committees for Natural Science and Technology (NENT), Oslo.
Nicholls, M (2005) Seeing the water for the trees, Ecosystem Marketplace, viewed 10 August 2005, <http://ecosystemmarketplace.net>
NMBIPP (2005) National Market-based Instruments Program Projects, Australian Government, viewed 14 August 2005, <http://www.napswq.gov.au/mbi/projects.html>
Nolt, J (2005) Arguments for and against obligations to future generations, University of Tennessee, viewed 10 July 2005, <http://web.utk.edu/~nolt/courses/346/futurgen.htm>
Nordhaus, W. & Tobin, J. (1972) *Is Growth Obsolete?*, Proceedings of the 50th Anniversary Colloquium of the National Bureau of Economic Research, New York, pp.1–80.
Norgaard, RB (2001) Dana Meadows and the limits to growth, *Ecological Economics*, 38:

167–9.

Norton, B (1988) Commodity, amenity and morality: the limits of quantification in valuing biodiversity. In EO Wilson (ed.) *Biodiversity*, National Academy Press, Washington DC.

—— (1999) Ecology and opportunity: intergenerational equity and sustainable options. In A Dobson (ed.) *Fairness and Futurity: Essays on Environmental Sustainability and Social Justice*, Oxford University Press, Oxford, pp. 118–50.

NSW Farmers (2004) *Water for Life*, Sydney, August.

NWC (2005) National Water Initiative, National Water Commission, viewed 21 October 2005, <http://www.nwc.gov.au/NWI/index.cfm>

NWF (1997) *Latest EPA Plan to Reduce Water Pollution Is Unenforceable*, National Wildlife Federation, Reston, VA, April 1997.

O'Donnell, M (2005) 11 states challenge break on mercury for coal power plants, *New York Times*, 19 May.

OECD (1974) *The Implementation of the Polluter-Pays Principle*, C(74)223, 14 November.

—— (1989) *Economic Instruments for Environmental Protection*, Organisation for Economic Co-operation and Development, Paris.

—— (1989b) *Recommendation of the Council Concerning the Application of the Polluter-Pays Principle to Accidental Pollution*, Organisation for Economic Co-operation and Development, Paris,7 July.

—— (1996) *Recommendation of the Council on Implementing Pollutant Release and Transfer Registers*, Organisation for Economic Co-operation and Development, Paris, 21 March.

—— (2000) *PRTR Implementation: Member Country Progress*, Organisation for Economic Co-operation and Development, Organisation for Economic Co-operation and Development, Paris,12 July.

Olszewska, J (2001) Turning water into gold: water trading rights in Western Australia, FindLaw Australia, viewed 15 March 2006, <http://www.findlaw.com.au/articles/default.asp?task=read&id=1746&site=GN

OMB Watch (2001) *A Citizen's Platform for our Environmental Right-to-know*, OMB Watch, Washington DC, March.

O'Neill, J (1996) Cost–benefit analysis, rationality and the plurality of values, *The Ecologist*, 26(3): 98–103.

O'Riordan, T & J Cameron (eds) (1994) *Interpreting the Precautionary Principle*, Earthscan, London.

Orum, P & D Heminway (2005) *Give the Public and Workers the Full Right-to-know and Participate*, The Louisville Charter for Safer Chemicals, September.

Ott, HE & W Sachs (2000) Ethical aspects of emissions trading, *Wuppertal Papers* (110).

Pace, D (2005) More blacks live with pollution, *New York News Day*, 13 December, <http://abcnews.go.com/Health/wireStory?id=1402790&CMP=OTC-RSSFeeds0312>

Parravano, P & L Crockett (2000) Who should own the oceans? *San Francisco Chronicle*, 25 September, <http://www.commondreams.org/views/092500-103.htm>

Partridge, E (1981) Why care about the future? In E Partridge (ed.) *Responsibilities to Future Generations: Environmental Ethics*, Prometheus, Buffalo, NY, pp. 203–20.

—— (1990) On the rights of future generations. In D Scherer (ed.) *Upstream/Downstream: Issues in Environmental Ethics*, Temple University Press, Philadelphia, PA, pp. 40–66.

—— (2001) Future generations. In D Jamieson (ed.) *A Companion to Environmental Philosophy*, Blackwell, Oxford, pp. 377–89.

Pauw, J (2003) *Metered to Death: How a Water Experiment Caused Riots and a Cholera Epidemic*, The Center for Public Integrity, 4 February.

Pearce, D (1983) *Cost–Benefit Analysis*, 2nd edn, Macmillan, London.

—— (1994) The precautionary principle and economic analysis. In T O'Riordan & J Cameron (eds) *Interpreting the Precautionary Principle*, Earthscan, London, pp.

132–51.
Pearce, D, A Markandya & E Barbier (1989) *Blueprint for a Green Economy*, Earthscan, London.
Pearce, D (ed.) (1991) *Blueprint2: Greening the World Economy*, Earthscan, London.
Pearce, F (1992) Why it's cheaper to poison the poor, *New Scientist*, 1 February.
—— (1997) Countdown to chaos, *New Scientist*, 29 November, p. 22.
—— (1999) That sinking feeling, *New Scientist*, 23 October, p. 20.
—— (2000) Smokescreen exposed, *New Scientist*, 26 August, p. 18.
—— (2005a) A most precious commodity, *New Scientist*, 8 January, p. 6.
—— (2005b) Planting trees can create deserts, *New Scientist*, 29 July.
—— (2005c) Big game losers, *New Scientist*, 16 April.
Pearson, B & YS Loong (2003) *The CDM: Reducing Greenhouse Gas Emissions or Relabelling Business as Usual?* Third World Network and CDM Watch, March.
PENGO (2002) *Submission on Green Offsets for Sustainable Development Concept Paper*, Peak Environment Non-Government Organisations, Canberra, July.
Phillips, G, L Kriwoken & P Hay (2002) Private property and public interest in fisheries management: the Tasmanian rock lobster fishery, *Marine Policy*, 26: 459–69.
PIAC (1994) *Legislation for Community Right-to-know*, Public Interest Advocacy Centre, Sydney, March.
Picolotti, R (1999) *Agenda 21 and Human Rights: The Right to Participate*, Center for Human Rights and Environment (CEDHA), C{rdoba, Argentina,1999.
Planet Ark (2005) New Zealand scraps Kyoto carbon-tax plan, 22 December.
Principles of environmental justice (1991) Environmental Justice Net, viewed 15 March 2006, <http://www.ejnet.org/ej/principles.html>
Privatising Our Water (2004) *The Guardian*, 7 April.
Quiggan, J (2001) Environmental economics and the Murray–Darling river system, *The Australian Journal of Agricultural and Resource Economics*, 45(1): 67–94.
Raghavan, C (1995) Southern lives are cheaper, say climate change economists, *Third World Resurgence* (64): 2–4.
Ravetz, JR (1986) Usable ignorance: incomplete science with policy implications. In W Clark & RE Munn (eds) *Sustainable Development of the Biosphere*, Cambridge University Press, Cambridge, pp. 415–32.
Rayner, M (2005a) History of universal human rights – up to WW2, Universal Rights Network, viewed 25 April 2005, <http://www.universalrights.net/main/histof.htm>
—— (2005b) International Covenant on Civil and Political Rights, Universal Rights Network, viewed 25 April 2005, <http://www.universalrights.net/main/world.htm>
Rees, J (1988) Pollution control objectives and regulatory framework. In K Turner (ed.) *Sustainable Environmental Management: Principles and Practice*, Belhaven Press, London.
Rees, WE (1996) Revisiting carrying capacity: area-based indicators of sustainability, *Population and Environment*, 17(3).
—— (2002) Footprint: our impact on earth is getting heavier, *Nature*, 420: 267–8.
Reid, WV et al. Millennium Ecosystem Assessment (2005) *Ecosystems and Human Well-being: Synthesis*, Island Press, Washington DC.
Repetto, R (1989) Wasting assets: the need for national resource accounting, *Technology Review*, January, pp. 39–44.
Resnik, DB (2003) Is the precautionary principle unscientific? *Studies in History and Philosophy of Biological and Biomedical Sciences*, 34: 329–44.
Reuters (2005) US states sue EPA over mercury trading rules, *Planet Ark*, 19 May.
Ricco, V, *Human Rights and the Environment in the Americas*, Submission to Committee on Judicial and Political Affairs, Permanent Council of the Organization of American States, 2003.
Richard, G (2002) Human carrying capacity of the earth, *ILEA Leaf*, 13 September.

Richardson, A (1983) *Participation*, Routledge & Kegan Paul, London.
Richman, E (2003) Emissions trading and the development critique: exposing the threat to developing countries, *International Law and Politics*, 36: 133–76.
Rising Tide (2005a) State of the emerging carbon economy, viewed 24 July 2005, <http://www.risingtide.nl/greenpepper/climate/carboneconomy.html>
—— (2005b) Why is emissions trading inequitable? viewed 24 July 2005, <http://www.risingtide.nl/greenpepper/climate/inequity.html>
Roberts, L (1993) Wetlands trading a loser's game, say ecologists, *Science*, 260(5116): 1890–2.
Robins, N (2005) The coming carbon crunch, *Ethical Corporation*, 21 July.
Robinson, J and S Ryan (2002) *A Review of Economic Instruments for Environmental Management in Queensland*, CRC for Coastal Zone, Estuary and Waterway Management, Brisbane, June.
Robinson, M (2002) Human rights, sustainable development and environmental protection, Paper presented at the Civil Society Forum, World Summit on Sustainable Development, Johannesburg, South Africa, 1 September.
Rosen, R (2002) The day Ashcroft foiled FOIA, *San Francisco Chronicle*, 6 January.
Rowell, A (1996) *Green Backlash: Global Subversion of the Environment Movement*, Routledge, London & New York.
Rowinski, C (1993) *Wetland Mitigation Issues and Regulations Issues*, New Hampshire Coastal Program, Concord, NH.
The Royal Society (2002) *Economic Instruments for the Reduction of Carbon Dioxide Emissions*, November.
Ruch, J (2000) My week, *Grist Magazine*, 12 December.
Sachs, A (1997) A planet unfree, *Sierra Magazine*, November/December.
Sachs, W (1992a) Development: a guide to the ruins, *New Internationalist*, June, pp. 4–6.
—— (1992b) Whose environment? *New Internationalist*, June, pp. 20–2.
Saladin, C & BV Dyke (1998) *Implementing the Principles of the Public Participation Convention in International Organizations*, Center for International Environmental Law, Washington DC, June.
Salvin, S (2000) *Developing a Market in Biodiversity Credits*, Nature Conservation Council, Sydney, 23 June.
Sample, I (2005) Climate change will fuel disease among poor, *Sydney Morning Herald*, 18 November, p. 12.
Schärer, B (1999) Tradable emission permits in Germany's clean air policy: considerations on the efficiency of environmental policy instruments. In S Sorrell & J Skea (eds) *Pollution for Sale: Emissions Trading and Joint Implementation*, Edward Elgar, Cheltenham, UK, pp. 141–53.
Scheer, R (2005) UN predicts 50 million environmental refugees by 2010, *E Magazine*, 19 October.
Schelling, T, ed. (1983) *Incentives for Environmental Protection*, MIT Press, Cambridge, MA.
Schulz, C (1994) National pollution inventory and financial liability for contaminated sites, *Australian Business Law Review*, 22(6): 441–4.
Securing the Future: Delivering UK Sustainable Development Strategy (2005) HM Government, London, March.
Self, P (1990) Market ideology and good government, *Current Affairs Bulletin*, 67(4): 4–10.
Seneca, J & M Taussig (1984) *Environmental Economics*, Prentice-Hall, Englewood Cliffs, New Jersey.
SFN (2003) The ITQ experience in New Zealand, *Shetland Fishing News*, 28 July.
SFP Sustainable Fisheries Programme (2004) *Quota Management Reform*, DEFRA, DARDNI, Welsh Assembly, Scottish Executive, August.
Shanahan, J (1993) *How to Help the Environment without Destroying Jobs, Memo to President-elect Clinton #14*, The Heritage Foundation, Washington DC, January 19.

Shelton, D (1999) A rights-based approach to public participation and local management of natural resources, Paper presented at the 3rd IGES International Workshop on Forest Conservation Strategies for the Asia and Pacific Region, 7–9 September.

Shrader-Frechette, K (2002) *Environmental Justice: Creating Equality, Reclaiming Democracy*, Oxford University Press, Oxford.

Sierra Club (2005) Mitigation banking guidelines, viewed 18 September 2005, <http://www.sierraclub.org/wetlands/resources/mitigation.asp>

Simon, JL (1981) *The Ultimate Resource*, Martin Robertson, Oxford.

Sinks Watch (2005) Flaws of the concept, Sinks Watch, viewed 24 July 2005, <http://www.sinkswatch.org/flaws.html>

—— (2006) Climate change: the forest connection, Sinks Watch, viewed 9 March 2005, <http://www.sinkswatch.org/fortext.html>

Smets, H (1994) The polluter pays principle in the early 1990s. In L Campiglio, L Pineschi & D Siniscalco Treves (eds) *The Environment after Rio: International Law and Economics*, Graham & Trotman, London, pp. 131–47.

Sokulsky, J (2005) National forum on synergies between water quality trading and wetland mitigation, Ecosystem Marketplace, viewed 27 July 2005, <http://ecosystemmarketplace.net>

Sonneborne, C (2002) Emissions trading developments in the US, *AETF Review*, August-September, pp. 2–3.

Sorrell, S & J Skea (eds) (1999) *Pollution for Sale: Emissions Trading and Joint Implementation*, Edward Elgar, Cheltenham, UK.

Sowman, M (2005) Subsistence and small-scale fisheries in South Africa: a 10-year review, *Marine Policy*, in press.

Stavins, R & B Whitehead (1992) Dealing with pollution: market-based incentives for environmental protection, *Environment*, 34(7): 7–11, 29–42.

Stockholm Declaration (1972) Declaration of the United Nations Conference on the Human Environment, <http://www.internationallawhelp.com/stockholm-decl.txt>

Sundstrom, A (2000) *Salinity Control Credits: A Comment*, Nature Conservation Council, 22 June.

Sustainable Development Unit (1999) *A Strategy for Sustainable Development for the United Kingdom*, DEFRA, London.

Suter, K (1999) The Club of Rome: the global conscience, *Contemporary Review*, 275(1602): 1–5.

Swedish National Board of Fisheries (1995) *Precautionary Approach to Fisheries Part 1: Guidelines on the Precautionary Approach to Capture Fisheries and Species Introductions*, Food and Agriculture Organization of the UN (FAO), Rome.

SWS (2005) Wetland mitigation banking, Society of Wetland Scientists, viewed 18 September 2005, <http://www.sws.org/wetlandconcerns/banking.html>

Taillant, JD (2004) A nascent agenda for the Americas, *Human Rights Dialogue*, 2(11): 28–9.

Taliman, V (1992) The toxic waste of Indian lives, *CovertAction*, Spring, pp. 16–22.

TCS (2002a) Fishing quota moratorium expires, Taxpayers for Common Sense, viewed 30 September 2005, <http://www.taxpayer.net/TCS/PressReleases/09-30-02ifq.htm>

—— (2002b) Protect taxpayers against fisheries giveaway, says group, Taxpayers for Common Sense, viewed 13 February 2006, <http://www.taxpayer.net/TCS/PressReleases/02-13-02ifq.htm>

Templet, PH (2001) *Defending the Public Domain: Pollution, Subsidies and Poverty*, Political Economy Research Institute, University of Massachusetts, Amherst, MA.

Thampapillai, DJ (1991) *Environmental Economics*, Oxford University Press, Melbourne.

Tindale, S & C Hewett (1999) Must the poor pay more? Sustainable development, social justice, and environmental taxation. In A Dobson (ed.) *Fairness and Futurity: Essays on Environmental Sustainability and Social Justice*, Oxford University Press, Oxford, pp. 233–48.

Trading Water (2003) *Ecos*, April-June, pp. 24–6.

Trainer, T (1985) *Abandon Affluence!* Zed Books, London.

Trindade, AAC (1998) Human rights and the environment. In J Symonides (ed.) *Human Rights: New Dimensions and Challenges*, Ashgate, Brookfield, VT, pp. 117–53.

Twyman, AS (2002) Jersey spiking Whitman plan, *Star-Ledger*, 17 September.

UDHR (1948) Universal Declaration of Human Rights, Office of the High Commissioner for Human Rights, <http://www.unhchr.ch/udhr/lang/eng.htm>

UN (1982), World Charter for Nature, UN General Assembly, <http://www.un.org/documents/ga/res/37/a37r007.htm>

—— (1992) Agenda 21, UN Department of Economic and Social Affairs, <http://www.un.org/esa/sustdev/documents/agenda21/english/agenda21chapter8.htm>

UN/ECE (1999) Protocol on Water and Health to the 1992 Convention on the Protection and Use of Transboundary Watercourses and International Lakes, International Water Law Project, <http://www.internationalwaterlaw.org/RegionalDocs/UN_ECE_Protocol.htm>

UNHCHR (2002) *Final Text: Meeting of Experts on Human Rights and the Environment*, UN High Commission on Human Rights, 14–15 January 2002.

UNHRC (1982) *Communication No. 67/1980: Canada*, UN Human Rights Committee, 27 October.

UNICEF (1989) Convention on the Rights of the Child, <http://www.ohchr.org/english/law/pdf/crc.pdf>

USEPA (1995) *Federal Guidance for the Establishment, Use and Operation of Mitigation Banks*, US Environmental Protection Agency, 1995.

—— (1996) Effluent trading in watersheds: policy statement, US Environmental Protection Agency, viewed 15 March 2006, <http://www.epa.gov/owowwtr1/watershed/tradetbl.html>

—— (2002a) *Clearing the Air: The Facts about Capping and Trading Emissions*, US Environmental Protection Agency, 30 October.

—— (2002b) Three forms of emissions trading, *Clean Air Markets Update*, Winter, pp. 1–3.

—— (2004) What is Toxics Release Inventory (TRI) Program? US Environmental Protection Agency, viewed 15 June 2005, <http://www.epa.gov/tri/whatis.htm>

—— (2004a) *Cap and Trade: Essentials*, US Environmental Protection Agency, 14 April.

—— (2004b) *Water Quality Trading*, US Environmental Protection Agency, viewed 17 December 2005, <http://www.epa.gov/owow/watershed/trading.htm>

—— (2005) *Clean Air Interstate Rule (CAIR): Fact Sheet*, US Environmental Protection Agency, 11 March.

van Sittert, L, G Branch, M Hauck & M Sowman (2005) Benchmarking the first decade of post-apartheid fisheries reform in South Africa, *Marine Policy*, in press.

Veit, PG & C Benson (2004) When parks and people collide, *Human Rights Dialogue*, 2(11): 13–4.

Venetoulis, J, D Chazan & C Gaudet (2004) Ecological footprint of nations, *Redefining Progress*, March.

Vidal, J (2005) Environmental decline killing poor, *The Age*, 7 October.

Vidal, J & T Radford (2005) One in six countries facing food shortage, *The Guardian*, 30 June.

Visser 't Hooft, HP (1999) *Justice to Future Generations and the Environment*, Kluwer Academic, Dordrecht.

Vogel, D (1989) *Fluctuating Fortunes: The Political Power of Business in America*, Basic

Books, New York.

WAEPA (2005) *Environmental Offsets: Preliminary Position Statement No. 9*, Environmental Protection Authority, Western Australia, June.

Wackernagel, M, Larry Onisto, Alejandro Callejas Linares, Ina Susana López Falfán, Jesus Méndez García, Ana Isabel Suárez Guerrero & Ma. Guadalupe Suárez Guerrero (1997) *Ecological Footprints of Nations*, Centro de Estudios para la Sustenabilidad, Mexico.

Wackernagel, M, NB Schulz, D Deumling, A Callejas Linares, M Jenkins, V Kapos, C Monfreda, J Loh, N Myers, R Norgaard, & J Randers (2002) Tracking the ecological overshoot of the human economy, *PNAS*, 99(14): 9266–71.

Wahlquist, A (2000) Salinity credits for sale, *The Australian*, 26 August, p. 2.

—— (2002) Salinity crisis blamed on water trading, *The Australian*, 13 July, p. 7.

—— (2005a) Let the cash flow, *The Australian*, 4 July, p. 29.

—— (2005b) Water trade is finding its own level, *The Australian*, 22 April, p. 27.

Walker, C (2005) Sustainable fisheries: can market-mechanisms help get us there? Ecosystem Marketplace, viewed 14 August 2005, <http://ecosystemmarketplace.net>

Waring, M (1988) *Counting for Nothing: What Men Value and What Women are Worth*, Allen & Unwin, New Zealand.

Waste Not (2002) *Business Europe*, 42(4): 6.

Water set to be the next 'big' investment (2003) EnviroInfo, viewed 19 September 2005, <http://www.halledit.com.au/onlineservices/enviroinfo/envinfo1990903.htm>

Watt-Cloutier, S (2004) Climate change and human rights, *Human Rights Dialogue*, 2(11): 10–1.

WCED: World Commission on Environment and Development (1990) *Our Common Future*, Australian edn, Oxford University Press, Melbourne.

Weinberg, A (1986) Science and its limits: the regulator's dilemma. In National Association of Engineering (ed.) *Hazards: Technology and Fairness*, National Academy Press, Washington DC, pp. 9–23.

Weiss, EB (1990) Intergenerational fairness and the rights of future generations, Foundation for the Rights of Future Generations, April, <http://www.srzg.de/ndeutsch/5publik/1gg/7jg2h3/weiss.html>

—— (1992) Intergenerational equity: a legal framework for global environmental change. In EB Weiss (ed.) *Environmental Change and International Law: New Challenges and Dimensions*, United Nations University Press, Tokyo, pp. 385–412.

Wilkinson, J, C Kennedy, K Mott, M Filbey & S King (2002) Banks and fees mitigation study reveals an industry transformed, *National Wetlands Newsletter*, 24(5): 5–6, 16–7.

The Wingspread Statement on the Precautionary Principle, Science and Environmental Health Network, 26 January 1998, <http://www.sehn.org/wing.html>

Winward, J (1991) Consumer preferences and the environment. In T Barker (ed.) *Green Futures for Economic Growth: Britain in 2010*, Cambridge Econometrics, Cambridge, pp. 107–20.

Worldwatch Institute (2005) *Worldwatch Global Trends*, Washington DC.

Yearley, S (1991) *The Green Case: A Sociology of Environmental Issues, Arguments and Politics*, HarperCollins, London.

Zedler, JB (2004) Compensating for wetland losses in the United States, *Ibis*(146): 92–100.

Zerner, C (2000) Toward a broader vision of justice and nature conservation. In C Zerner (ed.) *People, Plants, and Justice: The Politics of Nature Conservation*, Columbia University Press, New York, pp. 3–20.

Zinn, J (1997) *Wetland Mitigation Banking: Status and Prospects*, Congressional Research Service (CRS), Washington DC, 12 September.

INDEX